ABORTION, EXECUTION, AND THE CONSEQUENCES OF TAKING LIFE

James D. Slack

ABORTION, EXECUTION, AND THE CONSEQUENCES OF TAKING LIFE

Transaction Publishers
New Brunswick (U.S.A.) and London (U.K.)

This book is printed on acid-free paper that meets the American National Standard for Permanence of Paper for Printed Library Materials.

Library of Congress Catalog Number: 2011004901
ISBN: 978-1-4128-1021-0 (cloth); 978-1-4128-4222-8 (paper)
Printed in the United States of America

Library of Congress Cataloging-in-Publication Data

Slack, James D., 1952-
Abortion, execution, and the consequences of taking life / James D. Slack. -- Rev. ed.
p. cm.
ISBN 978-1-4128-4222-8
1. United States--Moral conditions. 2. Abortion--United States. 3. Capital punishment--United States. 4. Prison sentences--United States. I. Title.

HN90.M6S59 2011
261.8'30973--dc22

2011004901

The second printing remains dedicated to my beloved children,
Sarah Ashley and *Samuel Douglas Drake*
and my beloved wife,
Janis
I am truly blessed each day, for they are in my life and in my heart.

Tehillim 83:1
John 3:23
Al-Isra 182:80

Contents

Acknowledgments

A scholarly endeavor is never accomplished in isolation. While I take full blame for limitations, I want to acknowledge those who have invested tremendously in enhancing its value. Colleagues who added shape and voice: Hussam Ayloush, Executive Director, Council on American-Islamic Relations, Southern California; Jack DeSario, Mount Union College; Tom Duley, (retired) Executive Director of the Urban Ministry, United Methodist Church, Birmingham, Alabama; Michael Wayne "EZ" Eggers, death row inmate at Donaldson Correctional Facility, Bessemer, Alabama; Brian Glusman, (former) Rabbi of the Temple Beth-El, Birmingham, Alabama; Donna Handley, University of Alabama at Birmingham (UAB); Michael Howell-Moroney, UAB; Bill Humphreys, Chaplain, PCUSA, Carroll College; Rob Jackson, Vice President for Spiritual Life, Liberty University; Murray Jardine, Auburn University; James "J.J." Johnson, death row inmate at Donaldson; Joey Kennedy, Pulitzer Prize winning journalist and Commentary Editor for the *Birmingham News,* Alabama; Mark LaGory, (retired) UAB; Sr. Peg Maloney, R.S.M., Director of University Ministry, Regis University; Asthma Mobin-Uddin, M.D., (former) President of the Council on American Islamic Relations, Ohio; Mark Pruett-Barnet, Chaplain of the College, Wesley College; Gene Schandorff, University Chaplain, Northwest Nazarine University; Robert Schneider, University of North Carolina at Pembroke; Ashfaq Taufique, President of the Birmingham (Alabama) Islamic Society; Joanne Tetlow, Catholic University of America; Spencer Thury, Director of Campus Ministries, William Penn University; Rick L. Williamson, Professor of Biblical Studies, Mount Vernon Nazarene University; and William H. Willimon, Bishop of the North Alabama Conference of the United Methodist Church, and former Dean of the Chapel and Professor of Christian Ministry at Duke University. I also want to thank those who gave advice regarding the interview agreement form: Terry Alexander, UAB; Jack DeSario, Mt.

Union College, Michael Howell-Moroney, UAB; Mark LaGory, UAB; and Debra McCullum, University of Alabama, Tuscaloosa.

Several scholars helped shape portions of earlier drafts when various chapters were either conference papers, manuscripts-in-waiting, or simply ideas-in-infancy: Gregory Butler, New Mexico State University; Kevin denDulk, Grand Valley State University; Wendy Gunther-Canada, UAB, Akhlaque Haque, UAB; Rebecca McCumbers, University of Notre Dame; Steven Millies, University of South Carolina, Aiken; and Walter Nicgorski, University of Notre Dame. Several colleagues were also kind enough to answer or ask specific questions: Franklin Gamwell, University of Chicago; John S. Grabowski, Catholic University of America; Gary R. Habermas, Liberty University; and John Hare, Yale University.

I wish to acknowledge the contribution of thoughtful debate made by several students in my courses: (1) UAB graduate seminars on "Morality and Ethics in the Public Service": Adrienne Brown, Andre Davis, Jennifer Henderson, Gloria Howard, Vickie Love, Mark Naggar, Amy Philips, Territa Poole, Griffith Still, and Carl Thomas; (2) a Samford University undergraduate seminar in "Politics of Death": Nick Agnello, Kathryn Barnes, Robin Bishop, Zach Brooks, Ashley Hinton, Emily Hollady, Chris Johnston, Hannah McCurdy, John Rochell, and Cameron Searcy; and (3) Donaldson inmate-students in my "Morality and Integrity" classes: Michael Betts, James Campbell, Bruce Carroll, Paul Handley, Alex Hood, Michael Lang, James Martin, Tomas Snyder, Michael Thompson, and Kenneth Wiliford. I want to thank my graduate assistants for helping with this book: Meghan Ann Hauswirth, Susan McCarroll, Jennifer Garstka, Jennifer Henderson, Bashan Holt, Kamna Lal, Amy Philips, and Nuzhat Yasmin. I am grateful to Fred Shepherd, chair of the Department of Political Science at Samford University, for allowing me to teach a course on "Politics of Death," in which logic and argument about the sanctity of life was honed.

I am grateful for assistance to various groups and individuals for opening doors and assisting in the completion of this work: Billy Brown, Community Director, Kairos Prison Ministry at Donaldson; Reid Crotty, Senior Minister, Bluff Park United Methodist Church, Hoover, Alabama; the Ethics Section of the American Society for Public Administration; Kairos-Outside Ministry; Georgette Forney, President, Noel-for-Life and Co-Founder of Silent-No-More; Wanda Jones of the Birmingham, Alabama, Chapter of Victims of Crime and Leniency (VOCAL); the Living Waters Emmaus Community; Carol Melton of VOCAL; Serena

Mitchell, past Alabama Regional Coordinator, Silent-No-More; Herbert M. Newell IV, Executive Director, Lifeline Children's Services, Inc.; Don Roser, Pastor, Bryan Memorial Presbyterian Church (PCUSA), Birmingham, Alabama; and the anonymous owner, "Michelle," of an abortion clinic, which I call in this book "Omega Breeze" in the city of "South Amherst." Michelle has been most helpful in bringing me to a greater understanding of the complexity of abortion.

I am also grateful to the Alabama Department of Corrections (DOC) for approving my project proposal and facilitating its completion. Specifically I want to thank Brian Corbett, Public Information Manager; past and current Wardens: Grantt Culliver at Holman Correctional Facility; Gary Hetzel and Kenneth L. Jones at Donaldson; Correctional Officers at Donaldson: James Beachem, Kenneth Clark (Lieutenant), Thaddeus Clarke, Pamela Davis, Gary L. Holder, James Hudson, Spurgeon Johnson, Eddie Jones, Joe Tew (Captain), Eddie Watts, and Tony Williams; chaplains: Chris Summers at Holman, and Bill Lindsey and (associate chaplain) David Bucher at Donaldson. I am particularly grateful for Chris Summer's intellect, knowledge and time which he invested so generously in reviewing portions of the manuscript. This project could not have been completed without DOC support. On any given day, the men and women of the DOC are the finest public servants in the state of Alabama.

Finally I want to thank my family—Janis, Sarah, and Sammy—for faithfully tolerating an academic husband and father who too frequently spends more time on the construction of meaningless words and phrases than on the crafting of meaningful experiences and memories with those whom he most dearly loves.

James D. Slack, Ph.D.

Preface to the Paperback Edition

This book is about the intimate consequences of public action and moral truth. I define morality as absolute and constant norms, found in sacred documents, through which we strive to live our lives. These timeless values are important because we are expected to measure ourselves by them. When we do not, they scatter into the mix of temporal priorities. Our moral compass tarnishes, and we become lost as individuals and as a community.

At the time of the first printing, I had no idea how the above words would come home to roost. I have found that while college campuses speak robustly about the *concept* of academic freedom, collective and individual voices lean toward silence when theocentric (God-based) morality enters the substance of debate. In the case of pro-life positions on certain issues, the "baby" of First Amendment rights is quietly thrown out with the "bath water" of comfort. Too many in academia do not like linking opposition to abortion with support for the sanctity of all human life. So on days when executions occur in Alabama, anti-death penalty advocates are often bothered by the words on my pro-life placard proclaiming: "Murder, Execution, Abortion = The Same Thing."

I am not the only one in academia to experience first-hand intimate consequences from the sanctity of life debate. A colleague at the "University of South Amherst" (USA) placed a pro-life poster on her own hallway bulletin board. (The poster gave counseling information for post-abortion mothers.) A graduate assistant shouted that the display should not be protected by academic freedom because it "offends all women." If the poster were not removed, the student vowed, women at USA would take matters into their own hands. In an effort to accommodate, this colleague removed the placard and placed it in her twentieth-floor office windowsill. She then put another display on her hallway bulletin board—two (one black, one white) rubber figures of eight-week old babies in the womb. Next to them, she posed a question: "Should they not also have a right of choice?"

A vice president ranted that the display, if not removed, was going to "send every woman who has had an abortion into counseling." He asked the professor, "Is that your intent?" (The administrator was candid enough to admit that if the display were pro-choice, there would be no problem.) He then complained that the pro-life poster in my colleague's fifth-floor window hurt student recruitment efforts because prospective freshmen and parents could see the poster from the street below and would be prone to reconsider the decision to enroll at USA. She took the pro-life poster out of her window.

Her bulletin board display remained but was vandalized, not once, but twice. She found everything removed each time except for the thumb tacks, which were placed neatly in a row. Whoever committed the public acts of theft to property and the violation of academic freedom obviously felt no hurry to escape from the scene. The voice of protest was pretty quiet in those hallowed halls of USA. Public action, for which we are all ultimately responsible, deafened the simple whisper of moral truth found on a bulletin board and in a windowsill. My colleague was forced to retire shortly thereafter.

On any college campus it seems that academic freedom is the primary victim when individuals and institutions feel they have the license to tarnish the moral compass. Personal comfort and shared denial of what Bonhoeffer will call "the real" become highly valued within the mix of temporal priorities. As a result, the postmodern academy (like its societal counterpart) becomes a little more lost.

This is also true when applying theocentric morality to the question posed at the beginning of Chapter 5, "What do you do with a murderer?" Just as the first printing was completed, I became the spiritual advisor to condemned Alabama inmate Jack Trawick. I spent the entire execution week in fellowship with Jack, urging him to offer healing to his victims' loved-ones, as well as readying him to kneel before God at his death, which would occur at 6:17 p.m. on Thursday, June 11, 2009. Knowing about the activities behind the scenes, described in Chapter 4, gave me added reason to keep Jack focused throughout each day. I also discovered many different acts of agape love offered to him by execution team members and the warden—unselfishness that taught Jack a great deal about the sanctity of life in his last hours of this world.

By just about every account, Jack Trawick was a monster. He had a long history of raping, strangling, and mutilating young women. On the Monday of his execution week, he felt anger towards the victims' families because, from his perspective, they "rushed" the appellate process so that he would end up in the death chamber sooner than other inmates. Jack plotted to hurt them terribly with his final words in the death chamber. He had absolutely no remorse for murdering his victims and wished he could continue to murder other young women. On Tuesday, he joked that if he could only escape, he would be "back in business in a matter of minutes." On Wednesday, he commented that all the female correctional officers and nurses "who had been smiling at [him] for the last fifteen years" on death row would never have done so if they knew what he was thinking as he smiled back. Even on Thursday—his execution day—Jack insisted on telling me more "war stories" of prowling for victims near the University of Alabama at Birmingham (UAB) campus and Birmingham's South Side, as well as several "near-misses" with young girls hitch-hiking in California.

Sitting in Jack's death cell minutes before his execution, I again reminded him that his last words would be the beginning of a conversation that would conclude at the foot of the Throne. We prayed that he would choose words of healing for the victims' families, ones that would help him in that latter conversation. I kissed him and said "I love you." He was then extracted from the death cell and escorted to the death chamber. This monster ultimately chose healing in his last words. Jack finally discovered a linkage between moral truth and his own public actions.

Mary Kate Gach is the mother of Stephanie, one of Jack Trawick's victims. She did not attend his execution. For the post-execution press conference, Mrs. Gach wrote, "[T]he murder of my child is so hurtful that only my own death will bring closure ... I am thankful that I outlived this demon and that he did not continue breathing our air for another day longer." A week later, I was introduced to Mrs. Gach at a monthly meeting of Victims of Crime and Leniency (VOCAL). She insisted that I resign my membership to VOCAL because, by opposing the death penalty, I "cannot possibly be a supporter" of VOCAL. For nearly two hours in a sweltering Birmingham parking lot, she unleashed her rage on me for being the spiritual advisor to "that monster."

What can you say in response to a mother in so much pain? Nothing. I just listened. When she appeared to exhaust her hurt, I quietly said "I love you"—the same words I whispered to Jack.

Since the first printing of this book, I have seen the intimacy of pain and suffering in the heart of Mrs. Gach and occasionally, during the execution week, I gained a glimpse of the pain in the heart of "that monster." I saw that same suffering and pain among members of Jack's family, as well as in the victims' family members, who witnessed his execution. All truly wished for some sweeter outcome than what the past offered. No one wanted to move toward that uncertain future where pain remained for everyone except Jack.

Such are some of the intimate consequences of public action and moral truth. The same intimate consequence is found regardless of whether the issue centers on the unborn or the born. Ultimately *Imago Dei* is *Imago Dei.* I fear I would not have realized this simple truth had I not written this book. I hope the following pages affirm your faith in this same truth. Perhaps together, we might untarnish our moral compass and become a little less lost.

Public Morality and Public Action

As with the first printing, I am not concerned with private morality—the kind involving a personal relationship between the self and God or, in the case of secularists, the relationship with some other important entity. While choices stemming from that private relationship may have a secondary impact on others, the brunt of the consequences rests on the self. Public morality, on the other hand, is concerned with sacred norms and values that tend to have a more sweeping impact on society. We damage the moral compass of the entire political community when we choose to ignore the truth in situations that involve more than just the self—whether it be attempts to thwart academic freedom when it comes to feelings about abortion or attempts to deny humanity when it comes to feelings about murder and execution.

Public action is both cause and consequence of the application or neglect of public morality. Here I use the word "public action" in two ways. Collective public action—public policy—can have an impact on all of us because it permits or prevents us from engaging in selective activities that either underscore or question the community's moral compass. Individual public action, in relation to prescribed public policy, can also have a positive or negative consequence on others because it demonstrates our willingness to pursue or ignore sacred morality. As with collective public actions, the mosaic pattern of individual public actions either advances or erodes the moral compass of the community.

Where and What?

Focus is placed on the American political community. A theocentric moral framework, based on Founding thought, is constructed and enhanced with the political thought of Dietrich Bonhoeffer. The resulting normative model underscores citizen obligations and government responsibilities in finding and confirming the truth found in two specific sources: Holy Scripture and empirical events, or what Bonhoeffer calls "the real." This model is applied to the taking of life in the United States.

I emphasize the *intimate* consequences of public action concerning the taking of life because intimacy harnesses our natural preference for distraction and distance from both sources of truth: scripture and the real. Intimacy forces involvement and underscores obligation. Specifically, I examine the taking of life when it concerns abortion and the murder/capital punishment sequence of events. The act of murder is a public action because it questions the sanctity of someone else's life. Abortion and capital punishment also question the sanctity of the lives of others. Their intimate realities typically remain hidden, making it difficult to assess the consequences for the political community. As a result, it becomes even more difficult to link these kinds of public actions to the moral compass we profess to share.

Methodology

This is a theocentric phenomenological exploration and, as such, it is not a scientific study with a research design, hypothesis, dependent and independent variables, and statistical analysis. There is no random sample or control group. The methodology is one of direct observation and qualitative open-ended conversations, common in normative inquires (Kirk, 20003, Press and Cole, 1999, Neustatter, 1986; McLouth et al., 1984) and consistent with the expectations found within the literature on qualitative inquiry (McCracken, 1999; Kirk and Miller, 1986; Dexter, 1970). This normative strategy follows previous arguments of feminist scholars, beginning with Hope Landrine et al. (1995), that challenge the discerning value of "traditional" social science and call for a combination of behavioral approaches and other techniques that are more subjective in order to better capture nuances of reality.

To grasp the intimate consequences of taking of life, I talked with seventy-six people (of whom fourteen were African-American and three were Hispanic) about abortion and its alternatives, the death penalty and its alternatives, and justice in society. I also talked with Alabama Department of Corrections (DOC) officials about prison processes as well as technical and environmental issues. Literature on qualitative inquiry (Neustatter, 1986; and McLouth, 1984) underscores that scientific randomness is not a goal. Rather, it is more important that those selected speak “openly” and “honestly” so that what they have to say illuminates unique insights into experiences (Neustatter, 1986: 116).

The people with whom I talked were selected on this basis. A fictitious name was designated for each participant, with the exception of DOC officials. In order to further protect the identities of some people, geographic locations and background descriptions were altered. Conversations, which lasted typically from one to two hours, took place between 2007 and 2009 (most were “in-person” with a few via telephone and several “follow-up” conversations via e-mail). Each person received two copies of an interview agreement form before the beginning of their session, as well as a description of the nature and background of the project, selection process, potential risks or discomforts, potential benefits, confidentiality, and interviewee rights throughout the project. Each person also designated someone whom they could trust who would be available for post-conversation counseling, if needed. Contact information was also provided about the availability of pro bono counselors with whom they could talk, if needed.

Between 2007 and 2009, I visited several times the Holman Correctional Facility in Atmore, Alabama, which houses the largest death row unit and the state’s sole death chamber. Since 2000, I have visited Donaldson Correctional Facility in Bessemer, Alabama, on many occasions—both in the general population areas and the smaller death row unit. Between 2007 and 2009, I traveled to “South Amherst” and had tours of an abortion clinic I call “Omega Breeze.” (I have camouflaged the location and description of this abortion clinic because of the history of threats and actual violence committed by pro-life extremists.) I periodically observed activities outside this abortion clinic and digitally recorded the public exchanges that transacted between pro-life demonstrators on one side of the street and pro-choice advocates on the other. With recorder in sight for all to see, I typically listened from the middle of the street, and sometimes from either curb (when traffic was heavy), as public shouting took place. The names of the people who protested on either side of this street are not used, nor are their physical attributes described, allowing their identities to remain anonymous.

The Rest of the Book

Chapter 1 outlines the theocentric moral foundation envisioned by the Founders, and links it to the political thought of Dietrich Bonhoeffer.

It offers a normative model of seeking the truth about intimate consequences of public action. Chapter 2 explores the model's first source of truth, the Word of God, as it applies to the public actions of murder, abortion, and capital punishment. Chapter 3 explores the intimate consequences of abortion, and Chapter 4 does the same with murder and capital punishment. The realities are examined through phenomenological sketches of individuals and settings, all comprising a mosaic pattern of public action. Because of mixed scriptural messages about capital punishment, it is important to examine the reality of life in prison as an alternative to execution. This is done in Chapter 5. Chapter 6 underscores the importance of the government's task of providing outward justice, as well as the citizen's responsibility to be supportive of that task, in order to reconcile the reality of life-taking with the moral compass professed in the American political community.

1

Morality and the American Political Community

Causes and consequences of public actions do not occur in a vacuum. The focus here is on public actions concerning abortion and capital punishment that take place in a particular setting, the American political community. This is decisively a democratic environment and, as Montesquieu says in the *Spirit of Laws* (2005), it therefore requires much more virtue from its citizens and leaders than any other form of government. James W. Ceaser (1976) points out that, for this kind of political setting to sustain itself, citizens need to understand that democratic action is not unrelated to the moral actions of each individual.

Hence, the American political community is much more than democratic in nature. While its creation was aided instrumentally by John Locke (1689), Founders intended for the groundwork of this particular political community to be anchored firmly in a special kind of morality. Desired values and norms were to be theocentric and specifically based on the morality of the God of Abraham (Novak, 2004).

This is not to say that the Founders desired a theocratic government; that is, one where private actions and civic behavior would be determined and judged by laws requiring specific religious rituals and the adherence to a specific set of religious doctrine (Meacham, 2006). Early colonial documents proclaimed too much of that in the form of penalties for not praying at the appropriate time of day and for blasphemous speech against the church and God.[1] Specifically they feared two types of theocratic tendencies: (1) a national church as per those early documents and (2) legislative preferential treatment to various religious sects: Congregationalist in the New England colonies, Roman Catholic in Maryland, Episcopalian in Virginia, Methodist in Georgia, and Baptist in the Carolinas (Lonang Institute, 2006).

Rather than creating a secular moral foundation, Thomas Jefferson (1786) believed that religious tolerance was the appropriate antidote to combat theocratic tendencies. James Madison (1785; Muñoz, 2003) further argued in favor of religious tolerance by warning about the unintended consequences of officially placing Christianity above all other religions, as well as the adverse affects of placing one Christian sect above the others. Moreover, Madison (1785; Frohnen, 2002: 48) cautioned about passing laws to persecute non-believers, arguing that "we cannot deny an equal freedom to those whose minds have not yielded to the evidence which has convinced us. If this freedom be abused, it is an offence against God, not against man."

Religious tolerance was never meant to subjugate religious practices (Glenn, 1987). Jefferson (1820) fully supported separating the actions of government from the desires of individual sects or churches, but he never supported the building of a wall of separation between God and the political community (Church, 1989). In essence, the antidote to rid the political uterus of theocratic tendencies was not a prescription to murder or maim the infant republic also found inside that womb.

While fearful of theocratic governance, the Founders envisioned a political community where public action and its consequences would be based on theocentric moral principles. Certainly the Age of Enlightenment nurtured the primary Lockean value of individualism, as well as the need for equality in order to protect the pursuits of each rational person. This, after all, was the impetus for entering into the political community. But the idea of individualism and equality could not stand alone. The question became then, how do you regulate and control the civic engagement of entrepreneurs whose inherent Lockean self-interest may not always succumb to the basic need of living with one another?

Theocentric moral principles seemed the best answer. As reflected by John Adams, "the notion that a state and society could remain neutral and purged of any religion was ... a philosophical fiction. Absent a commonly adopted set of values and beliefs, politicians would invariably hold out their private convictions as public ones" (Witte, 2004: 25). The Founders were not necessarily concerned with everyone going to heaven, but rather how each person had to behave publically in this lifetime in order for the political community to work.

The resultant society would regulate itself through laws and expected behavior based on the morality found in the God of Abraham—and checked by the notion of a limited tolerance that is compatible with the God-based foundational values of the political community. These moral principles—of how to behave toward one another in this lifetime, not necessarily how to get to heaven for eternity—are found in sacred documents of the three religions which claim the God of Abraham: Judaism, Christianity, and Islam. While the Founders did not focus on either Judaism or Islam, this particular group of Christians opened the door for limited tolerance as long as moral values meshed with those of the God whom they worshipped.

A Model of Morality in the American Political Community

Theocentric, or God-based values, comprise the fundamental ingredient in the moral foundation of the community (See Figure 1). These values are *this-world* and not necessarily values related to eternity. Depicted at the apex is a weighted rod extending to the extremes, which symbolizes Founders' fears about two kinds of theocracy: (1) legalistic/fundamentalist theocratic tendencies, where government establishes a national religion and compels individuals to submit to specific worship practices and rituals and (2) sect-based theocratic tendencies, where a particular denomination captures government arenas and shapes public action to benefit its own position *vis-à-vis* other denominations.

Figure 1
Theocentric Moral Foundation of the American Political Community

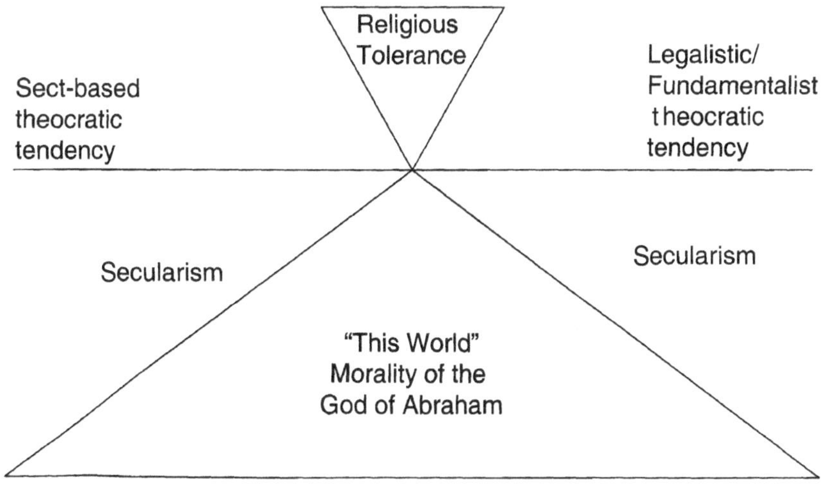

Because the weighted rod sits tenuously on the apex of the moral foundation, political gravity in either direction can pull the community into a state of theocracy. Or, if the rod is jettisoned completely off the apex, the entire political community might fall into a sea of secular values. To prevent this, it is essential that a weight of religious tolerance is affixed and remains steadfastly balanced at the apex of the theocentric foundation. This weight is depicted as an inverted triangle to reflect, in contrast to the theocentric foundation, its inherently non-stationary nature. If the weight of religious tolerance falters slightly in either direction, the community will lose its ability to negate the gravitational pull toward either kind of theocratic tendency. If it is knocked off completely, the community drowns in the stormy waters of secularism. Hence, the inverted triangle of religious tolerance keeps all contrary tendencies in check by requiring community acceptance of diverse interpretations of theological thought and church-based doctrine. It protects the inalienable right to worship and serve the God of Abraham in one's own way and prohibits public persecution of individuals who choose to do so. Such tolerance, therefore, requires the political community to accept the religious rights of all believers in the God of Abraham—Jews, Christians, and Muslims.

Maintenance of the theocentric moral foundation also requires tolerance toward non-believers because of the omnipresent slippery slope toward theocratic tendencies. But while the Founders argued that non-believers should suffer no persecution, there was also consensus that tolerance should not be construed as a permit for disrupting the carefully crafted balance which protects the theocentric moral foundation of the community. This is reflective of John Locke's idea that a state of *liberty* is not a state of *license*—and this is a prerequisite for a successful political community (1689 at 6.1-10). It also reflects the congressional consensus on the intent of the Establishment Clause: (1) to ensure that one religious sect does not interfere with the rights of other sects; (2) to guarantee that a government-based national religion would never be established; and (3) in the words of Representative Benjamin Huntington, with whom Madison concurred, to guard against the amendment being used to "patronize those who professed no religion at all" (Debate, 1789; Frohnen, 2002).

This is why the weight of religious tolerance is depicted as external to the theocentric moral foundation. The Founders, even Madison and Jefferson, never envisioned religious tolerance as the primary value of the community. As in so many areas of thought, they took their lead from John Locke's vision of the entrepreneurial dimensions of the community, as well as his devout Christian views on life (Nuovo, 2002; Higgins-Ciddle, 2000). Just as equality is considered an important yet secondary value needed to affirm the primary value of individualism, so too needed is the value of religious tolerance in its relationship to the value of theocentric morality. While never to be regulated by the social compact (Locke, 1689b), the value of religious tolerance lies within its utility to define and protect the parameters of the theocentric moral foundation and, thereby, to guide civic behavior and public action.

Symbolically depicted in smaller size (see Figure 1), the Founders never intended for the weight of tolerance to be so great as to crush the very foundation it is designed to protect. Furthermore, the Founders did not view the idea of religious tolerance as a catalyst for exchanging a God-based morality with one of secular humanism. As George Washington (1796) so eloquently underscored, "the public morality of the community cannot prevail in exclusion of religious principle." There was a very genuine concern that, in guarding against the threat of theocratic tendencies, the community might someday disembowel its theocentric moral base. If protected from a national religion (as was Madison's concern), would the Establishment Clause nevertheless become a tool used to patronize, in Huntington's words, "those who professed no religion at all"? The Founders thought otherwise and this is perhaps the reason Jefferson, in his letter to the Danbury Baptists, focused only on the fears of theocratic tendencies and neither diminished the value of theocentric morality nor implied that public officials must refrain from incorporating it into either the process or product of public actions. The constitutional wall which he correctly intended to build was one to prevent a national church (legalistic/fundamentalist theocracy) and to prevent specific churches from gaining government-sanctioned preferences in policy outcomes (sect-based theocracy). Separation of church and state never meant separation of community from God.

It is for this reason—to build and maintain a political community with a common moral compass guiding individual and collective public action—that the Founders entertained political questions about religion. Core moral values for civic engagement would be theocentric and derived specifically from the words of the God of Abraham. Given the concern for tolerance, along with Madison's particular caution that one religion should never dominate another, I argue that the Founders—if living in the twenty-first century—would feel philosophically comfortable with the moral values found in all three religions worshipping the God of Abraham: Judaism, Christianity, and Islam. But as Michael Novak (2004: xiii-xiv) astutely notes, "a commitment to religious liberty, or liberty of consciences, does not entail a commitment to the moral equivalence of any and all points of view." Other spiritual and secular values might be tolerated but would remain unwoven into the moral fabric of the community unless there was a demonstrated compatibility with *this-world* values of the God of Abraham.

So What?

Why is this important to know? We have forgotten much of the original intent of the Founders and, consequently, contemporary debate over many issues often renders two popular yet distorted caricatures of morality within the American political community. One is a Christian theocratic community where biblical doctrine dictates private lives and, ultimately, public action. If not a pure theocracy, government should have theocratic tendencies to monitor and judge behavior in an effort to maintain mosaic law within the community (Rosenblum, 2000). The second caricature is that of a completely secular political community where religious convictions of individuals are expelled from public display and expunged from public action in order to avoid both the perception and actuality of a theocratic state. At stake is the protection of the individual's right of conscience and the potential imposition of one's own moral compass upon the right of conscience of others. The argument, therefore, is that government should be completely free from the constraints of God and the concomitant sanctioned application of religious doctrine (Ivers, 1995).

The problem is that either stereotype renders a dichotomous and artificial set of truths for many contemporary political and social debates. Resultant policy positions are often skewed by inconsistencies within the original parameters for the political community as set forth by the Founders. For instance, if I advocate a theocratic ideal, then all of my truth will be derived from scripture. I will miss truth as it might be expressed in the reality of the world. If I advocate a secular ideal, then all of my truth—everything that I am willing to see as being truthful—will be based on anything *but* the morality found in the words of the God of Abraham. The lack of reconciliation between that which was intended by the Founders and that which is currently rationalized by contemporaries on both ideological sides is the crux of the problem in our collective attempt to seek, tell, and act upon the truth in the American political community.

The Political Thought of Dietrich Bonhoeffer and the American Political Community

Seeking truth about the intimate consequences of abortion and capital punishment in the American political community is a complicated task. It may seem strange to turn to a German theologian whose life experiences were anchored in a monarchy, then in a fledgling democracy, and ended in a totalitarian regime (Bethge, 2000). But Dietrich Bonhoeffer was heavily influenced by his American experience and, as such, became the most important (and least acknowledged) *political* philosopher of the twentieth century.[2] His words speak to the soul of all political communities in the twenty-first century that treasure democratic values in public action while acknowledging that the genesis of such public action must lie in the morality found in the God of Abraham. Given that the American Founders envisioned a democratic political community with a theocentric moral foundation, Dietrich Bonhoeffer speaks about the need for moral truth to govern our actions.

As background, Bonhoeffer and his twin sister Sabine were born in 1906 in the town of Breslau, Germany. He grew up well-educated and well-traveled, spending time in Barcelona, Rome, London, North Africa, and New York. In childhood he decided on a career as a minister *and* as a theologian—a practitioner and intellectual, if you will. He entered into theological studies at the University of Tubinger in 1923, and then at Berlin's prestigious Friedrich-Wilhelm University in 1924. In 1928 he earned a divinity degree.

On April 5, 1943 Bonhoeffer was arrested for espionage and involvement with financing the smuggling of Jews into Switzerland, as well as for his involvement in the plots to assassinate Adolf Hitler. Because of his international reputation, and that of his family, he spent eighteen months' incarceration at Berlin's Tegel Prison instead of being sent to a concentration camp. As the Russians approached Berlin, the decision was made to eradicate political prisoners whose deaths, up to this point, were deemed too cumbersome for the Nazi regime due to their respective international reputations. Dietrich Bonhoeffer's name was placed on the death list.

In April 1945 he was moved quickly, despite the crumbling transportation infrastructure, to Buchenwald and then to Schönberg for trial. Once a Nazi judge could commandeer a freight car to get to Schönberg, a perfunctory trial was convened on Saturday April 7. On Sunday, Bonhoeffer was moved to Flossenburg concentration camp.[3] On Monday April 9, he was stripped naked and paraded demeaningly to the gallows.

The details of his execution have been put in dispute. According to the attending physician, Bonhoeffer knelt and prayed at the gallows and then quietly died in a few minutes. However, one survivor claims that the deaths of those executed on that particular day took hours to complete. Since all were political prisoners involved in the plots against Hitler, the S.S. hung the victims on their tip-toes and revived them periodically prior to death so that the execution could be revisited several times (Slane, 2004: 28). But whatever happened, the attending physician (Bethge, 2000: 927-928) noted:

> before taking off his prison garb, [he knelt] on the floor praying fervently to his God. I was most deeply moved by the way this unusually lovable man prayed, so devout and so certain that God heard his prayer. At the place of execution, he again said a short prayer and then climbed the steps to the gallows, brave and composed.... In almost fifty years that I worked as a doctor, I have hardly ever seen a man die so entirely submissive to the will of God.

America and Bonhoeffer

Before all the horrors of Nazi Germany, Bonhoeffer came in 1930 to the United States to study as a post-graduate student at Union Theological Seminary in New York.[4] He examined American philosophy and the history of American theology in an effort to gain a better understanding of the role of individualism and its impact on both American culture and the American view of Christology. He also witnessed the reality of American life as it manifested during the early years of the Great Depression. He gradually became fixated with the concrete reality of the world of God and, while he did not waiver from his core theological beliefs, he grew "strongly motivated by an insatiable curiosity for every new reality" (Bethge, 2000: 165-166).

As such, he became a student of the conditions of African-Americans and grew frustrated by the condescension and counter-productiveness of white church intrusion into the black community. He also was alarmed by the loss of faith in the younger black generation. Bonhoeffer elected to expand his comfort level by grasping onto the reality of the situation.

With the help of an African-American seminarian at Union, he assisted in Sunday School classes at Harlem's Abyssinian Baptist Church. He also took excursions to Howard University and was an invited speaker to numerous secular and spiritual organizations. He read everything published by the National Association for the Advancement of Colored People. He became a fan of black gospel music and collected record albums which, in later years, would be used to introduce his German confirmation and seminarian students to Christianity and American culture.

The Social Gospel

Bonhoeffer came to America with a clear understanding of, and deep commitment to, the salvation gospel of Jesus Christ. This is captured in *John* 3:16, "For God so loved the world that he gave his one and only Son, that whoever believes in him shall not perish but have eternal life." It was his American experience, however, that brought Bonhoeffer closer to the social gospel of Jesus of Nazareth. This is best described in *Matthew* 25:31-46, portions of which read:

> Come, you are blessed by my Father; take your inheritance, the kingdom prepared for you since the creation of the world. For I was hungry and you gave me something to eat, I was thirsty and you gave me something to drink, I was a stranger and you invited me in, I needed clothes and you clothed me. I was sick and you looked after me. I was in prison and you came to visit me ... whatever you did for one of the least of these brothers of mine, you did for me.

Bonhoeffer began to fully realize that the community need for the *social gospel* in addressing the reality found in *this* world was as important as the individual need for the *salvation gospel* in preparing for the reality of the *next* world. In Bonhoeffer's mind and heart, the spiritual began to translate into the political, and the political merged with the spiritual. As a result, he grafted an enhanced understanding onto the concept of political community which rests upon a foundation of public action filtered through theocentric morality. I believe he did not view this in the vein of traditional Christian charity. Rather, it entailed a deeper, personal, and intimate involvement in the reality of God's world.

Social Gospel, Costly Grace, and Public Action

Upon returning to Germany, Bonhoeffer summoned Christians to witness the *real* (as he called it); to see the truth about the human condition and to use the words of God as moral measurement of that condition.[5] His words inferred an *intimate* involvement, one not dictated by distance or detachment, using scripture as the moral compass with which to navigate our personal and collective exploration and discovery of others in the political community. His sermons and addresses were poetic yet often blunt, especially those rendered to the German youth, calling for a social gospel based on "costly grace."

To Bonhoeffer, "costly grace is the gospel which must be sought again and again." It is costly because it costs people their lives; it is grace, because it thereby makes them live ... nothing can be cheap to us which is costly to God" (Bonhoeffer, 2003: 45). He argued that the social gospel of Jesus required one to make difficult and sacrificial choices about following Him in this world (Bonhoeffer, 2003: 43-198). Bonhoeffer juxtaposed costly grace with "cheap grace," which is the selfish act of seeking communion without offering confession; of just going through the motions of piety; of listening to Sunday sermons and not applying them throughout the week; of neglecting to seek truth in the real. He believed that cheap grace stemmed from an erroneous assumption: once a Christian's soul is saved, her work in this world is complete.

Costly grace offers no follower a "free ride." With forgiveness as a central tenant, salvation must still be acquired each and every day; it is based on keeping Christ in one's heart. Applied to the social gospel, it requires the follower to offer great sacrifice on behalf of other members of the political community and, this too, must be rendered each and every day.

Fear of Theocratic Tendencies and Secularization

Like the Founders, Bonhoeffer developed a fear of theocratic tendencies and, like them, it resulted more from experience than philosophy. For the Americans, it was in response to initial theocratic practices as well as preferential treatment given later to selected sects by various colonial legislatures. For Bonhoeffer, this fear crystallized out of the practice of, and preferential treatment given to, the Reich Church. Like Jefferson and Madison, therefore, he came to argue for a clear distinction between the boundaries of church and state (Roberts, 2005: 78). Like Jefferson and Madison, however, he also feared the consequences of the amorality and immorality ingrained in the secular world and, like them, he believed that there should be no wall between God and community.

In a series of manuscripts written between 1940 and 1943, now compiled in *Ethics* (1995), Bonhoeffer wrote "Government and Church are separate, but government and Church have the same field of action, man" (p. 346). He argued that "[t]he American democracy is not founded upon the emancipated man but, quite on the contrary, upon the kingdom of God and the limitation of all earthly powers by the sovereignty of God" (p. 105). He viewed the U.S. Constitution as a document "written by men who were conscious of original sin and of the wickedness of the human heart" (p. 105). He concluded: "the kingdom of God on earth cannot be built by the authority of the state but only by the congregation of the faithful" (p. 105).

Outward Justice

While the nature of government should not be theocratic, the task of government is more than simply a concern about secular activities in public life. He wrote, "the Church proclaims the principles of the social and political order, and the state makes available the technical means for putting them into effect" (1995: 105). In doing so, government maintains "by the power of the sword an outward justice in which life is preserved and is thus open for Christ" (Bonhoeffer, 1995: 336). Government serves God by establishing and maintaining this "outward justice," but does so in religiously neutral ways. Government leaders must reflect the moral values of God, "but the office of government [itself] remains independent of" the influence of church (Bonhoeffer, 1995: 343). He argued that "the dominion of Christ over all government does not by any means imply the dominion of church over government" and, therefore, the church cannot claim that "government should pursue a Christian policy, enact Christian laws, etc." (1995: 341, 342). Rather, the church must obey government and not interfere with government's central secular yet theocentric task of ensuring *outward justice* to advance the life of each individual who may then be "held open for Christ" (Bonhoeffer, 1995: 336).

Religious Tolerance

The seeds of religious tolerance in the political community might have been planted in the American garden, but for Bonhoeffer its fruits were cultivated and harvested in the imprisoned soil of Nazi Germany. This is reflected in one of his poems (Robertson, 1999: 51), *Christen und Heiden* (translated, *Christians and Others*).[6] While there is one line that separates Christians from others—Christians stand by God in His agony—it is clear that Bonhoeffer sees sanctity and compassion in the eyes of God for everyone, regardless of religion. In this poem (shown in Figure 2), Bonhoeffer even suggests that Christ, through His crucifixion and resurrection, removes the sins of all humankind, despite whether or not His act of salvation is acknowledged.

Figure 2
Christen und Heiden

All go to God in their distress,
seek help and pray for bread and happiness,
deliverance from pain, guilt and death.
All do, Christians and others.

All go to God in His distress,
find him poor, reviled without shelter or bread,
watch him tormented by sin, weakness, and death.
Christians stand by God in His agony.

God goes to all in their distress,
satisfies body and soul with His bread,
dies, crucified for all, Christians and others
and both alike forgiving.

In the final year of his life, Bonhoeffer expanded the idea of religious tolerance in his unfinished thoughts on "the nonreligious interpretation" of Christianity (Bethge, 2000: 853-892). He came to the realization that "the one-sided cry of 'the world for Christ' had to be counterbalanced by 'Christ for the world'" (Bethge, 2000: 856). In his unvarnished drafts, he continually probed "who Christ really is for us today" (Bethge, 2000: 864). At Tegel Prison he searched for a "universal Christ" who would have meaning for all people, but meaning in terms of where they truly live and meaning for how they truly bear responsibility for each other (Bethge, 2000: 857). This "Christ" would be non-sectarian and would not be seen through the "arcane disciplines" of individual churches (Bethge, 1997: 300).

The growing awareness of the need for religious tolerance, as a key to the theocentric morality in the political community, becomes omnipresent throughout his imprisonment. According to Bethge (2000: 871), Bonhoeffer felt "that the Gospel should be free from its trammels, understood and passed on: that it should, in other words, continue to live on in a 'nonreligious' way." Bonhoeffer practiced what he preached, as was evident on his last Sunday on earth. A fellow prisoner asked him to conduct a worship service. He initially declined because he did not want to offend the diversity of faiths in the cell room as well as the young atheist Russian officer with whom Bonhoeffer had been exchanging views about Christianity for several days. He did not want to "ambush him with a church service and thereby place religion in the way of Christ" (Bethge, 2000: 926). His sensitivity to tolerance was matched only by the tolerance of his flock in that small "political community." All—especially the atheist—begged him to conduct the service. Bonhoeffer acquiesced. That afternoon many who had worshipped with him were transported to the Flossenburg concentration camp and, the next day, were summarily hanged.

Bonhoeffer's Elaboration of the Envisioned Political Community

Bonhoeffer brings clarity to the envisioned moral foundation in at least two ways. First, he delineates the kind of theocentric morality expected within the political community. To be sure, all verses in the sacred documents of the God of Abraham comprise the moral compass intended to direct human interaction, as do all other sacred documents which are consistent with His word. For example, the Jewish (and Christian Old Testament) concept of *lex talionis* (law of retribution) and the Islamic concept of *Al-Qisaas* (law of equality) are very much part of the theocentric moral foundation.

But at its core, a place that the Founders left vague, Bonhoeffer underscores the central moral role of an *intimate social gospel*. It is the *social gospel*—meaning love, protection, nurturing, and compassion for others as each travels individual routes and collective paths through this particular lifetime. It is *intimate* because, as Bonhoeffer realized in Harlem and as too many contemporary members of the American political community have forgotten, a social gospel morality requires close examination and engaged understanding of the human condition. Love, protection, nurturing, and compassion cannot be rendered from afar or in clinical fashion. It must be presented as an intimate gift from God through a democratic political community that, while desiring advantages of individualism, ultimately embraces His morality.

Certainly an intimate social gospel as the core moral value is affirmed by the Founders' implicit worry about the kind of human interaction desired and public action envisioned in the political community. Rather than being necessarily concerned about how each member got to heaven—the salvation gospel—they sought a theocentric morality which would regulate *this-world* behavior and keep all citizens free from harm and desperation as they pursue individualistic endeavors. This would require a balance of moral strength among everyone so that no one could justify the infliction of injury or suffering upon another as a byproduct of striving to accomplish one's own dreams. While too infrequently stated as such, hence the utility of Bonhoeffer's contribution, an intimate social gospel was always the *a priori* phenomenological assumption governing public action in the American political community.

Because of the importance of religious tolerance, the moral genesis for an intimate social gospel does not have to flow from *Matthew* 25:31-46. Its civic meaning might originate from the Islamic *zakat* (compulsory annual charity/giving) or *sadaqa* (daily duty of giving extemporaneously to those in need). It could also be derived from the Jewish *tsedakah* (righteousness) or the 613 *mitzvote* (commandments). It could come from the prophet Micah (*Neviim* 6:8) who proclaims God's expectation that we "act justly and love mercy." It could come from Christian parables, like the Good Samaritan (*Luke* 10:25-37). Its civic value could derive from the Ten Commandments, moral values shared by each of the three religions of the God of Abraham. This moral expectation of a social gospel may be interpreted and implemented in a variety of ways, but its civic meaning nevertheless remains: an intimate engagement by members of the political community to understand, protect and nurture all other members.

Bonhoeffer's second contribution to the clarity of the envisioned American political community is the importance of *deliberate action*. Taken in regards to costly grace and outward justice, deliberate action does not imply a singular ideological path. For Bonhoeffer, it certainly did not require a leftist or rightist solution to the problems facing Germany. So too in the case of America; deliberate action may be pursued within the framework of liberalism or conservatism. Bonhoeffer reminds the citizen that, regardless of politics, all members of the theocentric democratic political community have the responsibility to take action regarding the fulfillment of their own duties to the community as well as the duties of their government. As Bonhoeffer realized in Tegel Prison, Germans have no one to blame but themselves when the theocentric moral foundation collapses. The same is true for Americans.

Figure 3 illustrates Bonhoeffer's contributions to the theocentric-democratic political community. Public action is regulated by intimate social gospel. Remaining at the apex is a carefully balanced rod proclaiming the task of citizenship (costly grace) and the task of government (outward justice). These obligations are inherently non-ideological; they may be performed from the political perspective of the Democratic or Republican parties. Both tasks, however, retain the civic purpose of the Founders (that of regulating public action), but they also have a clarified moral aim: regulation that advances the life of each person so that she may become open to her God or her conscience.

Because this rod rests tenuously, with the gravity of selfishness and indifference potentially casting it off the apex, the weight of deliberate action is affixed at the center. Like the weight of religious tolerance in Figure 1, this is depicted smaller and inverted to symbolize its inherently non-stationary nature. The weight could swing off keel toward total government domination and thereby translate citizens' efforts at costly grace into futile voices in the wilderness—something alien to a Lockean political community. It would turn public action into dictatorial action, and the ends of morality could easily get confused with the means of

Figure 3
Bonhoeffer's Elaboration of the Envisioned Political Community

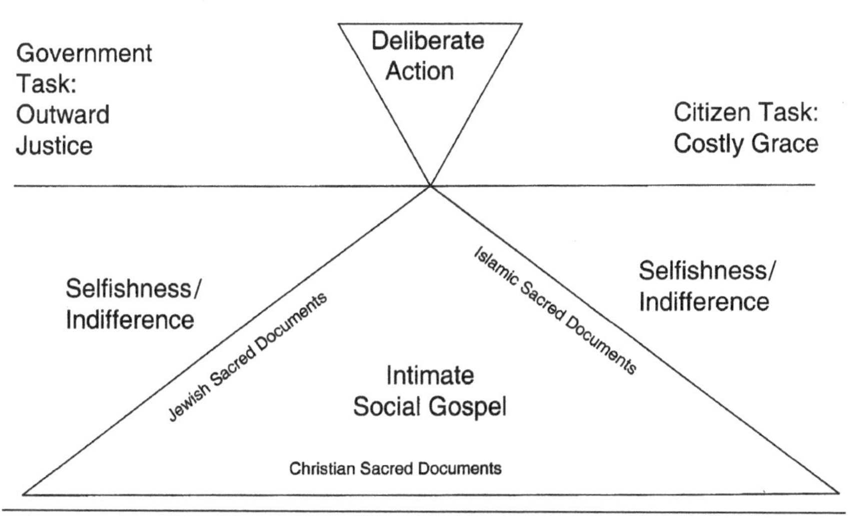

ideology. Or, it could slam in the other direction, turning the citizen task of costly grace into what John Locke described as a state of license rather than a state of liberty. A tumble in this direction would make government impotent in hearing the collective concerns of all citizens and securing a common plan for accomplishing outward justice. It would turn public action into public anarchy, the "morality" of which might also center on the means rather than the ends.

What Does It Mean to Tell the Truth?

Given Bonhoeffer's elaboration of the envisioned democratic political community, what can we learn from him about the truth in such an environment? His quest for the intimacy of truth was apparent in his reactions to experiences under the Nazi regime. His concern for the truth, as well as the shame he felt about the failure of truth's survival in the political community, is evident in excerpts from his poem *Nachtliche Stimmen* (translated, *Voices in the Night*), written in Tegel Prison in 1944 (Robertson, 1999: 62-63). This is illustrated in Figure 4.

Truth Defined

Bonhoeffer began to write on the issue of truth between 1940 and 1943. On December 5, 1943 Bonhoeffer wrote (Bethge, 1997: 158-159) "Speaking the truth ... means, in my opinion, saying *how something really is.*" But for Bonhoeffer, what "really is" must be placed within the context of theocentric morality. He writes (1995: 364, italics mine): "The assigned purpose of our words, *in unity with the word of God*, is to *express the real, as it exists in God....*"

Figure 4
"Nachtliche Stimmen"

...We learned to call lies just
uniting ourselves with the unjust.
When violence was done to the weak,
Our cold eyes did not speak...
...Shrinking from pain and poor in deeds,
We have betrayed Thee before men.
Though we saw lies raise their head,
We dishonored the truth instead.
We saw brothers dying while we had breath
and feared only our own death...

Since truth is that which "really is" only to God, what does it mean to speak untruthfully? To Bonhoeffer, lies and rationalizations are simply human reconstructions made to reflect what exists in the limited minds of their makers. Such mortal constructs represent a "denial of God" and the "deliberate destruction of the reality which is created by God" (Bonhoeffer, 1995: 364). According to Bonhoeffer (Bethge, 1997: 163-164) "'falsehood' is the destruction of, and hostility to, reality as it is in God." Hence, when we fail in telling or acting upon the truth, it is because we have sought not to find it through God. We forget that "one does not owe truthful speech to this or that individual, but solely to God" (Bonhoeffer, 1995: 359).

Bonhoeffer recognized the intricacies of his definition of truth—perhaps because of his indictment and pending trial, the testimony from which he knew may hurt many others. He noted (1995: 359) that

> Telling the truth ... is not solely a matter of moral character; it is also a matter of correct appreciation of real situations and of serious reflection upon them. The more complex the actual situations of a man's life, the more responsible and the more difficult will be his task of "telling the truth."

He recognized that "the truthful word is not in itself constant; it is as much alive as life itself" and that "every utterance or word lives and has its home in a particular environment" (1995: 360-361). However, all this is not to suggest that Bonhoeffer believed in a postmodern reconstructive truth. Far from it. He realized (1995: 361) that "the concept of a living truth is dangerous, and it gives rise to the suspicion that the truth can and may be adapted to each particular situation in a way which completely destroys the idea of truth." Hence, "when words become rootless and homeless, then the word loses truth" (Bonhoeffer, 1995: 362). While the spoken word is influenced by each set of circumstances, it nevertheless "is subject to the requirement that it shall be true" (Bonhoeffer 1995: 360).

Summary

Bonhoeffer reasoned that theocentric morality required two interrelated sources of truth. The first is Holy Scripture. Using Bonhoeffer's definition (1995: 364), truth must be found in "unity with the word of God." Truth must be found in the words of the sacred documents. The second source of truth is "the real, as it exists in God" (Bonhoeffer, 1995:

364). That is, truth must be found in the complete reality of the world as created by God.

The first source—the *Word of God*—is absolute and constant. The second source—the *real*—is absolute but remains in a state of flux and cannot be discerned simply by "throwing a religious veil over what already exists" (Bethge, 2000: 884). Reality, after all, is not "lifeless." From this second source, the truth found yesterday in God's reality may not be the same as the truth which will be found tomorrow.

The Intimacy of the Real

It is the second source of truth which is the most difficult to acquire because it requires *intimacy*. As noted by Bonhoeffer (Bethge, 1997: 369-370):

> I thought I could acquire faith by trying to live a holy life.... I discovered later, and I'm still discovering right up to this moment, that it is only by living completely in this world that one learns to have faith.... By this-worldliness I mean living unreservedly in life's duties, problems, successes and failures, experiences and perplexities. In so doing we throw ourselves completely into the arms of God, taking seriously, not our own sufferings, but those of God in the world.

Just as with faith, finding what is right and wrong from the second source of truth requires an intimate knowledge—of being "completely in this world" and wrapping ourselves "completely [in] the arms of God." But even doing that remains insufficient. Bonhoeffer requires an intimacy of others, not just ourselves. We must focus "not [on] our own sufferings, but those of God in the world." It is the *intimate social gospel* which underlies the second source of truth.

But just how can we discern truth via an intimate reality that is seen only through the eyes of God? Because mortals are made of clay, they must compensate for their frailty and pretentiousness of only *approximating* what "really is" to God. This explains Bonhoeffer's confession that he is "still discovering right up to this moment." If one can learn only by living completely in the world then the same method of inquiry must be applied to the search for a truth seen only by God. We must "unreservedly" search for the intimate evidence of truth in this world and not be tempted to rest at the point of proving our own political or theological bias or remaining at a detached and safe level of scientific inquiry.

Citizen-*Nachahmer*

How can mortals be entrusted to this search? For that matter, how can humans be entrusted to read all the applicable words of God without the bias of selectivity? Bonhoeffer's answer (2003: 288) is that the *Nachfolger des Gottes* (follower of God) must become the *Nachahmer des Gottes* (imitator of God). For Christians, it means to become "Christ-like," as described in Paul's letter to the Ephesians.[7] For non-Christian believers in the God of Abraham, *Nachahmer* means to become "God-like." While Jews and Christians believe humans are *created* in His image (*Imago Dei*), Bonhoeffer (2003: 282-283) wrote that "the aim and objective" is for us to

> *become* the image of God. Body, soul and spirit, that is, the form of being human in its totality, is to bear the image of God on earth. God is well pleased with nothing less than God's own perfect image (italics, mine).

To find the truth from God's two sources, then to speak it back to God—all of this requires mortals to imitate God, as He would have us do on His behalf in dealing with the suffering found in His world. To seek the truth about the intimate consequences of public action calls for the passive *citizen-nachfolger* (filled with a form of *civic cheap grace*) to be transformed into the deliberate *citizen-nachahmer* (filled with a form of *civic costly grace*).

A Framework for Finding the Truth about Public Action

A conceptualization of discerning truth is illustrated in Figure 5. The burden of determining truth about the intimate consequences of public action is placed directly on the shoulders of the private individual and government official. We seek truth about the *intimate* consequences of public action because the purpose of public action is to liberate members of the political community to better serve God (or the non-believer's conscience) through the social gospel. Hence, it is important to examine those intimacies in order to better understand the relationship between public action and the citizen.

Efforts to seek truth about the intimate consequences of public action are subject to harmony between two sources: sacred documents of God and "the real." If the weighted bar is unattended—if either the "word" or the "world" is neglected or abused—then the bar cascades and truth falls prey to human rationalization and lies. This is reflective of the Found-

Figure 5
Finding Truth About Public Action

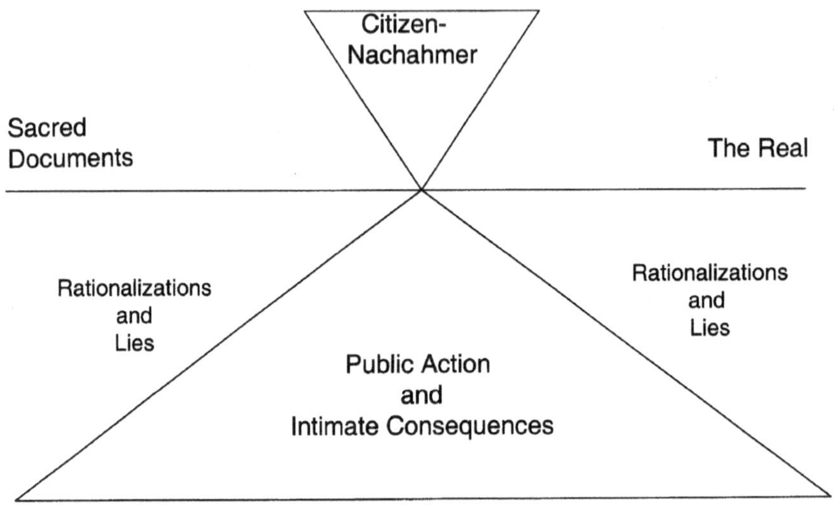

ers' fear about theocratic tendencies. People may read scripture with a selective eye toward what they want and thereby justify decisions not necessarily grounded in the word. The same is true about superficial or biased searches of the real—it can be used to limit one's perspective to fit comfortably into one's ideology or bigotry.

There is another reason to strive for harmony on that weighted bar. Recall Bonhoeffer's claim that truth found in the real must remain in unity with truth found in our sacred documents. This is a claim with which all followers of the God of Abraham certainly agree. In our search for the truth about the intimate consequences of public action, what happens when the discovered reality—the real that is created by God and presented to us each day—is not in unity with what God expects via scripture? We have three options. We can ignore scripture and view reality without a constant moral compass. We can selectively read portions of relevant scripture and thereby try to change the morality to fit each new situation. Or, we can modify the real—through the social gospel—so that its truth regains unity with the word of God. By choosing the third option, we present back to God a world of public actions and intimate consequences that is more pleasing to Him because it better reflects *Imago Dei.*

How can we ensure balance and unity? The weight which keeps in sync these two sources of truth is the requirement that each individual (private citizen and government official) become a *nachahmer des Gottes*, or imitator of God. In terms of public actions, this means each must become a *citizen-nachahmer.* Each must use *civic costly grace* to search deeply and intimately in an effort to find the truth known and presented by God—both in sacred documents and in the real. As with the balanced weight in the envisioned political community, it is inverted to indicate its tenuousness. Imitating God, after all, is risky business. It is fraught with the constant potential of human failure. Both the Founders and Bonhoeffer discovered this to be the case in their respective life experiences. Because of the prospects of human failure in seeking God's truth, the inverted triangle is smaller and detached and, hence, signifies that this mandate is not part of the theocentric moral fabric of the political community—it is a theocentric directive and a human process, but not a moral value in itself.

Summary of Conceptualization

A theocentric path to truth is chosen because it fits into the vision intended for the American political community. Cognizant of the relationship between man and God, the Founders envisioned this community to have as its foundation the morality of the God of Abraham. The Founders were not necessarily interested in how one might get to heaven, but rather how citizens should interact in this world and how public action should reflect the intended nature of interaction. Ever fearful of theocratic domination, the Founders embraced a real but limited degree of religious tolerance and right of conscience. Moral values pertaining to human interaction—from secular and non-Abrahamic sources—were allowed to prosper as long as those values did not conflict with the *this-world* morality given by Abraham's God.

Central to *this-world* morality is the *intimate social gospel*—an expression of servitude and agape love toward every member of the political community. Like the Founders, Bonhoeffer was less concerned about "heaven" in the 1940s world of death and destruction than he was in the comparatively pastoral times leading up to that period. The moral command of Jesus to "love your neighbor" as yourself is a command for *intimacy* requiring *deliberate action* by everyone in *this* lifetime, for *this* political community. Each member of the political community must expend *civic costly grace*—much more than a minimal effort and sacrifice—to ensure the image of God (*Imago Dei*) is loved, nurtured, and protected in this lifetime. Government officials have an obligation to apply proactively the concept of social gospel through policies that ensure *outward justice* for all citizens and, thereby, freeing each person to engage in tasks requiring *civic costly grace* on behalf of others.

Applying the social gospel in the democratic political community requires finding the intimacy of God's truth about public actions affecting the human condition. Bonhoeffer argues that this kind of truth can only be found through two sources: (1) the word of God, which is absolute and constant, and (2) the reality that is presented by God each day and is, therefore, absolute but always changing. In order to acquire and act upon this kind of truth, all who reside in the political community must accept the role of *citizen-nachahmer,* or "imitator of God," as it applies to public actions and their intimate consequences. When reality does not stand in unity with morality, it is the real which must be modified to match the word so that it can be presented back to God as a more pleasing and just reflection of Him. Doing so renders a morally stronger political community, one in which public action is well justified.

Notes

1. For instance, see: *Virginia Articles, Laws and Orders* (1610-1611) and *Pennsylvania Freedom of Conscience* (1682).
2. Unless otherwise cited, material pertaining to the life, death, and activities of Dietrich Bonhoeffer comes from Eberhard Bethge (2000), *Dietrich Bonhoeffer: A Biography.*
3. His final recorded words, spoken to the remaining inmates as guards came to transport him to Flossenburg, were: "This is the end—for me the beginning of life" (Bethge, 2000: 927).
4. At the age of twenty-four, his reputation as a theologian and scholar was growing. His *Habilitationschrift,* or scholarly qualifying thesis—*Akt und Sein* (translation, *Act and Being*)—rendered a faculty position at the prestigious Friedrich-Wilhelm University in Berlin, just like his father. (*Akt und Sein* would be published in 1931.) His licensing thesis, *Sactorum Communio*, was published in September of 1930.
5. Dietrich Bonhoeffer became a leading dissenter to the growing nazification of his country. He was involved in the Christian youth movement in Europe, and published *Nachfolge* (translated as *Discipleship*) which outlined the costs of being a Christian in contemporary German society. In 1934 Bonhoeffer helped create the *Bekennende Kirche* or Confessing Church in opposition to the *Gleichschaultung*—the Nazi reorganization law which placed all the Protestant sects into one governmental agency known as the *Reich Kirche*, or Reich Church. The *Gleichschaultung* required a pledge of allegiance by all clergy to Adolf Hitler as Head of Church. He also helped author the Barmen Declaration, written in response to the nazification of the Protestant churches, proclaiming the words of Christ to be above and before all politics and public policy. He continued to lecture at Confessing Church seminaries

until the Gestapo closed them. His sermons were then circulated underground by former students.

6. Edwin Robertson notes that the poem's German title, *Christen und Heiden*, is translated as Christians and Others, even though the German word *Heiden* means Pagan. This is done because the word "pagan" is used much more harshly in the English language than it is in German. He gives the example that Jews often refer to Christians as *Heiden* in German and it is interpreted not in pejorative fashion. Since the theme is "forgiveness" and "tolerance," the title is translated to match Bonhoeffer's meaning.
7. It is easy to misinterpret what Bonhoeffer (and Paul in *Ephesians*) means by "imitator." This does not mean competing with God or creating one's own God. The phrase, imitators of God, is a reminder that, regardless of station or situation, all members of the political community are precious in His sight and, consequently, we must "imitate" God by keeping them precious in our sight, too.

2

The Word of God and Other Reasoning

The conceptual framework requires members of the American political community to embrace the role of *citizen-nachahmer*, or "imitator" of God, in the pursuit of truth about public action and the intimate consequences from those actions. The community's moral foundation centers on *this-world* morality offered by the God of Abraham. The core value of that morality is an *intimate social gospel*, which the *citizen-nachahmer* is charged with seeking through a *civic costly grace*. The social gospel mandates nurturing and protecting all members in the political community as each one pursues her individual goals in life. The social gospel is, above all, the "golden rule" and is characterized by intimacy because it requires close and engaged accounting of the human condition.

Truth about public action and its intimate consequences is derived from two sources which must be concordant: the *Word of God* and, what Dietrich Bonhoeffer called, *the real*—the world created by God and presented to us each day. When the real and the word are not in sync, it is the responsibility of the *citizen-nachahmer* to modify the real so that it is in unity with the morality found in the sacred documents. This affords us an opportunity to present back to God a reality of public action which is pursuant of the social gospel and, subsequently, more pleasing to Him. We want to please God because of the theocentric moral foundation of the political community.

This chapter explores the first source of truth in the conceptual framework—the word of God as it applies to public action concerning abortion[1] and capital punishment.[2] The focus is on sacred documents of the three religions which claim the God of Abraham: Judaism, Christianity, and Islam. In order for the weight of religious tolerance to remain steadfastly balanced at the apex of the theocentric moral foundation (see Figure 1), the rights of the "non-believer" to exercise her free conscience in determining moral truth must be protected. Hence, secular reasoning about abortion and capital punishment is also examined.

Sanctity of Life in the Word of God

In Judeo-Christian tradition, the sanctity—or *holiness*—of human life can be traced to *Breisheet* (*Genesis*) 1:26-27. On the sixth day of creation, God said "Let us make man in our own image, in our likeness. So God created man in his own image, in the image of God he created him; male and female he created them." The idea of *Imago Dei*—men and women created *by* God and in *His* image—means that human beings are precious in His sight and, therefore, obligates everyone to hold all others as equally precious in their own sight.

Sanctity of life is also expressed throughout the Christian New Testament. Jesus calls each follower to "love your neighbor as yourself" (*Mark:* 12:31). The social gospel is based on the holiness of humanity; as Jesus said, "whatever you did for one of the least of these brothers of mine, you did for me" (*Matthew* 25:40). Jesus upholds that sanctity by declaring (*Matthew* 19:18): "Do not murder."

Although the *Qur'an* does not recognize human beings as *Imago Dei*, its scriptures indicate that humans are special in the eyes of God and are uniquely invested with His spirit. In the *surah* (chapter) *Al-Hijr* (*The Stoneland*) 29, God says "I have fashioned him and breathed into him My spirit." *Al-Isra* (*The Children of Israel*) 33 states: "Nor take a life—which God has made sacred—except for just cause." In *Al-An'am* (*The Cattle*) 151: "take not life, which God has made sacred, except by way of justice and law."

Abortion and Judaism

A *developed* human being may be sacred, but what about an unborn baby? While abortion is never explicitly discussed, Hebrew scriptures give more affirmation to the defense of the unborn than they do to the rights of the mother. In *Breisheet* 1:28, God shows His concern about the unborn and their role in the future of the earth: "be fruitful and increase in number, fill the earth and subdue it." In *Breisheet* 25:21-22, Rebekah becomes pregnant with Isaac's sons, Jacob and Esau, and "the *babies* jostled each other within her" and "two nations were within her womb." Note that Moses uses the word "*babies*" in reference to the embryos in Rebekah's womb. Even prior to the birth of Moses, *Shmot* (*Exodus*) 1:16 chronicles the Egyptian king's order to midwives: "When you help the

Hebrew women in childbirth and observe them on the delivery stool, if it is a boy, kill him; but if it is a girl, let her live." Hence, the king ordered the midwives to perform a kind of partial-birth abortion.[3] Because the midwives disobeyed the king, God rewarded them: "So God was kind to the midwives and ... because the midwives feared God, he gave them families of their own" (*Shmot* 120-21).

God says in *Yermiya* (*Jeremiah*) 1:5: "Before I formed you in the womb, I knew you." Even though He is talking specifically about Jeremiah, God does not indicate He knows more about *this* future prophet than He does about any other unborn person. Hence, scripture gives no reason to assume that God is unaware of the identity of *other* developing unborn human beings even before they enter the womb. This relationship between the unborn and God is affirmed further in *Yisheyah* (*Isaiah*) 49:16 where God says that He has carved, in the palm of His hand, the name of the person He creates and, therefore, He will never forget who is made in His image. Other *Tanakh* verses affirm God's knowledge of unborn babies. In *Iyov* (*Job*) 3:3, the Hebrew word *"gebher"*—a term typically reserved for a child—is used in reference to Job when he was in his mother's womb. At 10:8-12, Job reminds God that "Your hands shaped me and made me.... you molded me like clay ... clothe me with skin and flesh and knit me together with bones and sinews....You gave me life and showed me kindness, and in your providence watched over my spirit." *Qohelet* (*Ecclesiastes*) 11:5 states that "as you do not know ... how the body is formed in a mother's womb, so you cannot understand the work of God, the Maker of all things." *Tehilim* (*Psalms*) 22:10 reminds the believer that "from my mother's womb, you have been my God."

It is difficult to find Hebrew scripture that supports abortion. According to pro-choice advocate Laurie Zoloth (2003: 22), this "necessitates a call for reclaiming central rabbinic texts by creative reading." Accordingly in *Ba-Midbar* (*Numbers*) 5:11-30, if a husband suspects his wife of infidelity, then both must go to the rabbi and he gives her "bitter water that brings a curse." If she was faithful to her husband, then the drink will not harm her and she will still be able to have children. But if she has defiled herself, then the drink will "go into her and cause bitter suffering; her abdomen will swell and her thigh waste away, and she will become an accursed woman among her people." Zoloth argues that this passage justifies the use of medication (the bitter water) to induce abortion.

The argument is also made that Hebrew scripture shows God's concern with overpopulation, and this justifies abortion. Joel Cohen (1995: 6) claims that this is verified on a Hebrew tablet found in Babylon which required followers to limit fertility. Jack Miles (1995) argues that God has always been concerned with population control and points to the *Breisheet* account of the flood as proof. Whether or not His concern is with over-population or just sinful living within that population, God does say in *Breisheet* 6:7, "I will wipe mankind, whom I have created, from the face of the earth ... for I am grieved that I have made them." Hence the argument: if God created humans *Imago Dei* and God can destroy humans, then the God-granted power and freedom of choice should enable humans to destroy a human embryo or a fetus for the sake of environmental concerns.

Linda Myrsiades (2002) offers another creative reading of Hebrew scripture, one based on sexism. In 1 *Melakhim* (*Kings*) 3 we find King Solomon's dilemma about two women claiming one baby. Usually this passage is viewed as a pro-life message since Solomon's remedy is not to split the baby. However, Myrsiades argues that King Solomon simply limited the options to either life or death and, hence, drastically minimized the choices before the two women. In doing so, King Solomon "victimized not only the child but also the woman.... Indeed, both mothers ... have been erased as mothers" (p. 169).

Abortion and Jewish Interpretation

While Hebrew scriptures defend the embryo and fetus, the *halacha* (Jewish law) establishes one justification for abortion. If the unborn child presents a risk to the life of the mother, it is then regarded as a *rodef*—a pursuer of the mother with the intent to kill her (Eisenberg, 2007). The *Mishna* (*Oholot* 7:6) states that "if a woman has [life-threatening] difficulty in childbirth, the embryo within her must be dismembered limb by limb [if necessary], because her life [*hayyeha*] takes precedence over its life [*yayyav*]. Once its head (or its greater part) has emerged, it may not be touched, for we may not set aside one life [*nefesh*] for another." The life of the unborn is potential because it is not a *nefesh* and, consequently, the *halacha* says that potential life cannot compete with the actual human life. While full rights do not occur until the baby's head (or its greater part) exits the womb, *Oholot* 7:6 also indicates that the abortion must be precluded if the mother's life can be saved by perhaps severing just a limb of the fetus. Hence, every effort must be made to save the life of the unborn as well as the mother. Jewish scholars have long argued that when a baby is deliberately aborted without cause (*rodef*), punishment for the mother may include death (Jewish Encyclopedia, 1901-06).

Abortion and Christianity

Because much of the Christian faith stems from its Hebrew past, scriptures found in what is called the Old Testament (the *Tanakh*) are not necessarily repeated in the New Testament. As in the Old Testament, the word "abortion" is not mentioned in the New Testament. Still a pattern is borne of God knowing the unborn baby—and knowing her by name—even before she enters the womb. The first chapter of *Luke* indicates that Jesus entered this world as a conceived zygote, with the angel Gabriel telling Mary "you are to give him the name Jesus" (1:31). In *Luke* 1:13, an angel comes to Zechariah, the future father of John the Baptist, and says: "Your wife Elizabeth will bear you a son, and you are to give him the name John." God's knowledge of the unborn is also indicated in *Galatians* 1:15 where Paul claims that He knew him in the womb.

It is important to underscore that the above passages use the Greek word "*brephos*" in reference to the unborn babies known as Jesus of Nazareth and John the Baptist. At that time, *brephos* was usually reserved for describing newborn babies—as in *Acts* 7:19 and 1 *Peter* 2:2. Using *brephos* to describe babies in the womb is further indication that God's love for, or knowledge about, the unborn is equal to the born.

Christian scripture indicates that God has plans for the unborn, and He knows those plans prior to conception. In *Luke* 1:32, the angel Gabriel tells Mary that Jesus "will be great and will be called the Son of the Most High." In *Luke* 1:15, an angel tells Elizabeth that her yet conceived son, John the Baptist, "will be filled with the Holy Spirit even from birth." According to *Ephesians* 2:10, Paul argues that God has specific work "prepared in advance for us to do."

There is perhaps a casuistry of scriptural support for abortion in the New Testament. Jesus says to Judas in *Matthew* 26:24: "woe to that man who betrays the Son of Man! It would be better for him if he had not been born." This is often interpreted by pro-choice advocates as meaning that, in some circumstances, it might be better for a baby to be aborted. Brian Elroy McKinley (2003) argues that the births of Jesus and John the Baptist were exceptional, miraculous events, just as were the births of Old Testament prophets. Hence, the argument goes that scripture lessons about these men cannot be extrapolated to issues pertaining to the sanctity of life of all humankind.

Abortion and Early Christian Interpretation

Abortion was a concern in early Christian writings. The fourth-century *Didache* simply states: "you shall not murder a child by abortion" (Kirby, 2001). This duplicated the first century *Epistle* of Barnabas 19:5: "Thou shall not murder a child by abortion" (Lightfoot, 2007). The first-century *Tertullian's Apologeticum*, composed as a defense of Christianity against non-believers, states (Glover, 2007: 121):

> To us murder is once for all forbidden; so even the child in the womb, while yet the mother's blood is still being drawn on to form the human being, it is not lawful for us to destroy. To forbid birth is only quicker murder.... He is a man, who is to be a man; the fruit is always present in the seed.

Abortion and Islam

Abortion is not mentioned in the *Qur'an*, but it contains no scriptures which can be construed to justify that act. *An-Najm* (*The Star*) 32, states: "He knows you well when He brings you out of the earth, and when you are hidden in your mothers' wombs." God's role in procreation and human gestation processes are also affirmed. In *Al-Hijr* (*The Stoneland*) 28, God says to the angels, "I am about to create man from mud molded into shape." In *Az-Zumar* (*The Troops*) 6: "He makes you, in the wombs of your mothers, in stages, one after another, in three veils of darkness." In *Al-Muminun* (*The Believers*) 12-14:

> We created Man from a quintessence (of clay); then We placed him as (a drop of) sperm in a place of rest, firmly fixed. Then We made the sperm into a clot of congealed blood; then of that clot We made a (fetus) lump; then We made out of that lump bones and clothed the bones with flesh; then We developed out of it another creature. So blessed be God, the Best to create!

God's priority toward family and children runs throughout the *Qur'an*. *An-Nahl* (*The Bee*) 72: "And God has made for you mates (and companions) of your own nature, and made for you, out of them, sons and daughters and grandchildren...." Even in divorce, it is the responsibility of the parents to give the life of the unborn the highest priority. *At-Talaq* (*The Divorce*) 4 states: "Such of your women as have passed the age of monthly courses, for them the prescribed period, if you have any doubts, is three months ... for those who carry (life within their wombs), their period is until they deliver ... and for those who fear God, He will make their path easy." *At-Talaq* 6 reads: "they carry (life in their wombs), then spend (your substance) on them until they deliver ... and if they suckle your (offspring), give them their recompense."

Abortion and Islamic Interpretation

No Islamic source gives permission for abortion in the second trimester of pregnancy. According to Ebrahim (1989: 48), "the general teachings of the *Qur'an* and the *Sunnah* clearly establish that life in whatever form is to be preserved and is not to be destroyed except for a valid cause or reason." Are there valid Islamic reasons to justify abortion in the first trimester? Here there are several legal perspectives (Shaikh, 2003: 121-122; al-Haq, 1983: 3093-3109). The Zaydi school believes that abortion is permissible without any justification in the first trimester. The vast majority of scholars of the Hanafi and Shafi'i schools, however, believe first trimester abortion is permissible only if the mother's life is threatened. Most members of the Maliki school strongly disapprove of early abortions, and some Maliki scholars, as well as others from the (more minor) Zahiri, Ibadiyya, and Imamiyya schools, believe that abortion is absolutely prohibited in the first trimester.

Most Muslim authorities agree with either the Hanafi and Shafi'i schools, or with the Maliki scholars: "abortion is legal in one case only, and that is when the retention of the fetus or embryo in the uterus threatens the mother's life" (Shamsudden, 2007). The *nutfa amshajj* (fertilized egg) is to be protected and respected (Katme, 2007).

Capital Punishment and Judaism

If God created people *Imago Dei*, what guidance can Hebrew scripture give in regards to capital punishment? First of all, it says that murder is wrong—a point sometimes forgotten by advocates on both sides of the death penalty issue. In *Breisheet* 20:13, and then again in *Davarim* (*Deuteronomy*) 5:17, the Ten Commandments say "thou shall not murder." The Hebrew word used in this context is *ratsach*, meaning the intentional or premeditated killing of someone. The word *nakah* is reserved for situations where the killing of another person may not be premeditated or perhaps accidental. In *Shmot* 21:13, we read "if he does not do it [*nakah*] intentionally he is to flee to a place I will designate." What happens if murder, *ratsach*, is committed? Here the Hebrew message is a bit more mixed than in the case of abortion, permitting both sides of the death penalty issue to find some moral comfort. One finds scriptures that confirm the concept of *lex talionis*, or the law of retribution: *Breisheet* 9:6 "Whoever sheds the blood of a man, by man shall his blood be shed....''; *Va-Yikra* (*Leviticus*) 24:17 "If anyone takes (*ratsach*) the life of a human being, he must be put to death." *Ba-Madbar* 35:16-21 reveals the crimes that permit the death penalty: *ratsach* via an iron object, stoning, wooden objects, shoving, throwing something, or using fists. *Davarim* (*Deuteronomy*) 19:19-21 underscores the ultimate purpose of *lex talionis*: a warning to others who might also commit *ratsach*.

Yet there are also Hebrew scriptures which demonstrate *rachamin* (compassion), *chesed* (acts of lovingness), and an abstention from *lex talionis*. *Breisheet* 4 offers the story of Cain murdering (*ratsach*) his brother Abel. Rather than destroying Cain, God sentences him to a kind of life-without-the-possibility-of-parole: condemned to always being a "restless wanderer" and marked so that no one will end his misery. In *Shmot* 2:11-22, forgiveness is also shown to Moses after murdering an Egyptian guard. Despite the fact that Moses looked "this way and that and seeing no one," indicating a premeditation (*ratsach*), God still did not take his life.

Capital Punishment and Jewish Interpretation

The *halacha* leads to one basic conclusion: the death penalty is permissible but its imposition is never a requirement. *Makkot* (1:10) states that its use should be difficult and rare, and Jewish custom and law opposes its use if injustice results (Kermaier, 2007). When used, the *Talmud* requires a very high standard for conviction: (1) there must be at least two eyewitnesses who agree completely with the facts of the case, (2) there must be more than simply circumstantial evidence, (3) the murderer must be warned in advance about the consequences of his projected actions, and (4) the murderer must acknowledge that he understands the substance of the warning (Simmons, 2007).

Capital Punishment and Christianity

Notions of forgiveness and mercy are the hallmarks of the New Testament. In *John* 8:1-11, Pharisees brought an adulterous woman to Jesus and said, "In the Law Moses commanded us to stone such women. Now what do you say?" Jesus replied, "if any one of you is without sin, let him be the first to throw a stone at her." In *Matthew* 5:21-22, He affirms the belief that all earthly (non-blasphemous) sins are of equal gravity. In *Matthew* 5:7, Jesus says "Blessed are the merciful, for they will be shown mercy." In *Luke* 6:27-29, 36, He says, "But I tell you who hear me: Love your enemies ... pray for those who mistreat you ... if one strikes you on the cheek, turn to him the other also" and "Be merciful, just as your Father is merciful." In *Luke* 23:24, Jesus forgave his own execution team.

Yet several passages indicate an acceptance of *lex talionis*. In *Matthew* 26:52, Jesus warns one of his disciples "put your sword back in its place ... for all who draw the sword will die by the sword." In *Luke* 20:9-16, Jesus tells the parable of the tenant farmers who kill the land-owner's son. He concludes, "what then will the owner of the vineyard do to them? He will come and kill those tenants and give the vineyard to others." In the execution of John the Baptist, both *Mark* (6:14-29) and *Matthew* (14:1-12) fail to describe any opposition to capital punishment. No one, including Jesus, opposes the execution of the two criminals on crosses next to Him (*Luke*: 23:26-42). Jesus does not even question the Roman state's authority to try, sentence and execute Him (*John* 19:11). When Paul is tried before Festus, he says, "If, however, I am guilty of doing anything deserving death, I do not refuse to die" (*Acts* (25:11)). In *Romans* (13:1-4), Paul instructs Christians to submit to state authority:

> The authorities that exist have been established by God.... For rulers hold no terror for those who do right, but for those who do wrong ... if you do wrong, be afraid, for he does not bear the sword for nothing. He is God's servant, an agent of wrath to bring punishment on the wrongdoer.

Capital Punishment and Early Christian Interpretation

The Patristic texts underscore three basic beliefs: "(1) that civil rulers have morally legitimate authority over life and death; (2) that this authority has been conferred by God and is testified to in Scripture; and (3) that Christian discipleship is incompatible with participation in violence and bloodshed" (Brugger, 2003: 75). Christians were not permitted to be involved in capital punishment, not as jurists or executioners. Beginning in the fourth century, however, Constantine recognized the Christian church as a public institution and, by definition, made it a party to executions. Christian laity could participate in capital punishment, but decrees of the Council of Toledo (675 A.D.) and the Fourth Lateran (1215 A.D.) forbade clergy from any involvement (Surtis, 1995).

Capital Punishment and Islam

The equivalent to the Judeo-Christian concept of *lex talionis* is the Islamic concept of *Al-Qisaas*—the law of equality. *Al-Ma'ida* (*The Table*)

45 reads: "We ordained therein for them a life for a life, an eye for an eye, a nose for a nose, an ear for an ear, a tooth for a tooth, and wounds equal for equal as legal retribution."

Forgiveness, however, is always a potential outcome in Islamic belief. *Al-Ma'ida* 32 states, "But whosoever forgives it (in the way of charity), it shall be an act of atonement for him." *Ash-Shura* (*The Consultation*) 40: "the recompense for an injury is an injury equal thereto (in degree), but if a person forgives and makes reconciliation, his reward is due from God." According to *Al-Baqara* (*The Cow*) 179, "In the Law of Equality there is (saving of) Life to you, O you men of understanding; that you may restrain yourselves." In *Al-Isra* (*The Children of Israel*) 33, the decision for either *Al-Qisaas* or forgiveness rests with the victim's family: "if anyone is slain wrongfully, We have given his heir authority (to demand *Qisaas* or to forgive): but let him not exceed the bounds in the matter of taking life; for he is helped (by the Law)."

Capital Punishment and Islamic Interpretation

The principle of *Al-Qisaas* is underscored in the *hadith*. According to the *Hadith-Sahih Bukhari* (#26), "the Prophet said, 'the prescribed Law of God is the equality in punishment.'" The *Hadith-Abu Huraira* (9.83.19) reads: "And if somebody is killed, his closest relative has the right to choose one of two things, i.e., either blood money or retaliation by having the killer killed."

Summary of the Word

The three religions rely on scripture for finding moral truth about public action pertaining to life and death. Jewish *halacha*, early Christian documents, and Islamic *hadith* underscore scripture or explain when deviation is permitted. These are summarized in Table 1. Each religion places a high premium on the sacredness of human life. Scriptures do not support the practice of abortion, but hold the general but quintessential notions of love and forgiveness toward sinners who do. Moral truth from scriptures are mixed when it comes to capital punishment, showing both the right of equal retaliation as well as the necessity for love and its prerequisite of forgiveness.

Other Reasoning about the Sanctity of Life

Given the mixed lessons found in sacred texts, perhaps it is understandable that persons and groups struggling to abide by the God of

Table 1
Summary of Scripture and Other Theocentric Documents: Moral Truth about Life and Death

	Hebrew Scripture	**Hebrew Halacha**	**Christian Scripture**	**Early Christian Documents**	**Islamic Scripture**	**Islamic Hadith**
Sanctity of Life	Valued: *Imago Dei*	Valued: *Imago Dei*	Valued: *Imago Dei*	Valued: *Imago Dei*	Valued: with His Spirit	Valued: with His Spirit
Abortion	Not Supported	Opposed: unless mother will die or be severely injured from pregnancy	Not Supported	Opposed: no justification of deliberate killing of unborn	Not Supported	Opposed: unless mother will die from pregnancy
Capital Punishment	Mixed: *Lex Talionis*, with examples of forgiveness	Supported: but with restrictive qualifications	Mixed: commandment to love and forgive, but no opposition to executions; government is God's agent	Supported: Civil leaders had God-given authority to execute, but Christians could not participate	Mixed: *Al-Qisaas*, with possibility of forgiveness on part of victim's family	Supported: but with restrictive qualifications

Abraham on the issue of capital punishment fall prey to factions and subsequently search for additional reasoning to supplement the moral truth found in scriptures. Death penalty opponents offer arguments about the need to place Hebrew scriptures into historical context (Yoder, 1997) or the need to place greater emphasis on the New Testament (King, 2003; Megivern, 1997). Others focus on the community side effects of *lex talionis* (Beccaria, 1767; Stassen, 2002); its inability to deter capital crimes (Bedau, 2004); its total irreversibility as a punishment (Voltaire, 1770); the suffering of the condemned (Martinez, 2002; Johnson, 1998); its economics (Benthan, 1982); its lack of fairness and equality, especially in terms of race and class in the American political community (Stevenson, 2004; Dow, 2002); or the saliency of poor quality legal representation for those on death row (Bright, 2002). Given the security and safety afforded by modern-day prisons, current Roman Catholic policies support the possibility of capital punishment while opposing its actual implementation. The *Evangelium Vitae* (Chapter III at 56) states: "the nature and extent of the punishment must be carefully evaluated and decided upon, and ought not go to the extreme of executing the offender except in cases of absolute necessity: in other words, when it would not be possible otherwise to defend society."

Capital punishment supporters reason that scriptural clarity comes from the Old Testament (Endres, 1985) or that New Testament scriptures are misunderstood (Vellenga, 2002; Van Impe, 1973). Others focus on a number of dimensions of the "just dessert" argument, that the condemned is getting what he deserves (Burns, 1995; Hand, 1881). Some point out that, because of *Imago Dei*, murder is such an affront to God that the condemned deserves to die (House, 1997). Others base their reasoning on the horrible crimes committed and the need to protect the innocent from future acts of violence (Pojman, 2004; Montaque, 1995). Some argue that *lex talionis* deters future murderous acts (Cassell, 2004; Pojman, 2004). Still others argue that, even if we are uncertain about deterrence, the "best bet" is that capital punishment stops at least one criminal from committing additional murders (van der Haag, 1975 and 1968). There are also those who defend the judicial process in making extremely difficult decisions regarding the life and death of the convicted (Kozinki, 2004; Marquis, 2004).

It is also understandable that, given the trenchant politics of abortion in the contemporary American political community, pro-life advocates look to other, non-religious sources to supplement the moral truth found in scriptures. Some reason against abortion on the basis of reproductive sciences (Condic, 2003) and highlight that the unborn are the real victims—the only ones who "are not party to the debate" (McMahan, 2003: viii). Others speak about the manipulation of women into accepting the abortion option because of selfishness or self-centeredness (Kirk, 2003), the summary rejection of the adoption choice (Jackson, 2005), or a denial of post-abortion trauma (Burke and Reardon, 2002). It is argued that manipulation of women comes from a pro-feminist media (Press and Cole, 1999). Even some pro-choice advocates claim that feminism victimizes women by refusing to "acknowledge what abortion looks like and what abortions feel like" (Simonds, 1996: 93), as well as by propagating two myths (Wolf, 1995:183-186): that abortion does not end a life and that having an abortion reflects a "desire to be a good mother" to future fetuses. Speaking about her own abortion, feminist Naomi Wolf (1995:186) admits:

> If what was going on in my mind had been mostly about the well-being of the possible baby, that pill would never have been swallowed ... No: there were two columns in my mind—"Me"' and "'Baby"—and the first won out.... Essentially, this column came down to: I am not done being responsive only to myself yet.

Given the dearth of verses upon which a theocentric moral truth can be built in support of abortion, pro-choice advocates have no real choice but to supplant other reasoning in lieu of supplementing scripture-based belief. Richard Schoenig (2001: 225) argues that (a) if the purpose of salvation is eternal life and (b) earthly life means taking a chance that you may not find salvation, and (c) if you are an unborn child, then (d) wouldn't you want to have your life aborted to guarantee your place in heaven? He concludes that "abortion positively contributes to an end that God does desire." Some (Burns, 2005:13) call for a "minimalization of morality" on this issue, while others match Zoloth's (2003) call for "creative reading" of Hebrew scriptures by offering a different twist on the New Testament. It is argued that Christian tradition is unclear on abortion (Gudorg, 2003: 68) and that religion is forced upon the American political community (Zingler, 1985). According to Patricia Baird-Windle and Eleanor J. Bader (2001: 11-12), anti-abortionists "take power from their relationship to a God they believe speaks directly to them" and they are "intent on 'saving America' and imposing 'biblical authority' on its people, surrendering autonomy and the power of individual decision making ... submission to a judgmental and punishing God...."

The pro-choice archetype of reconstructive scripture stems from the Christian parable of the Good Samaritan (*Luke* 10:25-37), where a man traveling from Jerusalem to Jericho is attacked, robbed, and left injured alongside the road. Passers-by ignore the man's plight until a "lowly" Samaritan comes along. This "Good Samaritan" bandages the man, takes him to an inn for convalescence, and covers all costs. The parable teaches a lesson of how far God expects us to "travel" in showing love for our neighbor, in pursuing the intimacy of the social gospel.

Judith Jarvis Thomson (1971: 64-65) reconstructs this parable: Assume you awake in bed only to discover that someone (in her parable, a world-class violinist) with a potentially fatal ailment is attached to your kidneys. This musician has to remain for a nine-month period in order to have a chance at survival. The dilemma is this: If you permit this attachment, which means you must lay with her and curtail all your plans for the next nine months, she will survive and most likely produce wonderful music for humankind. If you choose to disconnect, and go about your life's business, she will certainly die. As much as you may like to help this violinist survive, and thereby benefit the world, the burden is so great that you decide to sever the attachment. Thomson argues that doing so is OK: "we are not morally required to be Good Samaritans—only Minimally Decent Samaritans." We are only required to do what is "minimally decent"—consider the consequences for both yourself and the other life and then make a decision based on the amount of effort you wish to invest. The fact that you considered all options makes you a "minimally" decent person.

Thomson (p. 65) argues that the same is true in the case of pregnancy: "If assuming responsibility for [a child] would require large sacrifices, then [the woman] may refuse." She has thought things through, weighed the pros and cons for both her and the unborn baby, and came to a rational conclusion. Morally she can claim to be a minimally decent Samaritan.

Leslie Cannold (2000: 134) advances Thomson's thesis in describing the "moral circle" of justifications given by pro-choice women who had abortions. At the circle's outer limits are self-centered reasons: "the athlete who becomes pregnant and has an abortion to improve her performance; women aborting an intended pregnancy to take up a contest winning of a trip overseas." As one gets closer to the center of this circle, the focus turns to the morality of killing out of love for the unborn: "each woman's abortion decision will be made thoughtfully, sorrowfully, and with respect for the sacredness of pregnancy and with love for the could-be child. That women's decision will be, in other words, responsible ones to kill from care."

Some base their reasoning on the tenets of science, both criticizing it for offering too great a glimpse of the unborn through ultrasound imagery (Solinger, 1998) but rejoicing in results which claim the lack of embryonic and fetal viability in the first trimester (Shrage, 2003; McKinley, 2003). Still others find morality in the service that abortion clinic owners and workers provide to women in America—a service which is performed in spite of the profound potential of violence by extremists in the pro-life movement (Press, 2006; Lyons, 2005). Others reason that abortion is an instrument of social justice, one capable of addressing such issues as overpopulation (Mc-quire, 2003), the consequences of rape (Saletan, 2003; Bitler and Zavodny, 2002), adverse emotional consequences of adoption (Cannold, 2000; Clair, 1995), and the financial limitations of woman who cannot afford to raise a child (Levine, 2004). Others reason that abortion is a way to ensure greater freedom, equality, and personal growth for women (Albrecht, 2003; Boyle, 1997). Another justification which underlies the feminist position on abortion stems from the gains made in the sexual revolution of the 1960s and 1970s. As Christina Page (2006: xiii) states, pro-choice advocates are "simply not sticking up for the right to an abortion. We are taking a stand on sex." Regardless of particular strategy, Gloria Albrecht (2003: 86) is correct in concluding that "the feminist reconstruction [of abortion] history was impressively accomplished."

Ideological justifications for abortion find their collective genesis in a publication authored by the Marquis de Sade (1795; 2006). *Philosophy in the Boudoir*, laden with graphic pornography, was widely read across Europe in the late eighteenth century, and shortly thereafter the number of abortions on that continent began to escalate (Farr, 1980: 9). Its popularity captured the thoughts of those who benefitted from the Enlightenment, especially the intellectual class, and there is no reason to assume that American visitors to the continent failed in returning home with copies of de Sade's masterpiece. Just as Dr. William Cooper (1772) presented the first clinical justifications for abortion (in lieu of caesarian sections) at that time, it was de Sade who became "the spiritual progenitor of the widespread use of induced abortion ... for social, economic, and political purposes, which is so evident today" (Farr, 1980: 9).

Philosophy in the Boudoir is actually written as a play about a group of "libertines" and their sexual activities during one single day. In between and often during various acts of sex, they also engage in philosophical discussions about religion and abortion. The plot begins as bisexual Madame De Saint-Ange becomes the "sex instructor" for a female child, Eugénie, whom she met by chance on a visit to a convent the prior year. Sparks flew but nothing could be done at that time because the nuns were watching. The Madame befriends Eugénie's parents (secretly having sex with her father) in order to gain their confidence and permission to invite their little girl to her house for an innocent "sleep over." Upon Eugénie's arrival to the Madame's house, they are joined by a bisexual man named Dolmancé, who is the story's primary philosopher as well as a "teacher's aide" to Madame De Saint-Ange. Their collective goal is to rid Eugénie of theocentric morality so that she can become a true "libertine" of the republic. Group and individual sex of all sorts is supported by the Madame's incestuous bisexual brother, known as "the Chevalier." These primary actors are also assisted by the Madame's butler and gardener. The encounters begin during the morning and, by the evening, Eugénie's mother, Madame De Mistival, arrives at the house of Madame De Saint-Ange because she suspects something's afoul and wants to retrieve her daughter. By this time, however, Eugénie has embraced completely the "philosophy in the boudoir," and she has practiced that philosophy in multiple ways with multiple combinations of partners throughout the day. She has become quite the eager little libertine of the republic—rejecting all morality except earthly values which bring immediate gratification. Upon her mother's intrusion, Eugénie orchestrates a gang rape of De Mistival. Finally, the Chevalier escorts the ravished woman home, without Eugénie, and gives her strict instructions never to interfere with her twelve-year-old daughter's libertinage. Upon the Chevalier's return, everyone enjoys a nice dinner and prepares for bed—a night of complete indulgence.

Why is this book important to the issue of abortion in the American political community? It is the first popular publication to damn the application of scripture-based morality to issues confronting citizens of a democratic society. Furthermore de Sade's viewpoints are the same as those taken by contemporary pro-choice advocates. Because the reasons they offer are rooted throughout his publication, the Marquis de Sade is actually the unsung poster boy of contemporary abortion defenders.

Through a series of barrages, De Sade attacks the role of religion in forming the moral basis of society. The character Dolmancé argues that "God is merely the ne plus ultra of human reason ... the product of either fear or weakness" (p. 24). He states: "Christian morality, too vague about inter-human relations, sets up doctrines so full of sophisms that we cannot possibly accept them..." (p. 118). To limit its moral impact, he begs, "with the greatest care, avoid mixing any religious fable whatsoever into the national education" (p. 112). He concludes that "[i]n this century, we are furthermore convinced that religion must be based on morality and not morality on religion" (p.104).

The seeds of the "Minimally Decent Samaritan" are planted firmly in the soil of Dolmancé's logic. He speaks about the concept of benevolence as being "more a vice of pride than a true virtue of the soul. A person comforts his fellow man purely in order to show off and never simply to do good" (p. 29). He reads from a libertine political flyer: "This absurd [Christian] morality tells us to love our neighbors as ourselves. Nothing would assuredly be more sublime if it were possible for deceit to bear the traits of beauty" (p. 118).

The characters Madame De Saint-Ange and Dolmancé teach freely, both to the young Eugénie as well as to the intellectual class reading de Sade's play, about the virtues of abortion. Dolmancé proclaims that abortion is an answer to overpopulation: "every individual who is born without the qualities needed to be valuable some day to the republic has no right to live. And the best we can do is to end his life the very instant he receives it" (pp. 144-145).

Contemporary values of self-centeredness and self-indulgence are also underscored. Madame proclaims to little Eugénie: "like men, you will enjoy all the delights that nature has made your obligations; you will not have to be constrained in any pleasure" (132). She promises: "A pretty girl should concentrate only on fucking, and never on bearing children ... and we will chiefly and uniquely align ourselves with the libertine delights, whose spirit never cares about breeding" (p. 16). The Madame promises "[t]here is no barrier to pleasure outside of your own strength and will; no exception beyond place, time, and person" (pp. 32-33). She explains to twelve-year-old Eugénie her right to an abortion: "a woman is always the mistress of what she carries in her womb, and there is as little wrong with destroying this kind of material as there is with purging the other kind of medicaments, if we feel the need" (p. 61). Dolmancé concurs: "we became as certain the masters of this lump of flesh—however animated—as we are the masters of the nails we cut from our fingers, or the outgrowths we remove from our bodies, or the digestives we expel from our innards; that's because they all come from us and they all belong to us, and we are the sole owners of whatever derives from us" (p. 62).

Conclusions

Standing on the gallows at Flossenburg concentration camp, Dietrich Bonhoeffer knew that applying the moral scriptures of God to the complexity of contemporary human life is not an easy task. Should the words of God be taken literally? Should scripture be interpreted to allow differences in conclusions? Should they be completely ignored—or even damned—when the message is not to our liking? There is a Hebrew saying: *Elu v'Elu Drivre Elohim Chayyim*, which roughly translates, "these and these words of the Living God." It means that all the words in scripture belong to Him, and no single verse holds greater moral truth than another. This is consistent with our model of theocentric moral truth.

While scriptures are not contradictory to the believer, some verses may speak more loudly to our pre-disposed political and ideological ears. It therefore becomes understandably difficult to accept the obligation of the *citizen-nachahmer*—that is, an imitator of God who expends deliberately a *civic costly grace* in the pursuit of moral truth about public action and its intimate consequences on the successes and failures of the social gospel in the American political community. If we are concerned with the relationship between public morality and public action, however, we have no choice but to accept the responsibilities of the *citizen-nachahmer*; we must do so regardless of degree of difficulty. To accept a lesser obligation means to fall prey to being a *nachfolger*—a follower, not of God, but of "truths" based on human rationalizations.

In the case of capital punishment, the fact that the *citizen-nachahmer* can choose different scriptural paths gives further credence of Bonhoeffer's call to seek His truth simultaneously in the real—the world as presented by God. Bonhoeffer (1995: 360) reminds us that if the truthful word "is detached from life and from its reference to the concrete other man ... then this truth has only the appearance of truth, but it lacks its essential character."

The problem is that both pro- and anti-death penalty forces, armed with an arsenal of moral truth from scripture, tend to seek and present only their view of the real—typically either through lop-sided statistics or one-sided examples—rather than strive to approximate God's view of the real. While this is a human trait, a more intimate and deliberate exploration of the real as presented by God each day is needed if we are to sincerely seek truth about the people who are affected by murder and capital punishment. The truth emanating from that exploration must then be reconciled with the truth found in the word.

But what about abortion? Scripture does not support abortion and, therefore, pro-choice followers—the *nachfolgers* of de Sade—must look elsewhere for a moral basis of truth. Without the affirmation of scripture, that truth is hard to find and harder to justify. Bonhoeffer (1995: 364) reminds us that the expression of the real must always be "in unity with the word of God." Their expression of "truth" is not, and there lies the rub.

When moral truth of scripture does not support our ideological positions, we tap the fears expressed by James Madison and Samuel Huntington in the debate (Debate 1789; Frohnen, 2002) over the First Amendment language: the right of conscience and religious tolerance might well end up patronizing "those who professed no religion at all" to the detriment of all believers in the God of Abraham. Within the pro-choice movement, there is proclivity to belittle biblical verse and damn those who proclaim it. They seek to exclude Holy Scripture from this great debate. As noted by Bonhoeffer (1995: 103), this kind of dynamic results in a "religion of hostility to God," and this is detrimental to the envisioned theocentric foundation of the American political community. It comes as no surprise, therefore, that the scripturally disarmed pro-choice movement seeks to limit access to the real of abortion, keeping its public action as private as possible and hiding its intimate consequences under a bushel. It is the real of abortion which we seek next.

Notes

1. Abortion is the termination of pregnancy through the voluntary and premature expulsion of a developing unborn human being. It is terminal because the process concludes with the ending of life. It is voluntary in the sense that a woman chooses to abort the embryo or fetus. It is premature because it occurs before the completion of the nine-month gestation period. It involves a developing unborn human being because that is the biological definition of a human embryo or human fetus. See Rauch, 2006; Percy, 1991.
2. Capital punishment occurs when government, through its collective and deliberate judicial decisions and resultant penal actions, intentionally but legally causes the death of a developed human being who has committed murder. Death of a developed human being is defined as permanent cessation of electrical activity in the brain. See Kerrigan, 2007; Kastenbaum, 2006; Novak, 2006.
3. Within Judaism, there is disagreement over this interpretation of whether or not this act constituted partial birth abortion or simply murder because of the head appearing. This verse is used by Christian Evangelicals to demonstrate similarity, not contrast, between partial-birth abortion and murder.

3

The Real of Abortion

In *Stages on the Way to Freedom* (Robertson, 1999: 73), Dietrich Bonhoeffer writes:

> Choose and do what is right, not what fancy takes,
> not weighing the possibilities, but bravely grasping for the real,
> not in the flight of ideas, but only in action is there freedom.
> Come away from your anxious hesitations into the storm of
> events, carried by God's command and your faith alone.
> Then freedom will embrace your spirit with rejoicing.

This chapter explores the *real* of abortion. The normative framework in Chapter 1 calls for members of the American political community to act as *citizens-nachahmer*—civic imitators of God—and seek truth about the intimate consequences of public action, like abortion, from the *Word* of God and the *World* of God. That is, truth found in scripture about abortion must be accompanied by truth found in the real about abortion as it is presented by God each day. The truth that comes from that reality must then be reconciled with the truth which flows from the word of God.

To the skeptic—theologian, atheist, or social scientist—I admit freely the obvious impossibility of capturing the totality of the world He creates about abortion. Neither theology nor science affords this opportunity. Bonhoeffer reminds us (1995: 70) that "to understand reality is not the same as to know about events. It is to perceive the essential nature of things." We can try to gain that phenomenological perception—of understanding "the essential nature of things"—by rejecting the safety of our physical, ideological, and scientific comfort zones—"coming away from [our] anxious hesitations"—and expanding what we normally see. We do this by paying closer attention to the intimacy of life which may otherwise fall to the wayside. If we do this, then we are equipped to plunge into the "storm of events" of public action. It is our actions, after all, not just our ideas, which "must bravely [grasp] for the real."

Abortion in the American Political Community

It was not until the late eighteenth century that abortion was referenced in professional medical documents. Given the limitations to the science of anesthesiology, Dr. William Cooper (1772) presented it as an alternative procedure to caesarean sections when the life of the mother was threatened. Truth is, abortion has been practiced since the early years of the American political community—although the degree to which it was embraced is widely disputed (Myrsiades, 2002; Mohr, 1978). Organized opposition to its practice emerged in the nineteenth century with founding feminists—Susan B. Anthony and Victoria Woodhull—arguing for abstinence and adoption in lieu of abortion. The American Medical Association (AMA) opposed abortion on the basis of morality (Brennan, 1983), safety (Herring, 2003), and to eliminate midwifery competition (Stormer, 2002). From these arguments emerged the first sets of laws banning or regulating abortion.

As urbanization and modernity continued, however, increasing numbers of women chose to have illegal abortions (Critchlow, 1999; Fuchs, 1991). Pro-abortion advocates greatly benefitted from the post-WWII civil rights and New Left movements. By the 1960s the AMA changed its policy, stating abortion "is a personal and moral consideration which in all cases must be faced according to the dictates of the conscience of the patient and her physician" (Brennan, 1983: 91). Advocacy groups, such as "Jane," emerged to empower women to make their own choices about abortion (Kaplan, 1998). In 1973 the U.S. Supreme Court issued a 7-2 ruling, *Roe v. Wade*, which deemed state laws prohibiting abortion as violating rights to privacy guaranteed under the Due Process Clause of the Fourteenth Amendment.

About fifty million abortions have been performed since *Roe*. Numbers rose to well over one million per year from the late 1970s through the 1990s, then tapered slightly and have since leveled above the 800,000 mark annually (U.S. Centers for Disease Control, 2007). Economics make it primarily a middle class affair, reflected in the locations of most abortion clinics. More than half of the abortions in America are performed on teenage girls and young women in their early 20s. Most are white, and about one-third are black.

Michelle

"Michelle" is a "simple country girl" in her early 50s, who hails from the mid-Atlantic region. She and her husband have no children, and they both work hard in keeping a long-distance marriage in tact. He watches their business interests from another state, which includes a ranch with Texas longhorn steers. Having reached that life plateau where realization sets in about the inevitable "onslaught" of age, Michelle desperately tries not to become "old." She is a chain smoker who engages in an on-going, yet unsuccessful, campaign to quit. Each time she tries, she then gains a few extra pounds which makes her turn back to the comfort of her menthol cigarettes.

Michelle is a very nice person with a kind heart. Raised first in the United Methodist Church and then in the United Church of Christ, she has "never had to 'find' the Lord as I was already 'found'." In Jeffersonian tradition, she says, "religion taught me to *think*.... I never believed Jesus walked on water, but that doesn't mean I don't believe in the parables." Her God "is not a vengeful God," but rather "a God that forgives, allows one to make mistakes ... does not punish."

She has a sense of humor and worries about people taking themselves too seriously, especially those associated with her industry. Being an extrovert, Michelle truly likes people. She is the type who engages strangers in genuine conversation while eating with close friends around a table at a Japanese steakhouse. She abstains from alcohol, but her humor and friendliness would place her on your "A" list for cocktail parties.

Michelle avidly loves dogs, which probably helps with the long-distance marriage and absence of children. She acquires them from animal shelters and rescue centers rather than from breeders. These animals are not just pets. With more than thirty dogs between their ranch and her local dwelling, they represent a need to take care of the vulnerable in our world. She is an animal rights advocate because animals "don't have a voice."

She is a shrewd financial investor. A victim of a car accident at the age of twenty, she used the settlement money to purchase a restaurant. Annual tax refunds from that endeavor were invested in buying rent houses. Profits from renters and the restaurant customers provided sufficient venture capital for her current business. While she is a dedicated service provider with a well-respected reputation within the industry, Michelle unashamedly admits that her interests would be elsewhere if not for the lucrative black ink. She finds profit or, if not, her natural business savvy looks elsewhere.

Michelle's business happens to be abortion. She profits from owning two clinics. Her clients follow national demographic trends in terms of race, age, and especially economics. "Poor women," she underscores, "don't have abortions. They have babies."

She has had two abortions, the second at one of her clinics. The first was when she was twenty years old and struggling to balance college and business. "It was a *parasite*. It *had* to be removed." Abortion was illegal then, so she found a backstreet doctor willing to break the law but received from him no compassion or professional caring. "I can still remember him saying, 'you didn't have a problem spreading your legs before. If you can't spread them now, I'm not going to see you.'" Providing compassion to her clients is one reason she entered the business.

By every definition, however, Michelle is the quintessential capitalist. She currently charges $500 for a medical (drug) abortion up to the seventh week; $425 for a first trimester surgical abortion with a light anesthetic and $475 for one with a heavy anesthetic; and for a second trimester abortion, about an additional $100 per week and maxing out at $1,100. After-hours (privacy) abortions start around $625, maxing out around $1,300. All fees are paid in advance. With an estimated 3,000 clients annually from just one of her clinics, some with second trimester abortions, it is likely that she grosses more than $1.5 million. Assuming business is the same at the "western" clinic, she probably grosses around $3 million yearly.

By any definition, Michelle is not a political ideologue. She is supported by local pro-choice advocates, and she takes advantage of pro-choice student volunteer escorts for the girls and women entering either facility. She learned quickly, however, that pro-choice politics hinders capitalism. Local feminist leaders don't always understand that she is running a business, not a political coffee klastch. In anticipation of a pro-life rally scheduled at one of her clinics, she laments:

> It'll be a *circus*. There will be pro-choice escorts, but there will also be those *pro-choice crazy ones* that just like to go to a demonstration. There's crazy groups in pro-choice: *socialists*. I mean, it will bring out every crazy in the world. And the only one who *suffers* is the *woman* [client]. That's the *bad* thing.

She believes that local and national pro-choice leaders misunderstand women who seek abortions by trying to make them look as heroes and defenders of feminism. "Women who walk in here ... do not view themselves as exercising their freedom of choice. This is not part of some political process. They're not interested in signing letters, signing postcards, signing up to be on mailing lists. They just want a medical procedure." It is not politics or constitutional rights, but simply issues of price and proximity, that determine if a woman gets an abortion at either of Michelle's abortion clinics.

Michelle is not sure when life begins, but she does not think a fertilized egg or embryo deserves protection. So many "fertilized eggs naturally abort.... So if that's true, God's the *biggest* abortionist there is!" She continues:

> I've thought through this issue, to do it as long as I have, and I have to sleep well at night ... but always think that, my God, if they were truly babies and human beings they'd just not be washed down with menstrual blood every month and flushed down the commode.... Is it *life*? *Clearly* it's life. Does it deserve *protection*? My answer is "*no*." The bottom line, you have two competing interests: the mother and the baby (or the embryo or the fertilized egg). And sometime during that nine-month gestation, a woman's rights are going to digress. At that point, I guess, rights can be ascribed to that fetus.

At her clinics, second trimester abortions are limited to the seventeenth week due to business liability and her own personal views about aborting a late second trimester unborn baby:

> I visited a clinic that did them routinely. I wanted to see what a twenty-four-week abortion looked like ... it looks like a *baby*. You know, you're getting too close. And I thought, how tragic that some women would wait until they were twenty-four weeks to have an abortion. How sad that we live in a society where that happens.

BJ

"BJ" is a semi-retired nurse who works as a counselor at one of Michelle's clinics. She is over 6' 4" in height, born on a Midwest farm, and was raised as a Southern Baptist. She rebelled from religion during her college years. Her first husband was Roman Catholic and insisted that they attend his church. "He never volunteered to go to the Baptist church, so that put a sour note on the Catholic religion." She resents the religious fervor of many pro-life advocates. They shout at her as she enters and exits the clinic and "choose to interpret [the Bible] to fit what they want. 'God won't forgive you for this.' Well, how do you know? It's everybody for themselves when it comes to this."

BJ has observed third-trimester abortions, and believes that life begins *only* at the moment of birth. There are two basic reasons why she entered the abortion industry. First, she believes that abortion is part of the professional duties of every nurse. "The women are [having abortions] because they feel it's the best thing for them.... It is a nurse's responsibility to provide that service." She regrets that many nurses avoid working in the area of abortion: "we don't get to pick and choose who we take care of ... that wasn't part of the oath taken when you got out of school." The second reason is personal. "I didn't *enjoy* my kids growing up. And that's been one of my things, that all women should not be mothers. And it took me a long time to realize that."

Omega Breeze in South Amherst

"Omega Breeze Women's Health Clinic" is the only abortion facility in "South Amherst," a community of about 200,000 inhabitants in a tri-state area. The city's commerce centers on tourism, with its nearby beaches, but white collar and high tech jobs are expanding. With several colleges, South Amherst is called the "Oxford" of the region.

Omega Breeze sits at the corner of Court and Union streets. These are relatively quiet, two-lane pathways, lined with palmetto trees, in a neighborhood of older homes, duplex apartments and modest businesses. It faces Court Street, directly across from a small shopping plaza. Directly across on Union is Tappan Square—part of the campus of the University of South Amherst (USA). On the other side of Tappan Square begins the famous "Slant Walk," which connects USA with several private colleges. At the end of Slant Walk is Peden Stadium, home to the USA Bobcat football team that competes in the Major American Conference (MAC).

Omega Breeze operates inside a large three-story house that has an ocean blue stucco exterior and a pastel red veranda stretching across its entire length. The clinic uses the first two floors, and the third has recently been renovated as Michelle's residence. From the third floor balcony, one can enjoy cool breezes drifting off the bay. Unlike the establishments across Court Street, there is no neon sign boasting the kind of business found within Omega Breeze. Clients come from word-of-mouth referrals, or from either Internet or Yellow Page advertisements. Students walking toward Tappan Square, as well as plaza customers, might easily remain unaware of the business conducted inside that stucco house.

A Matter of Privacy

The assumption is that an abortion is a private, confidential procedure. That is partially true. When a teenage girl or young woman contacts Omega Breeze, she is told of the need for three visits: a preliminary examination, the abortion, and a post-operative infection examination. The first visit entails watching a video, having an ultrasound, and receiving counseling. There are only thirty-one steps which separate the farthest parking place from the front door. The girl or woman enters a small lobby and waiting area. When her name is called, she crosses a hallway into a larger waiting room that holds twenty-eight chairs. In a room off to the side, with six chairs, she watches a video about abortion.

She then leaves the waiting room, makes a quick left, and walks five steps down a narrow hallway—passing an exit door which, for security reasons, always remains locked. Turning left again she climbs a flight of seventeen steps (there is no elevator) to another waiting room which has large windows overlooking Court Street and the bay. There are five chairs and two couches in this room, enough space for thirteen women to wait comfortably for the ultrasound.

When her name is called, she walks down a hallway to one of two examination rooms—the first is seven steps away and the second is fifteen steps away—for the ultrasound, which she is given the opportunity to view. (Michelle believes about 60 to 70 percent of the girls and women look at the ultrasound and, hence, "those who claim they don't know what they're carrying is bull!") Afterward she takes a left to the end of the hallway, and then down a back stairway to the large waiting room on the first floor. She meets with a counselor in an office arranged for three clients at a time. The counselor hands her a brochure about pregnancy and abortion, as well as a resource directory of South Amherst and tri-state social service agencies. The counselor answers questions and assesses the client's readiness for the procedure. Other options remain unmentioned unless the girl or woman appears to have doubts about having the abortion. According to Michelle and BJ, doubts are rare.

The second visit entails the abortion. This time the girl or woman is accompanied by someone to drive her home after the procedure. Her companion sits in the lobby while she goes to the hallway, takes a right, and walks to the front stairway which leads to the upstairs waiting room. Today, however, everyone in that room awaits abortions and not ultrasounds. When her name is called, she walks the few short steps to one of the same rooms where she had the ultra sound on the first visit. There she changes into hospital garb and, if she notices, there is a row of instruments and syringes neatly placed next to the examination table. Bundled individually in blue cloth, the number matches the expected number of abortions to be performed that day. A physician and nurse enter, give her an anesthetic, and perform the abortion.

The substance of the unborn baby travels through a hard plastic cannula and is suctioned (or in the case of D&C and D&E procedures, placed) into an 800 ml bottle with a filament-looking net inside. Cell tissue and fluids travel through the net into the bottle and larger body parts are caught in the net. Different diameters of cannula tubes are used depending on gestation: smallest for around six weeks and the largest at Omega Breeze is used for seventeen-week abortions.

At the conclusion of the procedure, the jar is taken into the sterile room next door—a 6 by 15 ft. room that contains three older sterilization machines, one of which does not work. It is here that a nurse accounts for all body parts. The contents of each jar are placed onto a metal pan, similar to shallow ones used for baking sheet cake. They are then outsourced to a pathology lab which generates a report for the clinic. The lab destroys the contents. The bottles are sterilized prior to further use.

Meanwhile the girl or woman walks down the hallway to a recovery area consisting of six brown recliner chairs in an outer room and four more in a smaller inner room. Each chair has thin white paper on its seat, identical to that which is found on examination tables, and this is changed for each new occupant. She remains in there for at least thirty minutes, and then exits down the front stairs. She meets her driving companion in the lobby. They exit the building and retrace their steps to the car.

A Public Affair

While everything *appears* confidential and private, the intimacy of the process of abortion is actually a public affair. Each teenage girl or young woman is never really alone, except for the ultrasound and abortion. There could be as many as twenty-eight women in the large waiting room downstairs, with each chair touching the next. It is not accidental that there are six chairs in the video room and three chairs (not including the counselor's) in the counseling room. The upstairs waiting room might have as many as thirteen clients staring at each other as they wait for their respective abortions. The recovery room is cramped, each recliner touching the next, which means no privacy after the abortion.

Each trip to Omega Breeze, even the third post-operative visit which most clients avoid, means likely exposure to many people. She will hear and see pro-life advocates as her car approaches the clinic. A volunteer pro-choice escort walks her to the clinic's entrance as the pro-life message becomes personal and intimate. Both pro-choice and pro-life people note her physical appearance, and they may comment about her after she enters the building. They may even notice, based on the license plate, whether she is local or from another county or state. When she exits, there will be more shouting, offering of prayers, and waving of posters. It is far from a private experience.

The Trenches of Court Street

The war over abortion is fought on a variety of fronts, but battle trenches can be found juxtaposed to many clinics. This is where advocates of pro-life and pro-choice square off over girls and women found in "no-man's land"—the space between their cars and the abortion clinic's entrance. Omega Breeze is no different. Trench lines form on Court Street: pro-choice on Omega Breeze's side of the street and pro-life along the sidewalk near the shopping plaza.

Cheerleaders of Death

The core of the pro-choice trench belongs to young student volunteers from "Cutler College," which is one of the liberal arts institutions just off of Slant Walk. They jokingly call themselves the "Cheerleaders of Death" because that is the name given to them by some of the pro-life demonstrators. They erupt in laughter about the nickname, and talk about getting black cheerleading uniforms (with skulls) and learning "death cheers." These are bright young students, excited about life, thrilled with the concept of new ideas, and all claiming to be atheists. Their task is to escort clients from the parking lot with the least amount of interference from the pro-life side. They are not security officers, just college kids with orange "street-crossing" tops. They offer only a symbolic presence.

The head cheerleader was recruited by a local feminist club; she then recruited the others. In the libertine spirit of de Sade (1795), she believes that "every person has the right to do whatever they want, including having sex with a million people and not have safe sex." She is convinced that children as young as twelve, just like de Sade's "Eugénie," should be allowed to engage in sex if that is their choice. If she were a parent, which she is not, "I would inform them of *safe* sex, but I would not tell them not to do it because that's not my right."

The Pro-Life Trench

On the other side of the street are "red-tapers," "rosarians," and "shouters." Red-tapers are usually teenagers who stand and pray motionlessly with their mouths covered with red tape labeled "LIFE." Rosarians are Roman Catholic men, women, and children who pray quietly and conclude with reciting the Rosary. Shouters are typically evangelical Protestant men who scream at the pro-choice trench and the teenage girls and young women in "no-man's land." They carry signs about abortion and some wear clothing with theo-political statements: "Homosexuality is a sin, Islam is a lie, Abortion is murder: Some issues are just black and white." They also take turns driving an old Ford truck around the block; its external speakers blaring funeral music and, on its sides, are posters of aborted unborn babies. On any given encounter, there may be as many as ten red-tapers, eight shouters, and twenty rosarians on Court Street. The cheerleaders focus their attention on the shouters.

Dynamics

At stake are the thirty to forty girls and women who routinely enter and exit Omega Breeze on the days abortions are performed. Waiting for the initial client to drive into the parking lot, there are first-name greetings across Court Street—similar to handshakes before the start of a MAC football game. Questions are raised about lunch plans as well as the health of "regulars" on the opposite side of the street who seem to be absent. But soon first-name pleasantries are replaced by personal taunts. Shouter: "God said 'thou shall not murder.' You are *defying* God!" Cheerleader: "Hey, what about [an abortion clinic terrorist] *Eric Rudolph*? Didn't *he* defy God and commit murder?" Shouter: "Why do you have a problem with Eric Rudolph killing one cop, when *that* [pointing to Omega Breeze] building murders thousands of babies?" Cheerleader: "Are you *kidding* me? You are defending the murderer of a police officer?" Shouter: "You can't complain about the murder of one policeman in one breath and in the next breath condone the murder of thousands of babies."

A couple arrives and a cheerleader performs his task. Shouter: "Ma'am, it's *not* too late! You can *still* stand up for the *life* of your child!

[Pointing toward the cheerleaders] Don't have blood on your hands like *those* people. Don't be a *murderer*! *Don't* turn yourself into a murderer! Don't be *afraid*. You can *save* the baby."

Another couple walks with a cheerleader toward the entrance and, because they appear Hispanic, one shouter opens in Spanish and another translates: "Its *murder, murder, murder*. You are walking into a *hell-hole*. *It* is truly a hell-hole. It's cold blooded *murder*. The Bible says that he who takes a life, his life will also be taken. When you get away from the word of God ... you end up in the wilderness." Now an older woman accompanies a teenager into the clinic. Shouter: "Grandmother, *please* don't let her murder your grandbaby. That baby *needs* you right now! Ma'am, *please* don't murder your baby!" A young woman sits outside, smoking a cigarette, awaiting the completion of a friend's abortion. She shouts to the pro-life demonstrators:

> You need to find *compassion* and *love*. My aunt had an abortion about twenty years ago, and she suffered a lot, feeling angry and ashamed and feeling like she couldn't tell anyone. I didn't know about it until a couple of weeks ago. She found a Sunday School class in her church for women who had abortions. She's much better now *because* she met some *nice* Christians who *cared*, not like you guys. You ought to find out what Christians *should* be doing!

Shouter: "We *are* doing what we should be doing. Read the *Bible*." Young woman: "You were out here about three weeks ago when I had *mine*, and you made me so mad! I'd do just the opposite you want, just because you made me *mad*!"

While the pro-life trench clearly has the uphill battle in convincing clients not to enter the clinic, there *are* victories. One shouter is renowned for his volume and velocity. On one occasion he was so loud that the police officer assigned to guard Omega Breeze actually cited him for violating the noise ordinance. His voice projected through the clinic's upstairs windows and gravitated to one of the second floor examination rooms. A client, waiting for the abortion to commence, heard him cry repeatedly: "Mommy, mommy, mommy, it's not too late. *Please* don't kill your baby!" She was so taken that she decided not to abort. Leaving the building, she and her boyfriend crossed Court Street and thanked this particular shouter. To the disamusement of the cheerleaders, the three kneeled and prayed together. A week later, the couple decided to marry and invited the shouter to the wedding. He also attended the baby's baptism.

Meanwhile a young woman exits who is obviously feeling the results of the abortion. She walks very slowly and is helped by her companion. The cheerleaders pay her no attention. Shouter: "See what you've *done* to yourself? You're *bleeding*, aren't you? You may be *bleeding* inside and don't even *know* it. You see what happens when you *kill* your baby? Go to *Jesus*! Go to *Jesus*!" She is clearly bothered by these remarks and, once at the car, scowls at the shouter and slams the door. The shouter is oblivious to her reaction, as he continues: "Satan's gonna rip you up. You need to go to *Jesus*."

Several men exit the clinic to smoke cigarettes while they wait for their companions to complete abortions. Shouter: "Men, do not be *cowards*. God did *not* make you to be cowards. He made you to be *courageous*. Do *not* be cowards today, men." Another shouter: "Cowards are *bullies*. Anyone who murders children is the epitome of a *bully*."

A young woman and an older female exit unnoticed by the escorts. She appears physically shaken and does not look at anyone. She walks stiltedly to her car, helped by the older woman. Soon a teenage girl comes out, escorted by an older man. It is a hot summer day, yet she wears a hooded jacket to cover her face. Meanwhile, another car pulls up. Shouter: "Abortion is *murder*!"

One shouter turns his attention to a male cheerleader: "If a bunch of guys came by and gang-banged you, you would be yelling *help, help*, but those babies *can't* yell *help*." The cheerleaders catch the shouter's slip of the tongue when he misused the term "gang-bang" for "ganging up." They taunt with laughter: "Did you say you want him *gang-banged*? You call yourself a *Christian*? Are you *gay*?"

Now a teenager walks toward the door. Shouter: "Mother, you *know* you can adopt out your child. *Someone* is *waiting* to love that child." Cheerleader: "*No one* can love a baby as much as the birth mother, so why should she give it up for adoption?" Shouter: "How can you take care of your baby if you're *murdering* him first?" Another woman comes out. Shouter: "You are *guilty* of the killing of a little child!" A teenager goes inside. Shouter: "*Cold* blooded murder! Cold blooded *murder*!"

One of the physicians at Omega Breeze, an African-American woman, comes outside for a cigarette. Shouter: "The KKK [Ku Klux Klan] never killed as many blacks as *you're* killing. The *KKK* never hurt as many *black women* as you're hurting. The *KKK* never murdered as many *black babies* as you're murdering." Simultaneously an African-American couple walks toward the door. Shouter: "Be a *man*." The woman's companion responds that he *is* a man. Shouter: "You're an *Uncle Tom*, an *Uncle Tom*!" Another shouter: "Do not be a *coward*! You're nothing but a yellow-bellied *coward*! You are a *coward*, man!"

One shouter turns to the police officer at Omega Breeze. "Why wear the *badge*? If you're not going to do what the badge stands for, if you're not going to protect the innocent, just take the badge off and throw it in the garbage!" Officer: "You don't understand, I'm protecting you right now. Because the other day there was somebody that was ready to come beat you up. And I didn't let him." They begin to banter about a police officer killed by a terrorist, Eric Rudolph. Shouter: "He wouldn't have been *killed* if he was not protecting a *murderer*!" Officer: "He wouldn't have been *killed* if a *crazy man with a bomb* didn't plant one." Shouter: "Why was he a *crazy person* when he was trying to *stop* murder by *committing* murder?"

A college student coming from Tappan Square approaches the shouters. With a skim-board under one arm, he is wearing a black T-shirt with a large human skull with two fists on either side showing the extended middle finger. Penetrating the top of the skull is a bleeding cross. On the cross are the numbers "666" and on either side is the Satanic pentagram. With his unencumbered arm, he gives the "finger" and yells "Fuck you and tell your congregation I said, fuck you also!" As one shouter and the student get into a discussion, the police officer quietly crosses Court Street to ensure the shouter's safety—an act of kindness and professionalism which goes unnoticed by all the shouters. "What is your name?" The college student responds, "What the fuck does it matter, what's my name?" Shouter: "*God* knows your name. He knew it while you were in your mother's *womb*." Response: "Actually, when I was in my mother's womb, I was just a zygote.... God had nothing to do with it.... You stand out here and do this to people, it's totally rude. You pro-life? Well, do you ever eat *meat*? Then you're not so much pro-life are you?" Shouter: "An animal and a human are the same?" Response: "They are both *equal*."

Meanwhile a woman comes up to the now parked truck and stares at the poster of a twenty-one-week aborted child who was allegedly retrieved from a garbage can in Houston. Her three daughters stand next to her. The mother wants her daughters to see the poster because she gave birth to one of them, the fourteen-year-old, at twenty-six weeks. She wanted to show that daughter what she looked like at that time. They are shocked to discover that in that beautiful house across the street is an abortion clinic.

Occasionally Michelle interacts with the shouters. (She does this because of all the violence directed toward other abortion clinics. "For me it's harder to kill someone you see as a *human being* than someone you ascribe as the *anti-Christ* or a *baby killer.*") Opening in the morning, shouters hint that it might be unsafe to touch the door or place a key into the lock. When she comes out for a smoke, they ask about profit from "blood money." She answers with humor: "No, my *car* I bought with *good* money. The *blood money* goes to my charities!" She once joked about making fetal-shaped cookies for the shouters because "all that shouting must make them hungry." Michelle thinks the shouters are funny, but "what pisses me off about them is the ownership of Jesus and God and that arrogance of 'only I know what's right for you.'" About the kinds of comments shouted to her clients: "to do that is to torture another human being and that's just unconscionable." She continues:

> I don't understand why they can't see the person standing in front of them. They only see the belly and what they visualize inside of her. For the pregnant woman, I see the *woman*, they just see the *baby*."

Michelle sees hypocrisy in some pro-life demonstrators. Those choosing abortions tend to "sneak in" on days when no one is protesting. Sometimes they pay the additional expense for a private after-hours appointment. She also sees hypocrisy in many other pro-life supporters. A state senator who, upon finding that Michelle owns abortion clinics, asked: "What would a pretty little thing like you be doing in a place like that?" Michelle responded jokingly with a fictitious story about how she was once attacked by a black man. The senator was aghast and told her he felt "abortion is OK if you are a white woman raped by a black man."

Ironically Michelle understands the intensity felt by the shouters. She relates to it through her own passion for animals. "If I *did* believe what *they* believe, then I would understand justifiable homicide. I understand that perfectly. Because I'm an animal rights activist, I can understand breaking into laboratories and removing the animals."

I Don't Hate You

Politics makes strange bedfellows, and abortion is no exception. One day Michelle walked near the rosarians and heard "Marge" break prayer and say, "I don't hate you." Michelle was surprised and asked Marge to repeat her words, which she did. As a result of that moment, both started to exchange pleasantries. Marge eventually invited Michelle to lunch. Michelle nervously accepted and secretly tape-recorded the lunch in case it turned out to be some kind of pro-life ploy. The experience was pleasant enough, and Michelle reciprocated—to the consternation of several pro-choice friends—with a dinner invitation.

Both disagree on the issue of abortion, but they have become good friends—a friendship that began with the words "I don't hate you." According to Marge, Michelle "has never disrespected me or tried to change me. She's not derogatory toward me or my beliefs, so that's one of the reasons that we get along so well." As for Marge, "I don't make any attempts to change her." Marge believes that "God's going to do what He's going to do" with their friendship. She believes that Jesus would have no problems "hanging" with Michelle, and that God will someday lead Michelle away from the abortion business—in His own time and in His own way. In the next life, she prays that Michelle finds God's *mercy*. "That is what I pray, God's *mercy* [for Michelle]. I hope that is what *I* find."

An Abortion Story

"Ashley" is a graduate student at a state university in Alabama. At the age of fifteen she became sexually active and, living in the inner city of Los Angeles, she wanted to join the "Crips" gang. As part of the initiation rites, Ashley had to choose between being beaten-up or gang-raped. Although she eventually chose not to join this gang, she repeatedly practiced the rape with a "good" friend. This started her sexual odyssey and, in the space of just four years, Ashley had over thirty different partners.

Promiscuity continued during her freshman year at college. Without knowing the father's identity, Ashley had an abortion in the thirteenth week of pregnancy—on the Friday just prior to Christmas. She did not want the abortion, but could not see the feasibility of feeding a baby and staying in school. Her college friends, many of whom use abortion as contraception, urged her to terminate the life of her unborn child. Her mother, a welfare recipient in Georgia who is dependent on a portion of Ashley's scholarship money to make ends meet, was concerned about the baby draining scarce resources. She insisted that Ashley come home and have the abortion. Ashley:

> There's a *bad* chain in my family. Like my sister, her dad left when she was a baby. *My* dad left when I was a baby. God knows what would happen to my child. I'm

in *college* trying to do something with my life so that when I have a child, I'd be prepared.

Ashley and her mother went to an abortion clinic which charged her a greater sum than expected. Her mother contributed part of next month's rent money to make up the difference. Ashley: "when I woke up ... when I realized it was *gone*, I was bleeding like really heavy." She wonders: "what do they do with all those dead babies?"

Intimate Consequences of Public Action

What is the *real* for individuals who associate with the act of abortion? This is an important question because, according to Dietrich Bonhoeffer, the primary philosophical task of democratic government is to ensure *outward justice* for all citizens so that each may be liberated to serve God in his or her own way. This freedom is critical to what the Founders envisioned because it reaffirms the theocentric moral foundation of the American political community. Does the real of abortion hinder this kind of moral freedom?

The answer is hotly contested within a highly politicized scientific community. In its taxonomy of mental illnesses and disabilities, for instance, the American Psychological Association (APA) does not recognize post-abortion syndrome (PAS) as a subset of Post Traumatic Stress Disorder (PTSD) because it considers abortion a benign procedure and a civil right for women (Throckmorton, 2005).There is also a large body of scientific research which substantiates this perspective (Gold-Steinbery and Stewart, 1998; Lemkau, 1988). One study concludes that less than two percent of women experience adverse consequences from abortions (Major et al., 2000). Another (Boyle, 1997) claims that the emotions experienced by (only a very few) women are actually the by-product of guilt brought on by religious beliefs rather than the act of abortion, itself.

Other scientific reports differ (Broen et al., 2005; Burke and Reardon, 2002). One indicates that abortive women, especially between the ages of fifteen and twenty-five, are significantly more likely to develop mental health problems than women who choose to give birth (Fergasson, et al., 2006). Another (Rue, et al., 2004) indicates that 65 percent of abortive women suffer from PTSD, and another (Gomez, et al., 2005) found that *100 percent* of the women studied did experience PTSD. Studies also indicate that abortive women are much more likely to be admitted to psychiatric facilities (David, 1985) and have significantly higher rates of suicide and suicide attempts (Reardon, et al., 2002; Gissler et al., 1996).

Scientific studies provide one perspective, but anecdotal evidence also reveals an important part of the real of abortion. Robert Spencer, who performed over 30,000 abortions in his lifetime, believed very few of his patients dealt with any kind of negative consequence (Lader, 1973). "THB," a volunteer counselor at an abortion clinic about an hour north of South Amherst, feels that the counseling process sufficiently screens out those who are emotionally unfit for abortion. THB admits, however, that "it depends also a lot on the counselor and the insight *into* the individual." Michelle and BJ agree, citing "only a handful" of clients each year who have been screened out. They also point to the minuscule number of clients who have called the clinic for emotional counseling at any time after their abortions. BJ remembers only two such phone calls over the last four years.

Some pro-choice advocates admit that problems arise. THB believes that some women experience trauma, "but they're usually not the ones that you hear about [at abortion clinics] because for some it appears so much later because they have repressed it for so long." Pro-choice social scientist Angela Neustatter (1986: 1-2) acknowledges what she experienced with her own abortion:

> Although I have always marched and campaigned for a woman's right to choose ... when it came to deciding to end a pregnancy, I was shocked by the distress and confusion I felt. I did not like having to take personal responsibility for ending a life.

"Sarah," a psychiatrist in a city approximately one hour to the east of South Amherst, is pro-choice and believes that life does not begin until a personality develops—a minimum of three months *after* the birth of the child. She treats a lot of women who have had abortions. "Every single one of them has suffered horribly. They never forgive themselves." She sees no difference between post-abortive women who are deeply religious and those who are not. "There may be more *fear* with the women who are very religious.... But the level of grief for women who are even *atheist* is about the same."

Sketches from the Real of Abortion

The fact that science cannot definitively answer the question about the real of abortion is not of concern here. It provides a valid perspective, but such thinking has led us (at least, several generations of college students) to believe that the world we see phenomenologically or even spiritually is not as legitimate as the world seen through the lens of myopic hypotheses, confirmed or disconfirmed. The religion of science offers a kind of methodological "cheap grace" in that it permits distance from the real without an obligation to investigate it intimately from one's own vantage point. One purpose of this book is to convince the reader to engage the real as a *citizen-nachahmer* and accept the price of civic costly grace by searching intimately for what is *seen* through *Gods* eyes in *this* world. That is, to seek the "real" for yourself when it comes to public action and morality.

No Problems Whatsoever

Certainly pro-choice researchers must be correct in that many women—perhaps 98 percent of them—continue with their lives unaffected by abortion. "KC" believes she fits this bill. A twenty-five-year-old student at "McGuffey Law School," off of Slant Walk in South Amherst, she is unmarried but lives with her boyfriend and their five-year-old son. For her, life begins with conception and, moreover, abortion constitutes murder. Nevertheless, KC strongly believes in the right of the mother to murder her unborn. Her college friends are not bothered by abortion either. Many use it as a contraceptive; three of her closest friends have had a total of six abortions. When KC aborted her twins, the counselor asked why she wanted to have an abortion. "It was something I knew I *had* to do because ... we really didn't need another child."

"Jessica," a twenty-three-year-old biology masters student at USA, also believes her abortion is not affecting her life. Her dream is to earn a Ph.D. and return to teach at USA. When she was a freshman, those plans were threatened. Having just broken up with her long-time boyfriend, she went on a date with a co-worker. They snorted cocaine before dinner and, afterwards, returned to his home to listen to music; he claimed his mother and grandmother were in other rooms. The boy tried unsuccessfully to grope her and eventually offered her a drink laced with drugs. He raped her. Eight weeks later the pregnancy was confirmed. A Roman Catholic, she was pro-life before the rape. Now she is pro-choice:

> I thought abortion was *bad* because babies have life at conception. I really didn't take into consideration the flip-side. Then I had an abortion. I realized I wasn't ready to handle the pressure of having a baby.

Jessica remembers the pro-life demonstrators outside Omega Breeze. Her old boyfriend (they got back together after the rape) escorted her, and they were accosted by shouters.

> They don't *know* my situation and I'm pretty sure *everyone's* situation. They thought that I messed up and we had to get rid of this baby, or that I couldn't tell my mom, or something like that. They didn't know about the *rape*. They didn't know that it wasn't my *fault*. And they didn't know my boyfriend had *nothing* to do with it. They tried to make him feel like a *bad guy*, and he was the only *supportive* person.

She recalls her experience inside. In the waiting room, one woman said she had too many kids. Another was pregnant with twins. Others gave the impression that this was not their first abortion. The counselor was "just really impersonal and did not try to determine whether or not you were psychologically ready to have an abortion." She remembers that "the physician wore weird shorts and boots and I thought, 'is this really the physician?' He wasn't really presentable." She continues: "the environment is kind of strange if you're not initially prepared for what the business is about."

As the boyfriend of "Wendy," who has had two abortions, "Christopher" also has no regrets. Wendy and he are from Birmingham, Alabama and have known each other for about five years. She is forty-years-old and was raised as a Roman Catholic. Christopher is thirty-two years old and grew up in a Baptist family. She is an artist, and Christopher hopes to get into law school. Both have rejected Christianity and, three years ago, converted to Buddhism. They are pro-choice. He jokingly says life begins "when you're in my *phone book*!" He continues:

> Let's face it, there's a lot of *selfishness* that goes on. But who am I to tell people not to be *selfish*? If a woman feels like she should have an abortion, then she should *have* one!

Wendy's first abortion was the result of a rape when she was twenty years old. The second one occurred in the ninth week of pregnancy, and Christopher was the father. His role in the decision making: "I wasn't *against* it, don't get me wrong.... I'm pretty *selfish* and I admit it. I want some good things in *my* life for *me* before I start having to give to somebody else."

So Christopher and Wendy went to a clinic and split the cost for the drug, mifepristone, or RU486. They received no counseling, except advice that the effects of RU486 would be slightly discomforting. They returned home and Wendy took the dosage. The next day Christopher took the LSAT exam, required for law school admission, but he asked Wendy to save the remains because he was "kind of interested in the process." For him, "it was more of a scientific curiosity. I wanted to see it."

While he was taking the exam, Wendy suffered through tremendous pain rather than the promised "slight discomfort." Christopher: "It was quite a *big* thing, like giving *birth*, so I wish that I had *been* there for her. It was a *bloody mess*. Wendy went through contractions, just like a pregnancy. We didn't think it would be quite like *that*."

Text messaging at breaks, he thought about Wendy throughout the day. "I got done with the LSAT as quickly as I could.... I felt bad for her, because she was not doing well." He returned home to find Wendy terribly weak, but his thoughts turned to his performance on the LSAT: "One of the things I wondered was would I've scored *higher* on the LSAT. I guess that's kind of *selfish*, but it really wasn't the best I could do.... It was a stressful day in every sense of the word." He noticed something in a pint jar on the kitchen table which Wendy had saved for him: "It was a lot bigger than I thought it would be." Christopher:

> I do think about [the abortion] occasionally ... but I don't feel *bad* about it.... Having looked at it [in the jar], I didn't feel like I was throwing away some miracle.

Silence and Secrecy

Jessica and KC have not told their respective families. Now pursuing only monogamous relationships, Ashley has not been able to tell any boyfriend. "Crystal," a forty-three-year-old Roman Catholic from South Florida, has also kept things quiet. At the age of sixteen, she had an abortion: "I felt like a piece of meat at a slaughter house. They had it arranged so it would be like an assembly line." Since having the abortion, she has told only her husband and her sister. She still has difficulty using the word "abortion" in describing what she did.

"Dawn" is a single forty-five-year-old Southern Baptist from Chicago, Illinois, and she too has kept the secret. At the age of twenty-eight, she started to date several married men and had abortions in four consecutive years. She recalls her first experience at an abortion clinic: "I remember some of the women just squalling, just absolutely lost their minds, just crying. And I remember shaking constantly. It was just like you were a herd of cattle ... women were crying before they went in and they were crying after." For her fourth abortion, Dawn chose the more expensive private appointment because she wanted to avoid all the women crying: "If I'm gonna do this, I wanna do this by myself. I wanted to be the *only* one that's *crying*."

"Nicole," a thirty-one-year-old with a master's degree in chemistry, and her husband, "Bryan," a Ph.D. in biochemistry, also live in silence. Both grew up in Birmingham, Alabama. She was raised Baptist but joined the Church of Christ because that was her husband's sect. They became pregnant when they were dating at an Alabama undergraduate college and, because of their devout Christian upbringing, both were afraid to tell their parents. We "already knew that abortion is *wrong*. But, I guess when you're put in that situation, what you *should* be thinking isn't necessarily the first thing that comes to your mind." At eight weeks, Bryan and Nicole traveled to an abortion clinic. Nicole:

> We got up early that morning. I was crying. I was a wreck. Didn't sleep the night before. I knew that this was wrong from the beginning. I *knew* that inside of me there was life. It wasn't just a clump of cells like everybody would like to *believe*.... I'm a chemist and it's not like I didn't already *know*.

Like Jessica, Nicole's experience within an abortion clinic was not as private as she might have desired. She found herself with a group of women. There was no counseling or screening, and "the lady that did the video said, 'Well, I have had an abortion, so it's not a big deal.'" As the physician started to insert the speculum, Nicole started crying: "I *don't* want to do this." The nurse grabbed her arm and tried to comfort her: "It's OK. It'll be over in a few minutes." Nicole heard the suctioning and "I looked at this tube and saw a whole lot of blood." She thought, "oh, my God, that's my *child*. What have I *done*?"

It took a lot of alcohol for "Rosa" to have her three abortions slip out in conversation at a bar one night to her husband of over twenty years. "I drank more than a normal person on the weekends so not to think about it." A forty-three-year-old Roman Catholic from Tennessee, the third abortion occurred when she was an eighteen-year-old first-year student at a Catholic nursing school. The abortion clinic did not take clients after sixteen weeks, and she was closer to the end of the second trimester. So, "although I know they knew," she lied about the length of pregnancy. The only counseling that occurred was when the physician walked in: "he patted me on my thigh and said, 'you know what you're doing, don't you?' And I just looked at him with a blank stare on my face thinking to myself, 'No, I *don't*.'" The abortion procedure "was horrible. Very painful, just very painful. I remember them having to give me more sedation than usual and I remember I bled a *lot* with that abortion."

The day after, Rosa ate dinner with her family and realized that "my milk came down and it saturated my blouse." She "had conniptions because I didn't know what was going on. I went to the bathroom and padded my bra so that my mother and family wouldn't notice." After dinner she began to feel infected and shortly thereafter was hospitalized. This was Easter Sunday. Rosa's abortion took place on Holy Saturday. She never told her parents.

"Hannah" grew up in South Amherst and remembers the one time she confided in her dormitory floor's prayer-leader (at "Evangelical College") about the abortion she had the summer prior to her freshman year. After that, her prayer-leader "wouldn't have anything to do with me." Now a twenty-five-year-old social worker, she still worries about saying anything that would tip her hand to friends or coworkers. Only recently did she tell her mother, but her father is still unaware. (Her mother confided that, because Hannah was an unexpected pregnancy, *she* was nearly aborted.)

When she was pregnant, Hannah's primary concern was going to that college on Slant Walk, and not the life of the unborn:

> I couldn't throw a wrench in that. I didn't even think straight. I didn't realize that I could put my child up for adoption. I just found myself in a position where I didn't know what else to do. I just knew that I couldn't handle that right now.

Only her boyfriend and his mother knew of the pregnancy at the time, and it was his mother who escorted Hannah to Omega Breeze and paid the fee. On the first visit, she came in contact with shouters. "A woman yelled, 'you better repent, you're going to hell!'" On the second visit, she waited for her name to be called. Then to her surprise, "things were done as a *group* of women," rather than on a private basis. They all met a counselor: "She sat behind a very big desk ... she was unsympathetic, very direct, very business-like." Hannah was concerned about a cyst in her uterus that was initially detected in childhood. In the group meeting, she asked whether that cyst would be a problem. The counselor responded that the cyst may no longer be there, but Hannah said "the girl who did the ultrasound said that she *saw* it." To this, the counselor responded, "that girl didn't know what she was doing anyway." Hannah: "I was in shock and scared at the same time, just wishing it would be over with ... so I said 'OK'."

With the exception of one very close friend, "Caoimhe" has kept her abortion a dark secret. She is a forty-five-year-old Southern Baptist from Birmingham, Alabama. She has two grown children, was married for twenty years, divorced, and re-married four years ago. Caoimhe had the potential to be a world-class violinist, perhaps like the musician in Judith Jarvis Thomson's (1971) reconstructed parable. At the age of eighteen she received a full scholarship to one of the nation's top conservatories but, like Jessica, a pregnancy threatened those plans. Unlike Jessica, however, she wanted to keep the baby, marry the boyfriend "to give the baby a name," divorce him afterwards, and raise the baby while she went to college. Her boyfriend insisted on the abortion—saying that doing otherwise would be throwing away her career. "So he basically just bound me, gagged me, and dragged me to an abortion clinic." There,

> I told them that I did not *want* to have an abortion. I had changed my mind. They stuck a needle in my arm immediately to knock me out.... I screamed and cried, that's all I can remember.... The other women that were in there, they were staring at me. I told them again, I'm not gonna *do* this. The women looked very *scared* when I left. I guess they heard me *screaming*.

According to "Robin," "I tried to pretend it never happened." She is a thirty-five-year-old Mississippian, married with three boys and worships at a United Methodist Church. Her husband and oldest son are the only ones who know about the two abortions she had in high school—both times, she was eight weeks pregnant. She remembers the abortion clinic as cold and impersonal. "You could hear crying in the holding room ... crying of women who already had the abortion. I remember the sounds, the smells, the suction ... you could hear the sound of the motor of the pump, the suction when the baby was being withdrawn, the clinking of the utensils." She recalls: "this *hurts* so *bad*'" and then she thought, "this is what I *get*, of course it's gonna hurt ... look what I'm *doing*." Afterwards, she was wheeled into a recovery room with many other girls and women. "I just remember the *crying* ... so many people *crying*."

According to "Denise," a fifty-one-year-old Roman Catholic who grew up in Key West, "you bury it from your mind for many, many years. You absolutely squelch the whole thing." At the age of twenty, she had an abortion. "I cried while they were doing it until it was over." "Cynthia," a thirty-five-year-old Southern Baptist single mother who had three abortions while married in the military, just discovered that her long-time best friend also once had an abortion.

> Because women do have abortions, it's not something that is talked about. You're already beating yourself up. You're telling yourself, 'What kind of a *monster* are you to kill an innocent *child*?' You don't want people to say that, too. To *keep* that from happening, it's like a trash bag. You put it as far to the bottom of the bag as you can and you shove every other thing on top of it so that it won't come out.

Things that Go Bump in the Night

For some women, perhaps even 98 percent of the women who have had abortions, nothing seems to go "bump in the night" with respect to the choices they made about abortion. However, others mention various events that cause a re-visitation of the abortion experience. For Cynthia, long drives by herself are reminiscent of the drive from Boston to the abortion clinic in New Hampshire. As on that drive, she still has to pull off the road to cry. In addition, "every time I would go to the dentist, even for a cleaning, I would just be in tears. It was the sound from the instruments they were using." "Emily" (see below) feels the same: "I shake when I sit in the chair because you know that little wand of suction dentists put in your mouth? I had three suction abortions." She also cannot drink orange juice or eat Ritz crackers because these were given to her in the recovery area after the abortion. Nicole revisits her abortion on its anniversary, as well as when she sees her nieces and nephews. For Hannah, seeing other children and babies also makes her revisit the abortion. For Rosa, the birth of a grandchild now triggers nightmares about that child drowning. Nightmares of this kind started after the abortion and were initially directed at her children. For Crystal, the suction noise is revisited each time she turns on her vacuum cleaner. She gets the same feeling with the noise from espresso machines at coffee houses. "Many things tug at my heart: crackers because they gave us crackers and Tang. I will *never* have Tang again."

Worries, Guilt, and Self-Esteem

"Emily" is a forty-nine-year-old Californian. She grew up Roman Catholic but recently became a Southern Baptist. She had three abortions between the ages of eighteen and twenty.

> When I walked out of that clinic, I thought all my problems are over.... I don't have to deal with my father. I don't have to worry about getting married. I can go back to my job. They were *right*. I went back to my life as normal. Those feelings of shame and regret are not immediate. It's something that comes on you later in life.

Crystal believes she is a murderer. "And murderers belong in prison. The prison is my *life*." Cynthia believes she is as "filthy as someone on death row." Denise convinced herself that she was not worthy of ever giving birth. "It wasn't that I didn't love children ... but the truth of the matter was, I knew I already destroyed a life, so what right did I have to bring any *more* in?"

KC has not had adverse experiences from the abortion, but she is afraid of the decades to come when she will approach the apex of her career. "When you do something *wrong*, maybe it comes back on you. Maybe you just don't see it." *Wrong*? "Yeah, it was *wrong*. I don't justify it. It was *wrong*, but it was a decision I had to *make*." Nevertheless KC believes she murdered her twins "because that's what it *is* when you terminate a pregnancy." She remains pro-choice, but rejects its adage that the zygote and embryo are just clumps of cells.

> It really doesn't make sense because it *is* life and its growing *into* a life, so why would it be considered just cells? You have *cells* all over your body, regardless of being pregnant, so that really doesn't make sense.... It's breathing, it's moving, it's eating the things you're eating.

Caoimhe "just felt so *worthless*. I never went to college, like I *should* have. I started at [a state university near her hometown] a few years later, but I just took some music classes and volunteered in their little orchestra. I started a science major, but I didn't finish it." That feeling of worthlessness has remained since the abortion. "I felt like I didn't deserve any man, except [the boyfriend who forced the abortion]. I deserved to be *married* to that man." She did and "was married very unhappily for twenty years."

Hannah has experienced some physical problems since the abortion: "I never had cramps a day in my life 'til the abortion. Now I do. Sometimes I'm in so much pain as a direct repercussion of that abortion." Evangelical College holds an annual "pro-life" week. As a freshman, she was also required to take a two-semester course on life ethics. "Every time [someone] said something or I read something about abortion, it hurt. It was like a stab in my heart. I just felt very *wrong*. There was just a lot of hurt, a lot of *shame* about what I did." As part of her social work major, Hannah interned as a "God mother" at a home for unwed mothers. "The entire time I would keep saying that I wished I knew about this, I wished I took this opportunity to be like these girls. They're having a hard time and they're struggling, but they're still getting help, counseling, and they made the right decision." She remembers how crippled she felt each time the college president recited at weekly vespers *Psalm* 139: 15-16: "My frame was not hidden from you when I was made in the secret place. When I was woven together in the depths of the earth, your eyes saw my unformed body. All the days ordained for me were written in your book before one of them came to be."

Like KC, Jessica has not experienced negative consequences from her abortion. Yet she too has trepidations. Even though she is now pro-choice, Jessica realizes that the morality gleaned from her family and Catholic high school constitutes the correct values. "It *is* wrong to stop a life. I could have given it up for *adoption*. There were *other* choices." She has tried to strike a bargain with God by pledging to earn that desired Ph.D. degree and "improve every aspect of my life." Her bargaining is "one thing that is probably helping me out … it is my penitence and my reconciliation for what I've done [because I've] deprived somebody (the fetus) of the possibility of doing something great."

What about Wendy? According to Christopher, her behavior changed after the abortion. In the finest tradition of de Sade,

> She started acting out sexually ... and drinking heavily. There was some nineteen-year-old boy working on the air conditioner at the next apartment and she just went over to him and said "come over here and have sex with me and then leave." There was another guy, she was given a phone number and just pursued this. It was like some kind of "S&M" thing that she was in to.

Anger and Violence

"Armida" is a thirty-five-year-old Roman Catholic from eastern Alabama. She is now married with five children. When she was twenty and a single mom of two children, she had an abortion at eight weeks. She became repetitively violent toward her partner after the abortion. "I would throw things at him and push him or scratch him and try to hit him." Nicole still becomes very angry at Bryan. She believes he should have been like the shouter at Omega Breeze: calling out to convince her to leave the clinic. She also gets angry when friends get pregnant. She and Bryan have given birth, but the eight week ultrasound brought back the anger over the abortion. Fundamentally Nicole is angry at herself:

> People who are murderers, and I consider myself as a murderer, they can say, 'Oh, you know, I just did it, it doesn't mean anything.' To me, if you go back to Cain

> and Abel, when the brother was slain, Cain *knew* what he'd done. He knew it immediately. He knew it was *wrong*. Now he tried to *hide* it from himself, tried to hide it from *God*. Man cannot look inwardly, only God can do that.... So I truly believe that even women who say it doesn't matter and they claim not to think about it at all, *they* do. They *do*.

Relationships

Since the abortion, Rosa lacks enjoyment during sexual intimacy with her husband. Hannah and her husband are having difficulty getting pregnant. Robin finds it difficult to be close to her children. "It wasn't a 'wall' between me and my three sons, but it was like a 'screen door.'" Since her abortion, Cynthia is not comfortable around men. She has had no relationships in fifteen years. She fears being around groups of men, even at the mall or on elevators. She grows anxious at grocery stores if a man comes down the aisle.

> I don't have any medical proof, but I never was like this before the abortions. I've built a cocoon around me and I don't do the things adults are supposed to do, because I'm not comfortable in that situation. And I am 100 percent sure that in *my* life all of this is because of what I went through.

Psychiatric Hospitalization

"Shep" is a seventy-one-year-old Episcopalian. A "good ole boy" who lives in a small town on an Alabama river, he is fun-loving and possesses a talent for painting verbal caricatures about himself and his life. Both physically and emotionally, he is a very strong individual. At the age of nineteen, Shep and "Barbara" were pregnant. They were in love and got married, but Barbara's parents did not like Shep and tried to circumvent their relationship. They convinced her to get an abortion behind Shep's back. This was in 1957, well before *Roe*, and an abortion was especially hard to acquire in rural areas.

> I haven't forgotten about it and I never *will*. [Abortion] is not a *woman* thing. [The baby] was *mine*. It just wasn't *hers*. I can speak to the *pain*. Every time I hear the word, "abortion," it's like a *dagger* going through my heart. So it's *not* just a woman thing.

Shep and Barbara remained married, much to the consternation of her parents. By the 1970s, however, Shep was diagnosed with depression and was treated with shock therapy. In 1977, he checked himself into a psychiatric hospital. He never got over the abortion.

Suicide

Upon her return to college after the Christmas abortion, Ashley tried unsuccessfully to commit suicide with a combination of alcohol and drugs. Roommates found her in time. "I didn't want to kill myself or my child. I got confused. It *does* hurt." Right after the Easter abortion, Rosa "took a bunch of sleeping pills and took some Quaaludes." Fortunately she panicked and, after calling a girl friend, was rushed to an emergency room before it was too late.

As Shep was being discharged from the psychiatric hospital, he learned that his beloved Barbara could no longer take the silent pain of abortion. Barbara found Shep's twelve-gauge automatic shotgun in a rack on the upper shelf of their walk-in bedroom closet. She was not a hunter, but somehow managed to lock and load. Barbara blew off her head. Shep had to rush home from the psychiatric facility to clean up the mess and burry his wife. In 2001, the guilt of both the abortion and Barbara's suicide caught up with her elderly mother. She, too, used a shotgun to blow off her head. While Shep is not absolute about cause and effect, he is certain that the unspoken pain from the abortion contributed greatly to the destruction of all their lives.

Sense of Loss

KC and Jessica have never thought about what their babies might have been or what they might have contributed to society. Michelle also does not dwell on that.

> Do I think now that I would have a child however old that would be? For me that's like looking at a *Norman Rockwell* thing—it's an ideal picture of what might have been and you know, whether I did the right thing or not is between me and God."

The painting Christopher draws is more from Rod Serling than Norman Rockwell. He laughingly says his aborted child would "probably [be] a criminal."

> I think the world feels a bit lighter without my little off-spring running around. Honestly, and not to make light of it, we always think we're going to lose the next Einstein or like the rebirth of Christ. There's a lot of criminals that are born.... Believe me, the world lost just an average kid. Just a kid.

Others believe differently. Robin: "Two very beautiful women who could have helped change the world for *God*. One person *can* make a difference, and those would have been *two*." Dawn: "Disciples for Him. It's pretty awesome what God can do, if you allow Him to do it!" For Emily, her aborted children would have become: "Something great. They would have made a huge contribution to this world. I just know this, and I robbed this world of something good." Ashley: "I think my child would have *been* my best friend. Someone that I would have been able to say, 'I don't care where I go, you're coming with me. And I'm gonna always love you, no matter what. I'll do *anything* for you.'" Through prayer and meditation, Armida believes she has met her aborted child. "I imagined her as a really strong person. Very caring and supportive and very, very, intelligent person. I think that she is somebody I could have really *leaned* on." Hannah takes a different brush to that Norman Rockwell painting.

> Of all the babies that have been aborted, he could have been the person who would have changed the world. He could have been the person who would have cured some ailment that affects a lot of people. My family has lost a grandchild and a great-nephew. I've lost a son ... my future children lost a brother. Future generations lost a grandfather or an uncle or a cousin. He would have had *joy* in his heart.

Lessons about the *Real* of Abortion

Remember the words of Dietrich Bonhoeffer (1995: 360): "If one is to say how a thing really is, i.e., if one is to speak truthfully, one's gaze and one's thought must be directed towards the way in which the real exists in God and through God and for God." Because the sanctity of life is a supreme value in the *Word* of God, the moral truth coming from scripture is that abortion is wrong and may be overlooked only in the extremely rare case of when the mother's life is at risk. From this one perspective, the world which God creates and presents to us each day—the *real* in Bonhoeffer's terms—is equally simple and straightforward.

Simplicity of the Real

When asked why women come to her clinics, Michelle gave a variety of reasons: "not ready" for motherhood, "can't afford another child," "deformative reasons," and "no emotional support." According to BJ:

> Most of them don't think [they] can take care of a child or *another* child or not *mentally* able at this time to take care of a child. Some are not the brightest light bulb. They're really kind of '"blank."' Others want something *better* in their life and they know that a child right now is not what will help them *get* to that point.

Neither Michelle nor BJ offer "life of the mother" as one possible explanation for any of the estimated 3,000 abortions occurring annually at Omega Breeze. Frankly, if lives were at risk, girls and women would seek procedures at hospitals and not at abortion clinics. Hence, the real of the abortions conducted at Omega Breeze is morally wrong. They cannot be reconciled—placed in unity—with the word of God. And if this is true for the 3,000 abortions at this clinic, is there any doubt that the same is true for the overwhelming majority of the fifty million abortions performed since the *Roe* decision? Certainly the real demonstrates an absence of balance in moral strength between the born and the unborn. Death is imposed upon the unborn as a by-product of the born's simple desire to accomplish libertine dreams.

The simple reality of assisting in these abortions is also bankrupt of moral justification. This is why, through the Hippocratic Oath, Christian and Jewish physicians pledge: "To please no one will I prescribe a deadly drug nor give advice which may cause his death. Nor will I give a woman a pessary to procure abortion." Muslim physicians make a similar pledge: "To regard God in carrying out my profession. To protect human life in all stages and under all circumstances." Those who perform abortions do so to please the politics of *our* times and not the morality of *all* time.

Recall BJ lamenting that some nurses refuse to involve themselves with abortion despite taking the Florence Nightingale Pledge at graduation? She forgets that the oath also states: "I solemnly pledge myself before God.... I will abstain from whatever is deleterious and mischievous and will not take or knowingly administer any harmful drug." Nurses take an oath before God not to hurt life. Those who abort, hurt life before God.

A pro-choice student activist once told me, "Sometimes I think God sits up there and says, 'don't put *my* name on *this* anymore!'" I respond by looking at de Sade's (1795: 23) rejection of God in favor of the libertine lifestyle. The character, Dolmancé, proclaims: "What can virtue mean for someone who does not believe in religion!" He is right; get God out of the equation, and you have the real completely void of the nuisance of moral virtue and theocentric pledge. For that student as well as BJ, here is the rub: God *has* already placed His name *against* abortion and He's *not* removing it. The pro-choice movement is therefore correct in noting that choice and its consequences affect women *because* of the virtues *imposed* by God. A great part of the real entails choosing between following moral precepts found through God or pursuing the libertine freedoms ascribed by de Sade. That is the simple reality of choice.

Complexity of the Real

Other aspects of the real of abortion are not so straightforward. Pro-choice scholar Linda Myrsiades (2002: viii) is correct in noting, "there is nothing neat about abortion. Its exercise, and resistance to that exercise, involves many different ways of seeing, feeling, and codifying it as an experience." "Juliane," a woman who aborted her child (Press and Cole, 1999:42), ponders: "Why can't there be truth in the matter? If people are to know the truth, then they need to be told the truth." Sitting in an ethics class at that Catholic nursing school just prior to her Easter abortion, Rosa also mulled: "What's the *answer*? I wanna know what the *answer* is!"

Part of the real is this: Abortion politics tries to deny complexity and defines the situation in denotative and dichotomous ways. Michelle is correct in that too many pro-life advocates point only at the belly of the woman rather than at the woman, herself. Contrary to the social gospel, they ignore a significant part of the real.

The shouters on Court Street are a case in point in their efforts to serve as *citizens-nachahmer.* While they rightfully adhere to the straight line roadmap of scripture, they fail to navigate the tortuous path of the real—a path which is as much a part of God as the word, itself. Jessica's point is well taken: shouters knew nothing about her circumstance nor that of her boyfriend. In the twenty-first century, an African-American man escorting a woman *anywhere* in the American political community—including into an abortion clinic—does not deserve to be called "Uncle Tom." Similarly an African-American physician does not deserve to be linked with the KKK. Nowhere in scripture does God call us to belittle others or use racially charged epithets in His name. For the one girl or woman within the abortion chamber who hears the shouter's cry for mercy, how many become enraged by both the invasion of presumed privacy and the abnegation of common civility? How many, like that young girl smoking a cigarette outside Omega Breeze, would have the abortion "just because you made me so *mad*." At that point, the intimacy of the social gospel is also aborted.

Ultimately the Christian shouter must ask, what would Jesus do in *this* reality? (The Jew and Muslim must ask, what would the God of

Abraham have me do *in this context*?) I believe He would either *quietly* pray with the rosarians or *silently* pray with the teenage red-tapers. This is how He would want the *citizen-nachahmer* in the pro-life trenches to convince girls and women to think twice about what they are about to do. Non-violence was the basis of the civil rights movement of the 1960s, and verbal non-violence should be the basis of the civil rights movement for the unborn in the twenty-first century.

Ironically, Michelle's critique also applies to those who man the pro-choice trenches on Court Street and throughout the American political community. Not one cheerleader has ever had an abortion, yet all are quick to encourage and applaud those who do. They too look only at the simplicity of the woman's belly as she enters the clinic, and they ignore the complexities of the pain on her face and suffering in her body as she exits.

Some pro-choice counselors, steeped in personal baggage and armed with ideological agendas—addictions which apparently can only be satisfied through the fix of another woman's choice—also focus on the simplicity of the belly rather than the complexity of indecisiveness found on the face and anguish found in the heart. Truth is, there is both physical pain and emotional discomfort with the abortion procedure. If this were not true, why would women cry in the waiting room as well as in the recovery room?

Too many pro-choice celebrities also choose to look simply at the belly and ignore the complex real of the woman. The Fall 2006 issue of *Ms. Magazine* (p. 38-41) is a case in point. The issue reveals the names of hundreds of women who have signed a petition celebrating their own abortions. Those brave *signataires*! How little comfort their actions offer women, like Emily and Caoimhe, who suffer badly from the complex real of abortion. Those brave libertines! How recklessly they abort the intimacy of the social gospel for the sake of justifying their own acts of selfishness.

Finally when the abortionist seeks profit, she too looks only at the simplicity of the belly. The "philosophy in the abortion clinic" is very similar to the "philosophy in the tattoo parlor." Waking up the next morning, wondering with Jimmy Buffett just how that "Mexican cutie" got there, you realize that it was truly your choice. You were asked if you wanted a tattoo, but it was not the tattoo artist's business to press you for a true answer and screen you out because of time of night or level of intoxication. Such is the case with the for-profit abortion chamber.

You are asked, but not necessarily screened. You are screened, but not necessarily asked. As with tattoos, capitalism is the real of the abortion clinic.

The complexity of the real is reflected positively in other aspects, as ironically exemplified with shouters on Court Street who act much like a group of "stooges." Like TV's *The Three Stooges*, these men are ostensibly clowns. They shout things that make God look foolish and His followers look like bunglers. But remember the TV episodes where the *Stooges* go up against Nazi spies? These bunglers were somehow transformed into heroes who quash the plans of evil for the greater good. So too is it with the shouters on Court Street. Each may fail at being an effective *citizen-nachahmer*, but nevertheless each is a committed soldier in His trench. As other Christians enjoy mornings at Slant Walk coffee shops—while Court Street is absent of Jew and Muslim—the shouters abide by the word of their Lord and apply it to the reality which He presents. Through deliberate action they attempt to change the intimate reality so that it is more pleasing to Him. Passion is displayed equally with frailties.

Perhaps the greatest complexity lies in people like Michelle. How can an abortionist be such a delightful human being? How can someone be so compassionate about animals, because they "don't have a voice," and simultaneously turn a blind "ear" to the ultrasounds of the unborn human? Michelle sees the complexity yet has no answer. And how can an abortionist and a rosarian become close friends? Michelle and Marge have differing answers, with the former stacking it up to luck and the latter attributing it to the hand of God. Regardless, the real found through Michelle is a reminder that humans are not made of unidimensional clay. In the eyes of God, the sins of Michelle are no greater than those of the shouter who inadvertently quickens the pace of a girl's step toward the clinic's door, or the shouter who tries to inject fear into Michelle's heart about her own safety as she unlocks that door, or the shouter who nurtures racism and religious bigotry in his heart or inscribes it on his T-shirt. The reality is that she and the shouter are both equally loved by God and, as per the social gospel, we must differentiate the sin from the sinner. When we fail to do this, the trenches on the abortion front become fixed, public discourse hardens, and the real of the American political community becomes irreconcilable with the word of God.

The complexity of the real among the women who choose to abort must also not be neglected. Ideological labels, such as "pro-choice" and "pro-life," do not reflect their reality. Each woman interviewed considers herself a feminist. All believe in equal pay, equal rights, and equal opportunity. Some believe in the right to choose, and some believe that the wrong choice leads to murder. Some vacillate between the trenches, and some believe in a continuum rather than a dichotomy. The real is such that women who abort, similar to most human beings, cannot be placed into scientific taxonomy.

The Real of Pain and Suffering

In the American political community, we tend to show pride in the exercise of our constitutional rights. Why? Because they are things that did not come cheaply. Citizens fought for them and, in many cases, died to ensure our rights. We therefore tend not to be ashamed when exercising them. Upon the casting of ballots, for instance, we receive "I voted!" stickers and proudly wear them as we return to the reality of our lives.

Is abortion a constitutional right? Yes, according to the Supreme Court. As such, why are we so ashamed about exercising that particular right? One student asked me rhetorically, "Would you *want* to tell your parents about an abortion?" Other questions abound. Why do abortion clinics disguise themselves as "women's health clinics" and shine no light over their doorways? Why are past abortions publically rejoiced only by pro-choice demonstrators and celebrity *signataires*? Why do best friends not tell best friends, and wives not tell husbands? Why aren't "I aborted!" stickers distributed to girls and women as they exit the abortion chamber so they can wear them proudly throughout the day?

Answers to these questions lie in the spiritual as well as worldly suffering found in the real. One shouter rightly asserts: an abortion probably affects *at least* twenty others, including those whom are unaware of the missing links of honesty and transparency in the relationship.

Some people, like Michelle and Christopher, try to avoid the pain and suffering through intellectual rationalization, and others through psychiatrists, like Sarah. Some women, like Emily and Hannah, seek help through Bible study groups and others, like Rosa and Crystal, attend weekend retreats—all designed and facilitated by women who have had abortions. Sometimes people like Shep entomb themselves in other kinds of ministries and service projects just to get through the day. Many have even named their aborted babies in an effort to bring closure to the suffering.

The Real of Irony

Just two blocks from Omega Breeze, on Court Street toward the bay, is a Ronald McDonald House. It is a sanctuary for families who need a place to stay while their children receive treatment at nearby hospitals and, consequently, this is where *another* battle over life ensues. Similar to the abortion clinic up the street, students from the colleges along Slant Walk volunteer to help staff the facility. Unlike the abortion clinic, however, there are electric signs welcoming its patrons.

On a day when forty girls and women entered Omega Breeze to terminate the life found growing in their wombs, other mothers were desperately seeking ways to keep *their* children healthy and alive. An elderly man and woman sat in a late-modeled Chevy truck, waiting for their daughter to exit the Ronald McDonald House. They drove four hours because their newborn grandchild, "Keon," was ill and not expected to live. Doctors wanted to discontinue life support, but the family did not. The grandfather: "only *God* knows when life is to end. *Man* doesn't know and Man doesn't have the *right* to guess." So we prayed together that God would not end the life of this child. The grandmother did not understand how women could choose to kill forty babies on a day when prayers were raised for one.

Inside the Ronald McDonald house is "Thesha," an unwed mother of two boys who lives in public housing several hours away. She is twenty-eight years old and worships at a Missionary Baptist church. She has a high school degree, but is unemployed due to health problems. She has two children, both out of wedlock and both with different fathers. Her oldest son is four years old, and his father is a soldier in Iraq. According to Thesha, he's a good father. Her second son, Chryston (she proudly explains his name is pronounced "*Christ* - on"), is only three months old and *his* father is a deadbeat. She repeats the old saying, "daddy *may* help you but mama's *always* gonna help you." She says,

> It don't matter about never being married and not having anything. As long as I got the good Lord on my side, *everything* will work out. I just pray and keep a strong head and thank Him constantly.

Chryston has had a hard life, weighing just 1 lb. 2 oz. at birth and delivered shortly after the second trimester at twenty-six weeks—the same week as the daughter whose mother ventured into the pro-life trench up the street earlier that day to look at the abortion poster. It might have been easier for Thesha to abort Chryston, given her lack of employment and marriage, and the fact that she already has one child out of wedlock. Some might argue that she is clogging the welfare system by not having had that abortion. When she thought she might be pregnant, Thesha went to a testing facility. Tests were positive, and she told the counselor: "I don't believe in abortion. Through my religion, we don't believe in killing kids." She reflects: "With Jesus on your side and God, what *can* you do? Nothing *but* keep 'em!" And, "If it happened [being pregnant] it was *meant* to happen and it was already wrote. And what we go through, He had already *seen*." About an abortion clinic just two blocks up Court Street, she says:

> People here going through things with their baby and hoping that they continue to live. And then right [up] there, just taking them out and doing *whatever* when we over here fighting to keep ours alive. I don't wanna be no where around it.

* * *

While little agreement exists over the number of women suffering, given the estimated 50 million abortions since 1973, a very low pro-choice anticipation of two percent projects that figure to be around one million. Each year there are about 850,000 additional abortions performed, which means at least an additional 17,000 women will most likely embark on a life journey toward spiritual and worldly pain. While this does not include men who also suffer, it is comparable to the annual number of women diagnosed with ovarian cancer. Feminist organizations rightfully place pressure on Congress to dedicate more funding for research in the case of ovarian cancer, and this is in unity with the social gospel. No such pressure, however, is felt from these groups in the name of the intimate consequences of abortion. This is contrary to the social gospel.

Bonhoeffer (1995: 174) acknowledged that abortion may be encouraged by "an act of despair, performed in circumstances of extreme human or economic destitution and misery" but those circumstances "cannot in any way alter the fact of murder." The twenty-first century is no different than the time in which Bonhoeffer lived. The medical reality of abortion remains the same: it ends the life of the unborn. The moral reality is also the same: because it is murder of human life, hence destroying *Imago Dei*, the act of abortion is not in unity with the moral words of God. The intimate reality of abortion also remains constant: it makes some people suffer, and it makes everyone selfish.

Getting out of our comfort zones and looking at the intimate consequences of public action—in this case, abortions in the American political community—we see that the real includes miracles: some girls and women changing their minds, friendships struck across trenches, and silent and quiet prayers transforming streets into sanctuaries. The real, however, also includes concealed abortion clinics, some counselors troubled about their own lives, the silenced and the secretive sufferers, the fearful ones anticipating potential consequences, the libertines and their selfishness, nice people just in the wrong business, equally nice people erring in their efforts to eliminate that business, and fifty million murders. This is incompatible with the social gospel. It provides no balance of moral strength and thereby permits the public action of inflicting death and suffering on others and ourselves as by-products of unharnessed desires.

We must also acknowledge that which is conspicuously absent from the real: the vast majority of Jews, Christians, and Muslims in the American political community who are either too fearful or too busy (as per Bonhoeffer's poem, *Stages on the Way to Freedom*) to "come away from [their] anxious hesitations into the storm of events, carried by God's command and [their] faith alone." Refusing to accept the obligation of the *citizen-nachahmer* to invest civic costly grace in deliberate action so that the intimate consequences of abortion may be uncovered and brought into unity with the word of God, they, too, stray from the social gospel. They add to the imbalance of moral strength between the born and the unborn as a by-product of their indifference. In doing so, they contribute to the real of taking life—each day as it is presented back to God.

4

The Real of Murder and Capital Punishment

Recall from Chapter 3 those who oppose the killing of the unborn. Here are their thoughts on the death penalty. Shouter: "How can you be *against* the death penalty for a convicted murderer, but you are *for* the death penalty for an innocent child? God pronounces the death penalty in both testaments." Thesha: "When you put it all together, you still *killing*. *The Lord* isn't doing it, so I don't think nobody else has the authority to take somebody's life." Nicole: "If a man ever touched my daughter, I would kill him." Denise: "Yes! If someone murdered someone...." Now recall those who support a woman's right to kill the unborn baby. Here are their views on capital punishment. Sarah: "I'm totally opposed to it. I'm really very uncomfortable with executing a fully grown, sentient person who doesn't want to die." Christopher: "I don't think we should give the government that kind of power." BJ: "If you do something so horrendous, so meticulously planned, you deserve [execution]." KC: "Slaughter my family? I support the death penalty." Jessica: "If individuals can't take lives, why should government be able to take life?"

As explored in Chapter 2, and perhaps demonstrated in the views above, the word of God is absolute but varied when it comes to the issue of capital punishment. On the one hand, we attribute the highest value to the sanctity of life and, consequently, murder is condemned universally. Yet when it comes to punishing the murderer, scriptures of the three Abrahamic faiths permit two paths to public action: one stemming from forgiveness and the other from the principle of *lex talionis* (law of retaliation) or its Islamic equivalent, *Al-Qisaas* (law of equality). Because scripture provides two options, it is paramount that the *citizen-nachahmer* examine closely the *real* of murder and capital punishment.

Capital Punishment in the American Political Community

Harsh punishments like the death penalty—based on *lex talionis* or *Al-Qisaas*—have been acceptable since the dawning of the Early Settlement Era in America (Ward, 2007; Steelwater, 2003). Whereas the process of abortion has gone from being a private affair to something more public, capital punishment has traveled a reverse course (Johnson, 1998; Masur, 1991). Efforts to reform capital punishment, including making it more private, began during Founding times (Bedau, 2004; Bohm, 2003). Reforms also brought changes in the methods of execution to make them more humane and less painful. In the 1972 *Furman v. Georgia* decision, the U.S. Supreme Court struck down capital punishment laws because they tended to be arbitrary, not matching the severity of the crime to punishment. In its 1976 *Gregg v. Georgia* decision, the Court permitted the reinstatement of capital punishment as long as laws incorporated the following: (1) sentencing guidelines which stipulate mitigating factors in determining punishment; (2) bifurcated trials, having the jury deliberate guilt separately before deliberating sentence; (3) automatic appellate reviews; and (4) proportionality review, allowing the jury and judge to compare the case in question with other similar cases in the state.

Since the days of the Founders, about 13,000 persons have been executed, always with a much higher proportion coming from the African-American community (Steelwater, 2003; Barken and Cohn, 1994.) Today a growing number of foreign-born Hispanics are on death row, but one-third remains black and almost 60 percent are white (NAACP, 2007); only eleven women have been executed since 1976 (Religious Tolerance, 2007). While there are very intelligent men on death row, typically the formal education level is the lowest within a state's prison population. Currently thirty-six states have the death penalty, along with the federal government and the military.[1]

Method of Execution

There are several ways to execute a condemned inmate, but since 1983 over 85 percent of executions have used lethal injection.[2] Procedures at Holman Correctional Facility in Alabama are typical. The condemned is strapped to a gurney and EKG wiring is attached to his chest. The gurney has arm extensions on either side so that intravenous (IV) lines can be inserted into both arms in case one vein causes the drugs to "back up" into the IV line. Lying on the gurney, the man faces the windows of three small witness rooms—to his left, his loved ones; at center, officials representing the Alabama Department of Corrections (DOC); and to his right, loved ones of those he has murdered. Three journalists, drawn by lottery, also observe in the witness room of his loved ones. There is one reporter representing the Associated Press, another is from a local newspaper, and one from a local television station from where the murder took place.

The wall behind the head of the gurney separates the death chamber from the control room. That wall has a two-foot square window so Holman's warden, who by law is Alabama's sole executioner, can view the death chamber. Near the gurney's head is a padlocked metal chute that can be opened to connect cables to a now warehoused electric chair called "Yellow Mama." The wall also has a small metal opening where IV tubing and EKG wiring connect the control room to the condemned man on the gurney. Similar to the blue bundles of abortion paraphernalia on the counter awaiting each abortion at Omega Breeze, there is a small stack of toe tags resting on the edge of the window within easy view of the condemned man as he is lifted onto the gurney.

The control room is narrow, almost storage-like, and runs the length of the death chamber. There is an intercom system connecting it to the death chamber and the DOC's witness room, which contains a direct phone line to the governor and attorney general. Beneath the window in the control room are two rows of extremely large tubes, each about nine inches long, comprising the top portion of a syringe mechanism. Each row has seven tubes filled with the needed chemicals, which arrive pre-mixed. Back row tubes are used in instances where the selected vein in one arm "backs-up," a result of aqueous pressure within the vein that cannot be surpassed by external pressure to allow injection, and a second vein is needed from the other arm. Veins are used, rather than arteries, because they pump blood toward (not away from) the heart and, therefore, quicken the consequences of injection.

The warden takes the tube, labeled "1," and screws it onto the bottom part of the syringe mechanism. "1" is filled with 50 cc's of sodium pentothal, a yellow water-soluble crystal—a short-term barbiturate commonly used in American medicine—which induces rapid unconsciousness by depressing the central nervous system, lowering the blood pressure and decreasing the heart rate.[3] He pushes the plunger at the top of the tube.[4] Once "1" is empty, he proceeds to affix the next tube, labeled "1A," filled with an additional 50 cc's of sodium pentothal. Upon its discharge, he affixes tube "2," which is filled with 60 cc's of saline solution to ensure that all the sodium pentothal washes out of the IV tubing and into the vein. At this point a correctional officer (CO) makes sure the condemned is unconscious by pinching him and then flicking his eye lashes. Then on to tube "3," filled with 50 cc's of pavulon, a muscle relaxant which paralyzes the lungs and ends breathing. Tube "4" sends another 60 cc dose of saline to ensure the pavulon reaches its destination. Then the warden connects and plunges tube "5," containing 60 cc's of potassium chloride, which induces heart failure. Tube "6," filled with 60 cc's of saline, ensures all of the potassium chloride is washed into the vein.

About twenty minutes after plunging the first syringe, two attending physicians certify death. The IV needles and EKG modules are removed, and his arms are returned to the body's sides. The ends and sides of a body bag, pre-positioned and hidden between the gurney pad and the linen sheets, are pulled away and everything, including the deceased, is zipped up. A toe tag from the window's edge is placed on the zipper puller of the body bag, and the gurney is rolled out for autopsy at the University of South Alabama Hospital.

A Murder Story

"Michael" was a twenty-three-year-old college student who lived in a small town outside Florence, Alabama. He rented a house just 1.1 miles from his mother's home. For about a year, he shared that house with "John Henry," a man who was twice his age and was known for partying. With graduation approaching and with five job offers, Michael felt confident about the future and proposed to his girlfriend.

In the early hours of the Saturday before Mother's Day in 2003, a very drunk and drugged John Henry put a gun to Michael's head and, in front of his fiancée, pulled the trigger. Blood and brain matter spattered out of the side of Michael's skull. His fiancée called 911 and held him until the police and EMS arrived. Michael died in her arms.

Michael's mother, "Leigh," was awakened by a phone call around 5 a.m. on that morning. Her son's fiancée kept repeating the word "mom" but was unable to say anything else. Finally a nurse took the phone and said "Your son has been shot. We need you to come down to the hospital as quick as you can." Leigh asked about Michael's condition, and the nurse responded, "have the police gotten there?" At that point, she heard a knock on the front door.

When Leigh got to the emergency room, she learned Michael was dead. "I insisted on seeing my son. I was allowed to touch his left hand, but couldn't hold him or touch any more because of 'evidence'." Michael wanted to be an organ donor, but the need to preserve evidence prevented much harvesting. Leigh:

> something *good* could have come out of his death, but didn't. Every one of his organs was perfect. He could have saved seven or eight lives, and the best I could do was to donate his eyes, skin tissue and heart valves. The rest was wasted.

John Henry was arrested on that Saturday morning and, by afternoon, he was out on bail. The district attorney's office never notified Leigh about the bail and, for almost two years prior to trial, John Henry was a free man. His mother lived just about a half mile away, and so John Henry would ride past Leigh's home every day. Every time Leigh saw him, her rage would escalate:

> I thought I showed tremendous amount of restraint letting that son of a bitch live and not kill him. He's a wormy little creep. I could have taken him.

It took twenty-two months and four days for the trial to begin, and it lasted for three days. John Henry's attorney initially claimed self-defense, but changed the plea to accidental death. He was found guilty of second-degree murder, receiving a sentence of life with the possibility of parole, and was removed from the court room in handcuffs. Leigh: "I sat there and I *clapped* as he walked by." He never apologized for taking Michael's life or causing Leigh unending pain. Leigh hopes to be alive in 2047, John Henry's first opportunity for parole, because she wants to testify against his release.

Intimate Consequences of Public Action: Sketches from the Real of Loved Ones

Unlike abortion, consensus exists in the fields of psychology and psychiatry about linking acts of murder (Lovrin, 1999), capital punishment verdicts (Prejean, 1993; Dicks, 1991), and imprisonment (Golden, 2005) to conditions of deep personal damage—whether we call it emotional distress, anxiety or post-traumatic stress disorder (PTSD). Such linkages have been made historically (Cohen, 1995), as well as in the context of contemporary society (Schiraldi, 2001).

Devastating Impact

For Leigh, Michael's murder was "the worst hell I'd ever thought I'd *live* through." It produces an "emptiness that never goes away. John

Henry didn't just take one life, he took several." The hardest thing was to call her daughter on the eve of Mother's Day and tell her of Michael's death. The second hardest thing remains having to cope with very basic activities, like driving past the hospital emergency entrance where Michael was taken, or driving past the rent house where he was murdered. She cannot bear to see John Henry's family, to drive past their house, or to have them drive past her house. Unfortunately these things must be done each day in order to go anywhere in town.

Leigh cannot stand being in her own home, since that is where the phone rang about Michael's murder. She spends a lot of time at work and, in order to detour around the void waiting for her at home, she took a second job. She also gardens a lot and planted an oak tree in his memory—the "Michael tree." Leigh: "If I stay busy, I don't start drinking. I'm still holding to two drinks per night, but boy sometimes I want more." Ultimately she blames herself for the murder: "I wasn't there when he *needed* me. He was my *son*." She would gladly have exchanged places with him on that Saturday morning before Mother's Day. "It would've been easier than surviving without him."

Carolyn

For "Carolyn," the murder of her daughter was also "the hardest thing you'd ever go through. The pain is so great." She had a wonderful relationship with her daughter, "Sue," a beautiful 5' 2" girl with long sandy hair. In high school a boy named "Tag" knew Sue, although they were never friends. He began to make annoying phone calls to her about a year after graduation and, unbeknownst to anyone, was stalking her. On a warm September evening in Birmingham, Alabama back in 1989, Sue came home from work and played with her son "Justin," whom she conceived in high school. After dinner, she had to pick up a friend from work and told Carolyn that she'd be home by 9 p.m. Carolyn asked her to be careful, and Sue said, "Mama, who'd hurt *me*? I've never hurt anybody in my life."

Sue never picked up her friend, and she never returned home that evening. Carolyn: "This is every parent's nightmare, when she didn't come home." After 10 p.m. Carolyn and her husband, "Jerry," began to worry. Carolyn spent the evening calling Sue's friends, and Jerry drove around to look. Eventually they called the police.

Late the next day her car was found in a ditch and her body in an apartment. She was mutilated to the point where the coroner would not permit

Carolyn to identify her. Tag had choked her with an extension cord. Much of her hair was pulled out in the struggle, her face bludgeoned, and she was stabbed multiple times through the heart. Then Tag raped her lifeless body. He took her jewelry and tried unsuccessfully to sever a finger for a keepsake ring that Jerry had given her. Tag then asked his mother to rent a carpet shampooer, which he took to the apartment to remove as many blood stains as possible.

Tag was apprehended seventy-two hours later and confessed to the crime. He never received bail but, for the year-and-a-half prior to trial, Carolyn lived in fear that his family or friends might try to hurt them. While some of Sue's jewelry was found in his possession, a keepsake necklace (also a gift from her father) was found in the courtroom at the time of trial—around the neck of Tag's mother. Like John Henry, Tag was not convicted of capital murder and he never apologized for Sue's murder.

Carolyn believes Jerry has buried his feelings since that evening in 1989. "He acts like he's forgot, but he *hasn't*. He doesn't say anything, just puts it back." His nightmare is that Sue probably cried out for him while she was being stabbed and raped, because "she was *daddy's* girl."

Tag's Family

The devastation caused by murder also affects the families of the murderer. At trial, Tag's father stormed out of the courtroom in disgust of what his son did to Sue. He never returned. Tag's grandfather, a Baptist minister, apologized profusely to Carolyn and said he would pray for her family every day for the rest of his life. For the next ten years until his death, he was seen each day in the Jefferson County criminal court building, sitting in the back row of courtrooms and praying silently for the families involved in each murder case.

Bubba's Family

"Bubba" learned quickly that the act of murder makes people question the whole family. "Is he one bad seed or is this a bad family?" He came from a good family, although he "dibbled and dabbled in drugs—trying to hang out with people who were *sold* to that kind of lifestyle." One summer evening in 1977, Bubba robbed a Birmingham grocery store for drug money. In the process, he attempted to thumb-cock a handgun to scare the clerk. The hammer slipped, and he shot the man in the chest. Bubba would have done anything to retrieve that bullet, but that was impossible. The clerk was dead, leaving a wife and two children without a father. Bubba was sent to death row at Holman prison but, in 1980, the Alabama Supreme Court overturned the verdict on the grounds of errors made during the trial. A new jury sentenced him to life-without-the-possibility-of-parole (LWOPP). About nine years later, that verdict was overturned and a new trial was ordered. A plea-bargain was accepted and Bubba's sentence was reduced to life *with* the possibility of parole. His good behavior in prison led to parole in 1990. In 1999 he received a pardon based on community-service work.

Nevertheless, his act of murder greatly impacted his family, especially while he was on death row. His wife, "Lucy," was fired once her employer found out that she was married to a murderer. "And it was hard for her to find *another* job. She had to use her maiden name." Handling the finances and home repairs were now her responsibility. Bubba: "When I left, she didn't know how to do anything. So she was thrust from not having to worry about *anything* to having to worry about *everything*." She was encouraged by friends and family to divorce Bubba. They would tell her, "You ain't got nothing to look forward to. He got the death penalty. What you gonna do? Wait around to the last minute and drug this thing out?"

Friends of Bubba's son would say, "your dad's done a bad thing" or "your dad's on death row." Newspaper articles would precede Bubba's several appeals, and these too would have consequences for his son. School mates would comment, "there's a man in the paper that looks just like you! That's the same *name* you got." Lucy's parents wanted their grandson to deny any relationship to the man in the newspapers and urged him to invent a story about his father dying in the Vietnam War.

Bubba's family also suffered the emotional and physical toll of many visits to Holman prison. Bubba: "There are no close prisons" in Alabama—all of them are strategically located away from urban populations. The family faced the arduous task of waiting in lines, which would stretch outside Holman's entrance building, in the hot summer sun of southern Alabama. They would go through a metal detector, always with the possibility of being stripped searched. While this may appear a simple routine, similar to the post-September 11 experience at American airports, in a prison there is a special emphasis on control—an emphasis to which most "free-world" people are unaccustomed. In addition to prolonged and unexplained delays by COs with varying levels of compassion, sometimes there were cancellations of visits due to unanticipated lockdowns. There were also consequences for unintentional violations of the free-world dress code. Bubba's family sometimes "had to go and buy another shirt or another pair of pants so they [didn't] waste all of this time spent driving down here. Now they have to spend money that they didn't intend on spending."

Angela

Even though "Wes" would eventually be exonerated from a capital murder charge after spending four-and-a-half years on death row, it took a toll on his mother, "Angela." While her son had some "drug issues," they basically lived the middle-class dream in north central Alabama. However, Wes was erroneously accused and convicted of murdering two brothers during a drug deal in 1995. It was on a Friday evening when Wes called his mother about having been arrested for burglary. She did not know how to post bond and, in any event, was told that Wes could not be released because of another investigation. It was unexpectedly cold that autumn and, during the phone call, Wes mentioned that the county jail had not yet distributed blankets for the winter season. Angela: "I hated to cover myself that night because he was cold. I didn't want to be warm if he couldn't be." On Sunday morning, Wes phoned her again with the news that he had now been charged with capital murder.

Someone accused of a capital crime has two options: *pro bono* representation by an often inexperienced, overworked and underpaid public defender, or expensive representation by an experienced criminal attorney willing to invest time, organization, and expertise in obtaining a favorable verdict. Angela opted for the latter. She got a second mortgage on her home and depleted her life savings in order to cover more than $100,000 in legal fees. But the costs went beyond finances. Angela:

> I've never received a speeding ticket. I've never smoked a cigarette or taken a drink. I've gone to church my whole life. And now, all of a sudden, my son was arrested for capital murder. *Culture shock*? It was a very *big* shock for me!

Angela remembers waiting for the jury to return a verdict. "I couldn't sit still. I'd go to the bathroom and I would pray." Then came the guilty verdict. She hugged the mothers of the two murdered boys and told them she was praying for them, but her son was really innocent.

> I went to the bathroom and I laid down on the floor and I felt like I was dying. A woman came in and said, "what's wrong?" And I said my son was just sentenced to death. I had all these thoughts going through my mind about when Wes was little and when he said his first word. I thought about all the trophies he won. All the special things that he had said and done. All the times I'd sit up and rocked him when he was sick. I just laid there for the longest time.

At sentencing, Angela had to plea for her son's life—an experience no mother should endure.

> It's the most helpless feeling in the world. I was asked to make a scrapbook about Wes, all the things that he did growing up. The women on the jury were crying as I showed and told about my son. I begged them, please don't sentence my son to death. Please don't do that.

Life did not return to any sense of normal for Angela once Wes was placed on death row at Holman.

> It's all I could do to make it through work each day. I'd come home, and I lay on the couch and I close my eyes. And I didn't eat. I'd go to bed and I finally got to sleep. And I would wake up and I think what a horrible nightmare I just had. And then I realized that, oh no, that's my *real life*. And then I'd cry. I'd cry every morning when I realize that this is the *truth*. And then I'd go into the bathroom and just sit in there and think, this is too much of a nightmare. This can't be *real*. This can't be happening.

Her death row visits were similar to those of Bubba's family. The four-hour-and-thirty-minute trip from the towns north of Birmingham to Holman became a numbing part of her life. On one occasion, a Kairos Prison Ministry volunteer introduced her to another death row inmate. She thought, "what a nice looking young man. How spiritual he was because he was praying and I could just see the Spirit around him." It was only when that inmate left the visitation area that the volunteer explained he would be executed in just two weeks. It was then that Bonhoeffer's *real* sunk in. Angela:

> It hit me real hard. Actually *real*. For the first time I realized that Wes will be executed some day. I started crying. I was losing my legs and I couldn't *breathe*.

The Execution Team

Those who are associated with the murderer's execution are also greatly impacted by events beyond their control. The need to find space and time for emotional adjustment (Abramson and Isay, 2002) prior to the start of the next day is why the time of executions in Alabama has been changed from midnight to 6:00 p.m. "Shep," the man who lost both a wife and unborn child to abortion, is a Kairos Prison Ministry volunteer who helps prepare the convicted for his time on the gurney. He sees how the execution team interacts with the condemned. "They know the inmates as *people*. They care and you can see it in their faces."

What on earth do you do after an execution? Each team member answers in his own way. For the warden, work helps him cope. By 7:00 p.m. he checks with the team captain to make sure all procedures were followed. He then prepares for the brief press conference. Afterwards he works on related paperwork into the late hours.

Other members of the execution team, including the chaplain, leave Holman around 7:00 p.m. Some may stop for a beer at either the Whistle Stop Grill or David's Catfish House, but most simply go home to unwind before tomorrow's shift. The chaplain prefers to take a twenty-mile bike ride but, in the winter months, the lowering sun typically prevents such excursions. On those nights he goes directly home to his wife. Pulling into the driveway, his Belgium Malinois—Rango and Bo-Pachen—bark loudly from kennels behind the backyard metal barn. Such greetings usually annoy him, but not so after executions. On those nights he counts every sound of life as a true blessing—even the nuisance barking of his beloved dogs.

Holidays

Carolyn: "You know you need to have Christmas for the living and you need to make it special for Justin [Sue's child]. But first I have to go to her grave and bring her something special." Each Christmas eve, Carolyn and Jerry take a Christmas tree and secure it in a stand at the foot of Sue's grave. Batteries permit the lights on the tree to glow warmly throughout the night until the arrival of Christmas morning. Carolyn: "I take angels out there for her," and hang them on the tree. They wrap up packages and place them under that tree, and they station a plastic Santa Clause at the side of her grave. Then, and only then, can Carolyn muster strength for Christmas at home.

Other holidays are no different. On Easter, Carolyn makes her own flower arrangements for Sue's grave. She never purchases them from a florist because the scent still reminds her of Sue's funeral. She places plastic butterflies on her grave during the summer and decorates it patriotically on the Fourth of July. She can render little strength to do anything on March 4, Sue's birthday, but to sit and visit with her daughter.

For Leigh, the misery she felt during the first Christmas was just a harbinger of what would follow. "The calendar said it was Christmas, but it really wasn't. It never will be *again*." Each Christmas she decorates the "Michael tree" with lights. On his birthday, December 7, the Michael tree is decorated with balloons. Because he died the day before Mother's Day, it is beyond Leigh's physical and emotional capacity to celebrate that holiday—even with her daughter. She hasn't a clue as to what she will do when her daughter gives birth and they will want to celebrate Mother's Day with grandmother.

For parents of children on death row, holidays are also unimaginably painful. Angela recalls that the:

> first few Christmases, I couldn't go to be with the family [visiting relatives]. I had to just stay at home. I would wait until everybody left, and I would just cry. I would remember all the fun I had in previous Christmases with Wes. Putting things on lay-away and paying 'em out, because we didn't have much money. Wes was so excited about Christmas, and he couldn't wait to go to bed and get up to see what's under the tree. And then all of a sudden, he's not here anymore.

As with many death row inmates, Bubba's family did not visit death row at Christmas time. Bubba:

> You want to really see family, but you hate to see them *leave*. And so, it is better *not* to see them [around Christmas]. There were times when I just lied and told them I could not have visitors because I got tired of it—seeing them leave and seeing the hurt in *their* faces and feeling the hurt inside.

Anger and Hatred

You hate people when someone is murdered. For two decades, Carolyn has hated Tag. She knows that he now resides at Donaldson Correctional Facility, and she hopes he is raped or murdered. "The best thing to do is wait for poetic justice."

Leigh's anger is much newer than Carolyn's. This petite woman says, "turn him over to me. What I'd love to do to him would make the Apaches look tame." Her rage extends beyond the death of her son to the loss of future grandchildren: "I'd been a grandma by now, at *least* once, if he'd lived." She is also angry at how the murder stopped the life of his fiancée who is still not dating. "I've encouraged her to do so.... I would love to go to her wedding someday." But she knows the girl's agony over the loss of her soul mate prevents her from doing so, fueling Leigh's hatred.

Even victims' loved ones who attend executions leave the death chamber with more hatred than closure. Holman's chaplain: "You see it in their faces. They don't get the revenge they want. They feel bitterness." Shep: "They come down here seeking *vengeance*, and that's not what they get. They leave there worse than when they came. The ultimate punishment of death ought to *satisfy* you, but it doesn't. There's no satisfaction in that person dying."

This kind of reaction occurred after one condemned man, "Orlando," sang "Amazing Grace" while strapped in the electric chair. Shep: "the victim's daughter said that 'Amazing Grace' was her favorite song and now she never wants to hear that song again." At another execution, one surviving victim felt the condemned did not die in a sufficiently gruesome manner: "If we had a guillotine or gallows we would have a lot less crying" (Diel, May 4, 2007).

Struggle with Forgiveness

For "Anthony," a Kairos Prison Ministry volunteer for death row:

> It doesn't matter if you take a pick-axe and kill him, if you put him to sleep, if you execute him by electric chair—*nothing* is going to bring you peace, but *forgiveness*. And that's a hard thing to do. Forgiveness is three things: (1) it's a *decision*, (2) it's a *process*, and (3) it's a *grace*.

While on death row, Bubba wanted to contact the family of the man he killed to apologize and seek forgiveness. The anger felt by the family prevented such redemption.

> They wouldn't have none of that. And I could understand that. If somebody had killed one of *my* parents, *what does "sorry" mean*? And so if I said it a thousand times, it wouldn't bring anybody back or it wouldn't make them feel OK about him being gone. But I tried. I wasn't able to bridge any gaps with them or to repair the breach.

Carolyn has made some progress. A couple of years ago, she turned to God and prayed: "You've got to help me. I tried to do this alone, and it's not working. I can't do it without You." However, the path of forgiveness has been more difficult for Leigh. Someone in her Sunday School class encouraged her to pray for John Henry because "Jesus *said* forgive those who trespass against you the way *you* would want to be forgiven." She realizes that "it is hard to hate someone you're praying for." Hence, every morning Leigh tries to pray for John Henry. "But its by rote. I'm praying because I *should*. I'm not praying because I really *want* to have blessings placed on him." The best she can do is to pray for his family, that their suffering and shame will be diminished. "That's as close as I can come to praying for him."

Intimate Consequences of Public Action: Sketches from the Real of Murderers

Anthony asks "what is the ultimate punishment for murder?" He says that most people tend to respond with *lex talionis*: "Life is the most valuable thing you *have*. Kill them, take *that* away from them." For Anthony, this does not seem to be an answer that truly fulfills the mission of retaliation. "Most men on death row *want* to die because they are *tired* of spending so much of their lives in prison. [We] do death row inmates a *favor* by executing them."

When a man is convicted of capital murder in Alabama, the county of prosecution usually sends him to the assigned institution as quickly as possible—typically within hours of sentencing. Male inmates are housed on death rows at two institutions. Holman Prison, near the town of Atmore in the southern part of the state, has the largest death row—consisting of seven units, each having two tiers of fourteen cells—and is the location of the death chamber. It currently houses 178 men. Death row at Donaldson Prison, located in rural west Jefferson County in the north central part of Alabama, consists of one block—two tiers of twelve cells. It currently houses twenty-three men.[5]

Orientation

Death row inmates receive an initial orientation within twenty-four hours of placement in the institution. Each condemned man appears distrait, no longer as a "tough guy" in control of his world. Facial expressions and body motions, twitching and flinching, indicate apprehension concerning this new environment. Waiting in cuffs and shackles in the warden's outer office at Holman, he may hear common conversations among the COs, the secretary, and others—frequently about the prospects of state football teams or the outcome of other sporting events. These conversations continue as if he was not in the room and, while the natural tendency may be to join in, he will not because of the uncertainty about his role. He may want to sit down in a vacant chair directly behind him, and his knees may appear to bend slightly as if in the process of sitting, but he will hesitate and conclude otherwise because no one has instructed him to occupy that chair.

Then the warden appears and enjoins him into his office, along with both captains of the prison, the psychologist, the classification supervisor, and the prison chaplain. The warden typically has music playing in an effort to calm the man, who is finally offered a seat. It is a comfortable office chair, yet its very nature reinforces the man's quiet anxiety. He is a condemned murderer and he finds himself in this peculiar environment—perhaps reminiscent of earlier times when he found himself in the principal's office. But here he lacks control, and now he will remain in that condition for the rest of his life. Uncertain, and regardless of whose voices he hears, the man's eyes remain affixed on the warden.

Rules and expectations are covered: meal times, laundry procedure, funds list and visitation process. The warden also probes the nature of the individual or, in the warden's words, if "they have other things twisting and turning in their heads." How was he treated at the county jail or, if this is a death row transfer from Donaldson, how was he treated there? Has he ever been in prison before this conviction? Is his family from out of state? He tries to both anticipate future issues and give reassurance about the realities of life on death row. Warden: "once you get back on the Row, guys are going to tell you all kinds of things, and this is why we try to tell you up front pretty much how it's going to be."

The warden ends the orientation by describing what life will be like in the single cell: twenty-three hours a day with a shower every other day. He explains that the CO is the inmate's life-line and, if he respects the CO, that respect will be returned. Afterwards the psychologist conducts a separate session. Then he is issued a "Z number" (if he is not a transfer from Donaldson's death row and, hence, already has one) and given clean white prison pants and shirt, underwear and socks, a toothbrush and toothpaste, a box for personal items, and a "legal kit" consisting of: ten sheets of paper, one sheet of carbon paper, two envelopes stamped "for legal use only," and one pen. He is then taken to death row.

The Significance of "Z"

Like Michelle standing outside of Omega Breeze so that protestors can place a face to a person, Bubba says "it's easy to kill a number. It's harder to kill a man." Upon entry into the Alabama penal system, all inmates are issued a six digit numeric code—an Alabama Institutional Serial (AIS) number—which accompanies him the entire time of incarceration. In the case of a death row inmate, however, the AIS number is three-digits (reflecting the total number of persons who have been sentenced to death) and has the prefix "Z" attached to it. As with all AIS numbers, Z classifications are issued in ascending order of entry into the system. Virgil W. Murphy had the dubious honor of receiving the first death row AIS number, Z1, in 1926. He was executed on April 8, 1927. As of February 2009, Donald Dwayne Whatley is the latest inmate to be placed on death row, and his AIS number is Z757.

The significance of Z cannot be exaggerated because it serves as a daily reminder to the inmate of his standing in the pecking order of human life. Z is at the bottom of the alphabet, and the inmate convicted of capital murder is at the bottom of deviants in the American political community. He has intentionally destroyed *Imago Dei* in the worst possible way and, subsequently, his human misconduct is unsurpassed in abusing the intimacy of the social gospel. He can be placed in no deeper pit of permanent ostracism—not only isolated from the free-world, but also segregated from all others in the prison facility. Barring case reversal, such as with Wes, or retrials resulting in changed sentences, such as with Bubba, the Z means that death row will be the last place on earth these individuals will eat, breathe, and exist.

"Z-1" status places temporarily the new death row inmate into even greater isolation. At first arrival on death row, each inmate is placed into this category for purposes of psychological assessment. They are in complete lockdown, and segregated from every other death row inmate, for a period of at least three months. While in Z-1 status, the inmate can only leave the cell to shower and to exercise daily as a "walk-alone" in the yard for sixty minutes during the workweek. All ventures out of the cell entail handcuffs and shackles, and the excursion corresponds with lockdown of every other death row inmate.

While in Z-1 status, the man continues to be disoriented. He asks questions that have already been answered countless times—questions about routine things, like when is store day or shower day. But he also learns quickly that, on death row, there is always an audience—if not eyes, certainly ears—which gauges him by what he says and how he says it. Will he be a "tough guy"—someone to fear or respect—as he was in previous settings? He may therefore ask for favors, like permission to get out of isolation and attend church services, in an effort to show manipulation and regain control.

Death Row Cells

Throughout the Z-1 status period, the condemned man becomes accustomed to his cell. Holman's are approximately eight feet deep and five feet wide, about the size of a small walk-in closet, permitting most inmates to touch both walls with their outstretched hands. Each cell is dominated by one metal bed, with a shallow mattress, that rests perpendicular to the hallway. This consumes about six feet of the cell's length and about three feet of its width. One end of the bed lies flush with the back wall, along with a stainless steel sink with two push buttons (one "cold" and one "hot"), in lieu of faucet knobs, so that the man cannot run water without holding the buttons. Below the sink is a stainless steel commode with neither a liftable seat nor a closeable cover. Unless you want to sleep with your ears close to hallway noise, your head is never more than a couple of inches from the open toilet.

The small space between the bed and commode has a single light fixture and, below that, a typically filthy air vent. There are no windows in the cell, which means that light is always artificial and the air is usually stagnant. The aroma of feces and gases ruminates long after flushing the commode. It captures the bed and seeps into the narrow hallway. Across the hallway from each row of cells is a series of industrial-looking filmed windows with exhaust fans. These provide the only source of natural light as well as a modicum of ventilation. Since the arrival of Warden Grantt Culliver, each death row cell has a six-inch fan. Each man is also allowed to purchase a twelve-inch non-cable television set from DOC, costing about $100.

There is about two feet of space between the other end of the bed and the bar doors that span the five-feet width of the cell. The space on the end of the bed is consumed with a metal slab, functioning as a desk, which is welded to the bars. The bed functions as the only chair in the cell. There is also a small (about 2 x 2 foot) box for personal belongings. All in all, there is a space about two feet wide and perhaps four feet in length for the inmate to stand and walk during the normal twenty-three hours of lockdown. Because the bar doors leave much transparency, stereotypical of those in movies, there is never privacy in the bed or at the commode. Cells on the second tier, however, offer a little more privacy since the bars have an additional layer of metal mesh over them to keep inmates from reaching out and grabbing at others who walk along the narrow balcony. (Outwardly slanted balcony railings also help in providing more space between passers-by and inmates in the second floor cells.) The only place an inmate can enjoy some privacy is down each hallway at the dingy one-person shower which is surrounded by a five-foot wall. But here, too, a guard stands close.

The day rooms and the exercise yard provide the only opportunities for human contact in the sixty minutes per day death row inmates are permitted out of their cells. At Holman there were originally four day rooms in the death row units. However, two are now used for other purposes: a counseling/multipurpose room (where death row inmates can talk with a psychologist and where faith-based groups, like the Kairos Prison Ministry, meet periodically) and, across the hallway, the shift commander's office. Of the remaining two day rooms, one serves as the law library. All four rooms are of identical size and are quite small: approximately twelve cement blocks wide and eighteen blocks long.

Strips of aging paint dangle from the ceilings and walls of the day rooms. The law library and multipurpose room walls have fading murals painted by Danny Siebert, a serial murderer who died in 2008 of pancreatic cancer in the hospice ward of death row. On the short back wall of the law library, one finds a wizardly magical mural portraying good and evil in opposition to each other. The human figures have angel-like wings and faces which greatly resemble those of his victims. Painted in the multipurpose room, on the lengthier sidewall, is a mural dedicated to the University of Alabama: a large mean-looking elephant, the copyrighted "A" logo, and a portrait of Bear Bryant in his hounds-tooth checkered hat. Along the other length of the room is a mural dedicated to Auburn University: a big tiger (the copyright logo of that university) and a football player wearing an Auburn uniform with number 40 on the jersey. The shorter width wall in the back of the room has a mural dedicated to hunting and wildlife and, above that, there are four windows too high to provide relief for any inmate. The walls of the other day room, across the hallway from the law library, are lined with hobby craft cabinets. Those cabinets, installed four years ago, have never been used for their intended purpose (or any other function), and this is because of staff shortages. No CO is available to monitor and supervise death row inmates in building hobby crafts.

The front width of each of these rooms has open bars. Only a wall phone rests inside the multipurpose room; neither in it nor the other day room nor the law library can one find a TV. In the case of an extra special sporting event, such as a championship game, an inmate who has purchased a TV set from DOC may be allowed to bring it into the law library for community showing. As in their own private cells, inmates using these rooms can hand microwavable products to a fellow death row inmate "runner," one chosen from each tier on the basis of good behavior.

Out of their cells for approximately fourteen hours per day, the assigned runners assist the other inmates by heating items in the microwave oven provided on each tier of the seven death row units.

Because of the small size, only 15 inmates are permitted to use either the day room or the law library at any one time. The shear number of men on death row means that groups must be rotated throughout the day for their mandatory time outside the cell. When weather permits, men go out to the exercise area with others from their own tier section. There you find weights, volleyball and basketball facilities, as well as an eighth-mile dirt running track.

In contrast, Donaldson's death row does not have an "open feel" to it. Entry from the main hallway into the access-way requires pounding on a large metal door, eleven cement blocks tall and two-and-a-half cement blocks wide, which opens electronically. You pound and wave your hands through the door's side window until someone sees you from inside an elevated "cube"—a five-sided structure which houses two or three monitoring COs and is surrounded on all sides by the twenty-four cells of death row, plus a twenty-four cell mental health segregation block and a forty-eight cell general population segregation block. The appropriate control box button is pushed and the door "buzzes," allowing you to open the door. You walk through and slam it shut. Then you walk toward the cube down the five-foot wide darkened access-way for about thirty paces. Along the walls are an early model of a personal computer, with access to law cases, and six book shelves of dilapidated penal code volumes—all of which constitutes death row's law library. At the end of the access-way, there is a twelve-section window, approximately twenty feet long and fifteen feet tall, which allows COs in the five-foot elevated cube to have a constant and full view of the men in the death row day room.

That single day room is comparatively large—about the size of a triple garage, forty cement blocks tall at its peak at the windows facing the cube. It has four metal tables with pressed-wood tops, each with four attached metal stools. There are two wooden benches where perhaps a total of eight men might sit comfortably. On one of the metal tables is a microwave oven and a large old-fashioned hundred-cup coffee pot which keeps water hot for instant coffee, hot chocolate, cereal, and soup. A beach cooler, filled with ice, rests next to the table. There is an old chess set and a packet of dominos on one table. There is no common television or wall phone, but there is an industrial-size portable fan purchased by

Kairos volunteers during an excruciating heat wave in 2007. The day room is adorned with more than fifty half-gallon plastic milk containers, each with the upper third removed. These are used to catch rain which seeps through the rusting metal roof. Ceiling lights remain on twenty-four hours a day, even when inmates are in lockdown during the night.

Two shower facilities, which together look like an old industrial elevator shaft, are stacked on top of each other—one for the ground row and one for the second tier. Each shower has one faucet and is five-and-a-half cement blocks deep and eleven cement blocks wide. Both can be locked to act as a temporary holding cell. Each has a large Plexiglas window with a grey strip that "clouds" the inmate's groin area, giving some privacy while letting cube officers monitor all movements inside the shower facility.

With the day room space as foreground, Donaldson's death row unit looks like the outside of a cheap motel. The two levels of cells are connected from the day room area by a seventeen-step metal stairway on either side. The walkway for the top tier has a five-rail metal fence between it and the edge. Each cell contains a white plastic "patio" chair, common issue in prisons; a transparent twelve-inch television set—non-cable with rabbit-ear antenna, purchased by Kairos volunteers; and a portable heater for the winter.

In contrast to Holman, these cells offer more privacy and are larger. Rather than transparent bars across the front, there is a solid metal door—the same size as the outer door—with a three-inch wide and six-inch tall window at face level and a food tray opening at waist level. Each cell is about ten feet deep and six feet wide. At the back of each cell, spanning the width, is a concrete slab which acts as the bed frame. A thin mattress is placed on the slab. A stainless steel toilet with an attached steel sink rests between the bed and the door. There is a very small window near the top of the outer wall, an overhead light, but no fan. There is a box for personal belongings, but no desk. Most cell floors are covered with boxes of documents pertaining to trial and appeals, and these suffice for a desk. The extra wall space provides each man with sufficient room for personalization: pictures, paintings, cards, and poems.

First Experience

Shep: "death row people are *frozen* to the moment of their crime." Each one's act becomes the focus of all thoughts and activities thereafter.

"Glenn," a pastor and Kairos volunteer, believes these guys never thought "they're gonna end up on death row."

> They think, "how'd I get here? Wait a minute! This wasn't supposed to *happen*." And it isn't just, "I wasn't supposed to get caught for *that* murder." It's more, "Wait a minute. This whole *thing* wasn't supposed to happen this way. I'm not supposed to kill people. I *sure* didn't set out to get to death row." It is an odd sort of thing. You'd think by the time they get to death row, they'd be over that shock a little bit.

"Perkins," who knifed and bludgeoned the life out of a store clerk, was on death row at Holman from 1978 to 1982 until a retrial and plea-bargain reduced his sentence to LWOPP. He arrived from county jail on a December afternoon and, upon completion of his orientation, was given his state-issued clothing. On the upper right section of his shirt was stenciled his "Z" number. It scared the hell out of him. COs walked him past the death chamber and the brightly colored electric chair en route to his cell. The sight of "Yellow Mama" made him nauseous—his head remained inside the toilet bowl for much of his first day on death row.

Prior to the change in sentence, Bubba came within a few days of his scheduled execution. When walked through parts of the general population area to get to death row, he recalls the sobering fear of hearing the officers scream: "Lock it down!" Bubba: "Everyone had to get out of the hall and find a secured door and get behind it."[6] As did Perkins, Bubba also passed by the electric chair en route to his cell. He, too, was sickened.

"Marion," who was convicted of murdering a man by helping to stab him seventy-eight times on Memorial Day 1987, was on death row at Holman for eight-and-a-half years—until a retrial and plea-bargain led to a reduced sentence of LWOPP. After the orientation, he was given a mattress and a wooden box for his belongings. "Even though I was handcuffed, I was told to 'grab this and drag it through the hall.'" He too passed the electric chair. The consequences of his crime hit home when he heard the officers scream to general population inmates: "Get out of the hall! *Dead man walking*!"

First Night

Perkins' first night on death row was his first night in any prison. "I cried a lot. I was twenty-one [years old]. I was scared, so very much so." He would continue to cry for many nights thereafter during his Z-1 status period, and he would continue to hear the muffled sounds of crying in other cells as night passed into day. He learned quickly that when the lights are off, all a man has are his thoughts and his conscience. "You lay there thinking about all the 'what ifs' and the 'why didn't I's'. You see all the goals in life that you wanted to accomplish. I used to cry [a lot]. I'd pray to God, but I didn't really know *how* to pray."

Bubba's initial night in prison was also on death row. A large man built like a linebacker, he felt afraid for the first time in his life. "You feel all alone. The cell is electronically locked and it also has a chain and a pad lock." He could not clear his mind of the image of the death chamber and his seemingly inevitable destiny to walk someday down the hallway towards it.

Marion also remembers his first night on death row. He was scared and lonely, with sweat pouring the entire night to the point where his mattress felt soaked. "I was so afraid. I felt like I was isolated from the whole world." Yet Marion believes that the second and consecutive nights get no better. "Between the hours of 11 p.m. and 4 a.m., when you *have* to be alone with yourself, that is the hard part." So Marion laid there and thought about what he did that Memorial Day weekend and, more importantly, what he should have done and would do—if he could simply take back that day.

Coming Off Z-1 Status

I first met "Lawton" at a Kairos death row gathering. This was shortly after he came off "Z-1" status and, in all likelihood, was the first time he saw free-world people since arriving at Donaldson. There were about thirty volunteers and fifteen death row inmates enjoying free-world cooked food, praise music, testimonies, and one-on-one conversations. Lawton looked rather young—perhaps in his mid 20s. He spoke and acted with "middle class" mannerisms: confidently articulating his views and able to ask socially probing questions to keep a conversation quick and interesting. His skin was just starting to pale and grow waxy and his touch, a bit clammy—all traits acquired by most death row inmates due, I presume, to an insufficient amount of vitamins and limited direct sun light.

Lawton was the proverbial "deer in the headlights." While enjoying human interaction, he was not comfortable in his immediate surroundings. He truly wanted to be some place else, or at least on the "free world" side of the equation in death row—visitors who would shortly walk out the main gate and resume the tasks and pleasures of the day.

The strain of everything was starting to show. Occasionally he would fold his arms so that his left hand crossed his chest to cover momentarily the "Z" number stenciled on his shirt—a constant reminder as to who he actually was and where he actually lived.

Lawton insisted on telling me about self-perceived injustices surrounding his conviction of killing a man during a theft: not being present at the actual murder, his own integrity in rejecting a plea-bargain in exchange for testifying against his accomplice, his accomplice's unethical act of accepting the same plea bargain against him, and how a county jail informant cut another deal in return for testifying about a confession Lawton allegedly made one night. (Whether or not true, the general details are common stock among death row inmates.) He shook his head at the irony that (from his perspective) the real murderer, his accomplice, received a lighter sentence and would be paroled long before Lawton would be executed. He wanted me to understand that, in his world view, he was very different from the other death row inmates—he simply did not belong there.

Then Lawton began to talk about his family life as if he were not incarcerated, let alone on death row. He used the present and future tenses to describe an alternate reality and told me about his son and how his daily letters help that boy with home work. He talked about his family's business and how respected they are in the community. He told me about their last vacation and how, in a year or two, he will once again join them. One would have thought we were chatting at a university cocktail reception, or perhaps standing in line at the Saturday night country club buffet—certainly not in the confines of the death row day room. In another setting Lawton might have joined me in wearing an aloha shirt and blue jeans—discussing with surprise our mutual admiration of Dietrich Bonhoeffer. But this was neither the setting nor the world we shared for that particular moment, and that reality seemed branded deep into his soul. Lawton was wearing DOC "white," and I was the one wearing the aloha shirt—anything *but* white as per the free-world dress code in Alabama prisons. He occasionally became visibly perturbed, as if he was trying desperately to push the "refresh" button on his internal internet only to find that the same old web page kept returning.

Monotony

Regardless of what "happens" on any given day, the "routine" on death row is similar to that of grass growing or paint drying—the only difference is that *you* are the grass; you are the *paint*. Life is slow and methodic. Laundry is an example: in the morning, Lawton places his dirty clothes in a white mesh bag and shoves it through the food tray slot. A CO picks it up, gives it to a general population inmate who takes it to the laundry room and returns it later in the afternoon. On death row, pants and shirts are washed on Mondays, underwear and towels on Wednesdays, and sheets, pillow cases and winter cotton cloth coats on Fridays. While a particular day may see modification—for instance, you may decide to wash your clothes in an old mop bucket rather than have them returned from the laundry still dirty—nothing really happens that would be classified as "new" and certainly nothing counts as "exciting."

Food is another example. Breakfast is always between 2:00 and 3:00 a.m., lunch is around 8:30 to 9:00 a.m., and dinner around 3:00 p.m. At Donaldson, a general population inmate wheels into the access-way a large enclosed stainless steel server, heated and capable of holding trays for the 96 cells which comprise the three cell blocks surrounding the cube. The inmate and several COs don latex gloves and proceed to distribute individual trays. The inmate places four trays on large thin metal sheet pans and each CO takes one in each hand and, like restaurant waiters, balances them from underneath. Each CO enters the block, and an inmate reaches out through his cell tray slot and takes a tray. Soon another CO wheels in a gigantic container of "Kool-Aid-like" mixture with two large pitchers which he dunks into the larger container for refills. He then carries both pitchers in one hand with the same grave gusto as over-sized maidens carry beer steins at Munich's Hofbrauhaus. An inmate places his cup on the tray slot's shelf to indicate he wants a drink. No eating utensils are distributed. Each inmate is given a supply of plastic spoons, which are kept in the cell. No plastic knives or forks are ever distributed since these could be recast as weapons. The men seem to complete a meal in less than ten minutes, most likely because the food is consistently dull and the menu eternally monotonous.

While Alabama death row inmates are allowed out of their cells for one hour per day, except for weekends and holidays, this rule can bend. Inmates may be collectively denied that time if there is an emergency, a shortage of staff, or if it interferes with other scheduled activities. At the discretion of the warden, a decision usually deferred to the CO in charge, death row inmates might receive more time out of the cells or more frequent showers—if they have good conduct or if staffing and space allow. Because of these factors, the rules are a bit more flexible at Donaldson than at Holman.

At times, however, death row inmates may never leave their cells. Such is the case on alternating Mondays when visitation occurs from 8 a.m. to 1 p.m. Inmates with guests in the visitation room are handcuffed and, as a break from the routine, most choose to wear their "best whites"—clean and pressed for the occasion. At Donaldson, if the COs feel comfortable with a particular inmate, they will allow him out of his cell and handcuff him in the day room. Otherwise they will insist that he stand with his back against his side of the locked cell door and extend his arms out the tray slot so that he is handcuffed prior to the electronic opening of the door. At Donaldson, each inmate is then escorted by a minimum of two COs through the day room door into the access-way, then to the end of the access-way and through the metal door into the outside hallway. He then turns left and walks sixty-five steps down the hallway, through the security entrance into a large air-conditioned visitation area (about the size of a fellowship hall at a large church) which is just across from the administration unit. Men who have visitors typically do not eat breakfast and are not worried about missing lunch. Guests bring coins which give inmates access to sodas, snacks and machine-dispensed sandwiches and burritos.

Typically about 85 percent of death row inmates will not have visitors and, hence, most are in lockdown that day. At Donaldson, this means they are dependent on a runner—like at Holman, a selected death row inmate who is allowed to stay out of his cell—to perform the task of making sure each man has either ice or hot water throughout the day, if his cup is placed on the tray slot shelf. COs permit the men to set up their own rotation for runners—the only requirement is that all runners have a history of good conduct. Given the alternative of lockdown, most men get on the rotation. A little after 8:00 a.m. on visitation Mondays, the runner normally flashes his cell light and waves a towel out of the tray slot because he is worried that the CO has forgotten that it is his turn.

Runners seem to enjoy the feeling of being "alone." It is perhaps the only time when he can sit at a day room table, drink a cup of instant coffee, and not have to talk with someone or have to absorb the odor of another man's body or breath. Perhaps momentarily it makes him feel like he did in the free-world. The runner can talk with the men in lockdown, but he can also choose just to sit and daydream. Some runners use the time to do things, such as wash clothes or bed sheets in a mop bucket and hang wet items to dry on his open door, or take a relaxing shower.

Others choose to power-walk, and some read books. At times they appear excited with their assigned tasks, yet at other times they look quite bored. In a couple of hours, another inmate becomes the runner for the rest of the lockdown.

What to Do?

Some men try to exercise in their cells. Marion did 500 push-ups, 500 sit-ups, and ran in place for an hour every day in his cell. Some read, and others play solitary chess. One man's walls are adorned with pictures of dogs. The walls of some cells are home to pictures of scantily clad women, and these are used for recreational masturbation despite their proximity to posted pictures of parents and children. Perkins had that hobby while on death row at Holman. During a period when DOC permitted hardcore pornography, he spent much of his day fantasizing about the pictures affixed to his walls. While the bar doors gave no privacy from on-looking passers-by, the numbing routine of death row meant that Perkins spent much time masturbating regardless of who was out there. One day a volunteer minister looked in his cell and said, "Little man, if I was in that cell, the porn would be the last thing on my mind."

Some men simply vegetate. Lights remain off and little activity is apparent in their cells. They may watch TV or play a radio, but many choose to just lie on their mattress pads and perhaps stare into dreams long lost. Still others do little because of physical or mental disabilities. As Warden Culliver walked through Holman's death row, a very old-looking inmate sat in a wheelchair next to another inmate mopping the floor. Warden: "Hey! Doing alright? How you feeling today?" The old man, who had suffered several strokes and could no longer speak, just smiled with his two remaining teeth while he held a bottle half filled with urine. As the warden stopped to chat, I noticed that the old man had a makeshift board with numbers from 0-9 and letters of the alphabet. His right index finger scrambled to point at various letters and numbers on that board. The warden seemed to follow with some ease. With a big smile, the old man "fingered" good news. The warden congratulated him for having another birthday coming up at the end of the month. The "old man" was just turning forty-six.

Art tends to break up the monotony of life, manifesting itself in a variety of ways. "Abe" had been on Donaldson's death row for nearly thirty years and, through those decades, became a devout Christian and a meaningful spiritual mentor to many of the men on death row. He lived by example, often giving whatever he purchased from the prison store to inmates in the mental health block. He always tried to show the other death row inmates how Christ expected them to live.

The day after the issuance of the death date, and Abe's subsequent unannounced and quick transfer to Holman, his former Donaldson neighbors created an agape poster card—twenty-one by fourteen inches when folded—to be delivered to him by Glenn, the Kairos volunteer and pastor. On the outside, two arms in chains hold a closed Christian Bible at the top of a mountain. The sky above is filled with dark ominous storm clouds and lightning. Inside the card: doves on either side rise to the heights of a cloudless heaven. In the center, a man with broken chains and leg irons climbs freely up a few stone steps and begins to knock on a partially opened door. Through the door, beams burst outwardly and surround the face of Jesus. At the bottom of the page is the Christian Bible, now opened. Its left side reads "*Matthew* 7:8." The right side: "and to him who knocks, the door will be opened." The men on Donaldson death row signed the card with individual notes of endearment and Bible verses to wish Abe God's speed to his home in heaven.

As another example, a death row inmate once mailed me a handmade bible marker. Out of a piece of card board and, without scissors, he perforated it neatly and precisely into a two-by-six-inch rectangle. On one side in pencil is a sketch of Jesus with a shepherd's staff. The other side reads:

> Slack, A picture of Christ does not make the artist a Christian, nor can the act suggest the same. It's a lifetime of acts which demonstrate a man's love for God and others, nor can one bad act erase a lifetime of good acts. "Follow!"

The Seasons

Bubba: "prison is a place of extremes. It's either extremely cold or extremely hot." The unbearable heat and humidity of the Alabama summer is exacerbated in a prison cell by fifteen to thirty degrees. At Holman, Marion would plug the toilet bowl and let the water overflow until it covered the floor. He would then lay down in it to cool off. Many men rip off pant legs to make shorts and go without socks in plastic sandals. Some frequently sleep on the hard concrete floor because it is cooler to the touch. At Donaldson, some use their shirts to block off the small window/vent in the back of the cell in an effort to avoid the sun's heat. Even in the day room, it is extremely difficult to breathe.

Alabama winters, while lacking the consistent intensity found in the Midwest, still produce cold temperatures which are especially felt by inmates whose immune systems are hindered by a prolonged absence of vitamins and the constant anxiety of both living and facing death. The average low temperature in January is in the mid-30s at Holman and, at Donaldson, it is in the low 30s. There are nights when it sinks down into the teens. Bubba: "I remember several winters that, during the real cold times, you couldn't even get out of bed. You'd sleep fully clothed." Perkins remembers that the hot water heater always seemed to fail during the winter time, resulting in cold showers. At the weekly Bible study sessions in Donaldson's day room, inmates wear jackets and knit hats, as well as several pairs of socks, to counter the inescapable chill emanating from always walking on concrete floors.

Holidays

For the majority of death row men, just as it is for their families and the loved ones of those they have murdered, Christmas is the most depressing time of the year. For Marion, being alone at this time was always a potent reminder as to "what I did and how much pain I caused my family and how much pain they must feel on Christmas." Bubba: "You remember the Christmases when you were outside. Now the only thing you experience is separation from everybody you care about." There are no death row church services on Christmas Eve or Day. Bubba: "The closest to a service is the volunteers that would come through and talk to you" as Christmas approached. This still happens at Donaldson with the annual Kairos visitation to death row on the Saturday before Christmas. At Holman, members of the Faith Crusade Ministry from Montgomery visit before Christmas, laying hands on the men as they press the tops of their heads against the bars.

From Bubba's perspective, Christmas became a reminder of the simple and more important aspects of the holiday.

> TV is playing the same Christmas shows everyone else watches [in the free world]. Same tunes on the radio. Only difference is, you're sitting next to someone who is going to be executed. If you think about the death chamber down the hall, Christmas is not a joyous time. But if the man next to you offers you a piece of candy and you can offer him something, then it really *is* Christmas. I've seen people sing Christmas carols and others join in on the song. Death Row becomes a family.

Constant and Unending Fear

Regardless of how hard they try to hide it, every inmate on death row lives in a constant state of fear. It is a fear of living as well as a fear about dying. You can see it in their faces. If men in general population age rapidly, men on death row age exponentially faster. The two-toothed forty-six-year-old man in the wheelchair appears to be in his 80s. Lawton looks so much older today than he did coming off Z-1 status about a decade ago. He has lost only a few teeth, but his hair has grayed, waxiness has become a permanent feature, and his eyes appear "deadened." The end of Z-1 status means "waking up" from a ninety-day nightmare only to find that the nightmare is *the real*. The "refresh" button cannot change the web page.

Some try to hide from the fear by becoming increasingly reclusive inside of their cells. Others try to accept the fear. After a Bible study session, one man remarked that being on death row is the same as being Jonah in the whale. God is the only thing you have left in which to trust. Another man tries to cope with fear through metaphor. In a letter:

> Death Row is like waiting for a bus that has no permanent schedule. A man is told that his bus is coming, so he sits and watches. Buses show up and take others away, but yours don't ever seem to show up. Everyone's eyes are wide from the report, "Hey, here comes another bus!" Some hope it's theirs, while others start praying that it is not!

Jimmey D's Last Christmas

Every couple of months, the Kairos volunteers at Donaldson provide a Saturday gathering for death row inmates. The one around Christmas is especially meaningful because it may be the only glimpse of celebration death row inmates see throughout that Holy Season. There is a full day of singing, testimonies, fellowship and the human touch of embracing other brothers-in-Christ. Volunteers bring homemade cookies and snacks, a wide variety of soft drinks, and a home-cooked breakfast and dinner.[7] It is not uncommon to find Shep and other free-world volunteers positioned near the prison entrance, long before daybreak, frying bologna sandwiches (with mayonnaise on white bread)—the inmates' favorite breakfast. Others will bring dinner, which may be home-made lasagna, barbecue chicken, or pizza.

One Christmas turned out to be the last Kairos gathering for "Jimmey D" prior to his execution. As a twenty-seven-year-old, he was convicted of second-degree murder in 1957. While in prison, he corresponded with an elderly woman who owned a convenience store. She was instrumental in getting him paroled in 1976. At the age of forty-six, Jimmey D rented a room from the lady. One drunken night, he robbed her store and, despite pleas for mercy, shot her three times—in her arm, head, and directly in the face. After claiming unsuccessfully that the woman had committed suicide, he was convicted of capital murder and remained on death row at Donaldson for almost three decades.

My impression of Jimmey D was that he was a crotchety old man. He was seventy-three years-old by free-world standards, but he looked and acted more like 103 years-old in prison time. He always had a complaint about someone who was just trying to help him. That particular morning it was my turn. My "job" was to serve the bologna sandwiches to the twenty-four death row inmates coming through the breakfast line in the day room. Perhaps it was the volunteer next to me who "improperly" spooned grits on his plate, or perhaps it was the one who placed strips of bacon incorrectly—regardless, I endured the wrath once I served his bologna sandwich. He looked at the sandwich and then scowled at me. He jerked the Styrofoam plate from my hand, rearranged all the food with his fingers so each portion was separate and distinct, grimaced at me once more, and then walked away uttering something unkind under his breath. At that moment I had trouble remembering that, as per *Matthew* 25:36, it was not "just" Jimmey D, but actually *Jesus,* whom I had served. Anthony reminded me that Jimmey D "was 'ornery' because he was just so tired." Anthony:

> He'd been there so long and he was so *old* and set in his ways. Any little thing would just set him off. He was just *tired*. He was tired of being jerked around by DOC and his lawyers. It seemed like everything was going *wrong*.

As he passed through the breakfast line, it was apparent that Jimmey D was ready for Christmas to end. He was waiting to catch his bus.

Execution

All death row inmates eventually end up at Holman Prison, where the death chamber is located. Some are there from the start, and others—like Jimmey D—are transferred from Donaldson once the death date certificate is issued—typically thirty to forty-five days prior to the execution. Holman sends three COs to transport the condemned man: a supervisor, a captain, and an assistant warden. The condemned man and all his personal possessions are extracted without notice to thwart escape plans. Regardless of how well they think they are prepared mentally, the actual transfer comes as a shock—not only to the man being transferred but also to his neighbors on death row. Truly, his bus has arrived.

Facing his cell door, the condemned man sticks both hands through the food tray slit. He is handcuffed in the front which allows more comfortable seating in a vehicle. The door is opened and, at that point, his legs are shackled. He is provided only a cursory opportunity to shout goodbye to others on death row who are in lockdown. He is escorted through the day room door into the narrow access-way. The hallway door is buzzed and opened. Instead of turning left, as he has done in the past to see visitors, he now turns to the right. The COs shout to clear the hallway of all general population inmates and free-world people. He takes 105 steps down the hallway. He passes the kitchen and canteen on his left, perhaps for the first time realizing the source of his meals for all these years. At the hallway's end, he turns left and exits at the kitchen's delivery dock. The stench of filled trash cans can be hideous as he steps down into the "South Side" yard. There he finds the DOC vehicle.

The supervisor and captain sit in the front seat, and the condemned man sits in the back behind a metal screen with seat belt on and still cuffed and shackled. The assistant warden typically follows in a chase vehicle.[8] The caravan drives 200 feet toward the rear exit of Donaldson. Here he gains some insight into life on the South Side and its general population inmates who reside there because of good behavior. To his left, he sees weights and press benches as well as a spiritual garden maintained by Native American inmates. He also sees old volleyball equipment and a circular dirt path that acts as a running track. To his right is the make-shift softball diamond and an open green area. He does not see inmates enjoying this part of Donaldson, however, for all are in lockdown until he passes. The caravan exits past a guard tower and through a sally port with razor wire. It turns left past the arsenal building and onto the perimeter road. Curving around to the front of Donaldson, the caravan takes a right onto Warrior Lane. For 0.9 miles, the man in the back seat sees wooded state-owned land and DOC housing; he may even hear dogs barking at the K-9 unit—perhaps the last sounds of dogs he will ever hear.

The caravan then turns on to a series of two-lane roads through the country side for about twenty-five miles. A right onto Taylors-Ferry Road, a left onto Warrior River Road, and a right onto Fifteenth Street. Given his many years on death row, the condemned sees, smells, and hears things that perhaps spark memories of another time in life, and also permit a glimpse into the contemporary world which he has only sensed through the twelve-inch screen of a non-cable television set: rural and urban dynamics, the technology of cell phones and electronic billboards, and the newest cars. He also sees sky and land and, if he is lucky to have the window cracked for cigarette smoke, he might catch a bit of fresh air.

Large semi-trucks, flatbeds filled with timber, pass him at high speeds. Slower moving dump trucks prolong the trip somewhat and, as in other cars, frustrate his driver. For the last time, the condemned sees small communities and volunteer fire department stations, barbecue stops and mini storage facilities, and churches with varying marquees—all inquiring about the role of God in the reader's life.

The caravan then enters the outskirts of Bessemer, a rusting industrial town. The condemned passes tattoo parlors, convenience stores, a child daycare facility in a former church, and the declining human and housing stock caused by poverty and a government unwilling to pursue the "outward justice" about which Bonhoeffer writes. The two cars take a quick right onto Eighteenth Avenue and then a left for a stretch on State Route (SR) 150. They reach the outskirts of upscale suburban sprawl and affluence found in the city of Hoover. There he sees the things he never had, and perhaps the kind of things he once coveted so badly that the temptation led him to death row.

A short distance on I-459, and then onto I-65 for over 180 miles—south through what Alabamians like to call, the "black belt." He catches a glimpse of billboards boasting Chilton County's peach groves, and he sees the oversized confederate flag which flies in Autauga County and maintained by the Alabama Division of the Sons of Confederate Veterans. As he approaches Montgomery, he sees new housing development which, in all likelihood, was not a fixture prior to him earning Z-1 status. In Montgomery he is afforded a quick view of the town's single tall building, the white-washed edifices of state government, and a Hyundai automobile plant which, surely he speculates, could have provided a decent job and kept him out of trouble if it had only been built in an earlier decade. Then, out of Montgomery, the view reverts back to pastures and pine forests.

After about four hours, the two cars exit I-65. If the caravan would only turn east on SR 21, he would see life. Past a Best Western motel and a Native American gambling casino, the four-lane road would quickly lead them through rolling hills and, to the right, he would see children playing at Escombia County Middle School. The odyssey would lead shortly to Atmore, a town of 7,500 people, where many Holman personnel live and raise families. He would see poster-flags, hanging on all telephone polls, celebrating the town's centennial. He would notice a quaint downtown standing surprisingly *embonpoint*, not unlike what is found in New Orleans' French Quarter: upper balconies framed in wrought iron supports and grand verandas with ferns swinging gently in gulf breezes. He would observe overly polite drivers at four-way stops, and a few older men riding to work on well-preserved 1960-vintage Schwinn bicycles. A watchful eye would also spot a "Sav-a-Life" center, like the one Thesha visited when she was pregnant with Chryston, just 9.9 miles from the front door of Holman.

However, the caravan does not travel east on SR 21. It turns west and travels a two-lane path toward death just 2.9 miles away. The condemned man quickly passes the Jefferson Davis Community College and, for the last time in this world, he sees beauty in what God has made that day: farm country, pine trees, and rolling hills. The two houses maintained for DOC officials on the Fountain / J.O. Davis prison ranch, adjacent to Holman, are the last two homes he will ever view. He might glance out the window and find cattle grazing, a herd of horses, or even a donkey. He might also see an inmate trustee sheaving the long weeds along the frontage of the prison ranch, or perhaps another trustee driving a tractor with an American flag flapping in the wind from its poll attached to the engine hood. The cars then turn onto Ross Road, which runs past Holman. He is on this two lane road for the remaining 0.8 miles and, if still looking, he might see spring wild flowers and a green pasture as far as his eyes will take him. In the winter, he might see through the leafless trees the Holman water tower. In so many ways, Ross Road is the last *green mile* of his life.

Suddenly there is a gully in the road and, upon coming up the other side, he sees to his right Holman prison. The caravan makes a right turn onto a dirt perimeter road to the back of the prison. There he enters a sally port that is ten steps wide and fifty-three steps long. One end of the sally port closes before the other end opens. As the caravan moves forward, he might see to his left the exercise yard for those on death row, eight cages for death row inmates on "walk-alone" status, and two wings of death row. To his right, he sees the metal fabrication plant and the license tag plant—both operated by inmates who are not on death row.

When the caravan stops, the condemned man is met by Holman death row COs and enters the building. He walks past the death chamber and death cell but, since the arrival of Warden Culliver, those doors remain shut so that he does not see the trappings. He walks down a central hallway, which is approximately 150 steps, past the death row units and the infirmary to the central CO station. If his orientation meeting with the warden is delayed, he is then assigned to a new cell; if not, he is processed at this station. He then takes a sharp left past the visitation "yard," then a right, another quick right, and then a left to the outer glass door. He then exits the prison building through a breeze-way and enters the small administration building. There he awaits the orientation meeting with Warden Culliver.

Execution Week

When Holman opened in 1969, the death cell and death chamber were located in the boiler room. After the *Gregg* decision reinstated the death penalty, a newer facility was built next to death row. In 2002 it was remodeled to accommodate lethal injections. In the state of Alabama, executions are always held on Thursdays.

Monday and Tuesday The execution team, usually consisting of six COs and the chaplain, practices Monday and Tuesday to ensure all procedures are followed and all contingencies anticipated. Practices are stressful, as stressful as the actual execution, and team members sometimes use humor as a coping mechanism—such as when the condemned is obese, thus requiring more effort lifting him on and off the gurney. When levity flares, the chaplain's task is to search for ways to communicate to team members that the sanctity of life needs to be honored at all times, even during execution practices. This is something, through professional training and personal spirituality, that each member already knows—so the chaplain's reminder is always gentle and reassuring to each man. Everyone on death row, the condemned as well as execution team members, is a reflection of God—*Imago Dei* (in the eyes of Jews and Christians) or His most precious gift (in the eyes of Muslims). It is something that each team member understands. Practice sessions end on Tuesday so that the man can be transferred to the death cell by early afternoon.

Also on Monday and Tuesday, as well as the week before the execution, the chaplain meets with the condemned man and explains the processes that he will incur from the time he arrives at the death cell to the time he is laid upon the gurney. He also relates his own experiences with previous executions as he tries to prepare the condemned for death. If the man is Christian, the chaplain tells him that he will be standing with Jesus and may well be watching the activities in the death chamber from outside his body even before he dies. If the man is not Christian, the chaplain invites others to assist who share the condemned man's faith.

For Christians, the chaplain reads *John* Chapter 11. Here Lazarus dies, but Jesus raises him from the dead. He underscores Jesus' comments to Lazarus' sister in verse 26: "He who believes in me will never die. Do you believe this?" At various times he will ask the condemned man that same question, "do you believe this?" The chaplain explains that Jesus told his disciples that death only takes place at the appointed time and, until then, all believers are required to focus on the "here and now." He encourages the condemned man to use the "here and now" to help the healing process for the victim's family and his own family. The chaplain stresses that, until the man is dead, he can "work the work of life" and that if there is anything needed to be said—during the execution week and in the death chamber—he must make those words part of that healing process for all involved.

Death Cell Around 2:00 p.m. on Tuesday, the condemned man moves down the hallway to the "death cell." In contrast to cells on death row, this is an enclosed, air-conditioned unit. This amenity can cause problems, however, especially to the old and those with arthritis. Jimmey D could not get used to the air conditioning because he simply had not experienced more than an hour or so of it at any one time since 1977. Now at the age of seventy-four, he had to endure fifty-two hours of continual air-conditioning.

The death cell is a very bright room with linoleum floors, pastel grey bars, and egg shell white walls. It is twelve cement blocks high, ten linoleum squares deep, and twelve linoleum squares wide. There is a semi-partition between the bed and the bathroom areas. The bed area consumes seven tiles of width, and the shower/toilet section takes up the remaining five tiles of width.

The metal bed is situated lengthwise and flushed against the back wall. At some point in time, a condemned man wrote in ink on its mattress: "THIS MATTRESS BELONGS TO THE WARDEN." There are two chairs and a table at the end of the bed. The shower has a clear curtain and, near the front of the cell, is a stainless steel commode. There is a row of open bars at the front of the cell. On the other side of the bars is a narrow walkway (a little more than five linoleum squares wide). Its overhead lights, like those in the death cell, remain on throughout the week. There is a table against the wall opposite the death cell. At either end of the table is a chair for two members of the execution team who rotate and stand watch day and night on Tuesday and Wednesday. On the table is a Christian *Bible*, (in the case of a Muslim or Jew, an appropriate substitution is made), a log book to record activities and requests, and a land-based phone. If the inmate had purchased a non-cable TV for his former cell, it will be placed on that table. COs turn it on and off and change channels to suit him.

No other personal belongings accompany him to the death cell. Those are confiscated prior to his departure from death row and are given to whomever he designates. If he wants to read something in the death cell, it's given to him by a member of the execution team and recorded in the log book. When he's done reading, it's returned through the bars and that act is also recorded.

Once situated in the death cell, the warden makes his first visit. He, too, explains the forthcoming procedures and answers questions. They may chat about incidentals, ranging from football games to the weather—whatever the condemned man has on his mind. Depending on the needs of the man, the warden may talk with him daily or simply wait until Thursday to return.

Visitors The condemned man meets with spiritual volunteers and loved ones in the visitation "yard." To get there, he stands with his back to the wall and sticks his hands through the bars. He is cuffed and, once the bars open, he is shackled. He is escorted by two members of the execution team. Once in the visitation yard, the handcuffs and shackles are removed. This "yard" is a small room, approximately thirty-two by thirty-two square tiles, near the front of the prison. During execution week, the room is dedicated to the condemned man's use, and the hours of visitation are expanded to cover most of the day. There is a limit of fifteen visitors at any one time, and Kairos spiritual volunteers tend to withdraw if the number of loved ones approaches that ceiling. Unlike during regular visitation, loved ones can touch, hug and kiss the man and do so as often as they like. Glenn says that this is a time of "swapping stories and laughing and praying. Just doing the things that you would do *normally* like at a family reunion."

When he is through visiting, he is again cuffed and shackled and exits through the small shake-down room which is adjacent to the visitation yard. There he is frisked to ensure no weapons or contraband are in his possession. He is returned the reverse route from which he came: out through the tiled hallway, to the right through the infirmary and toward death row. This route is taken to minimize lockdowns of general population inmates.

Fear, Doubt, and Anger Most men have fears as the end approaches. This was true with Abe—the man who received the card from the other Donaldson inmates once he was transferred to Holman for execution. In the cool morning hours in November 1978, Abe and a friend were drunk. They decided to rob a farmer. They broke into the house and, after the farmer initially convinced them to leave, they returned through the back door with guns and knives. They shot or stabbed everybody in the house; murdering the farmer and his wife, and wounding his three children and their grandmother. After being shot twice and left for dead, one son crawled to his parent's bedroom to find his younger brother and sister crying over their dead parents. Abe and his accomplice were convicted of capital murder in 1979. Abe's brother, who witnessed his execution, is a police officer.

During execution week, Abe was scared about dying. But fear, even though well-hidden in many, is quite natural. Shep was Abe's spiritual advisor:

> Hell, I'd be scared, too. I mean, man, you're fixin' to die. To me, it would be the *norm* to be scared. Course, we are Christians and so we believe we're going to heaven, and we're confident of our salvation. And Abe was confident of *his* salvation. And I'm confident of *my* salvation. But, God, don't tell me I'm gonna die at 6:00 p.m. this Thursday. I'd have a damned stroke!

Some men begin to doubt their faith in God. Shortly before his walk to the death chamber, Jimmey D struggled in that way. He told his spiritual advisor, Anthony, "I've accepted what I've got to do, but I don't want to die, and I don't like it." He became increasingly uncertain about the afterlife and simply concluded that "I'm gonna find out in a little bit."

Some men are very angry for a variety of reasons. "Robert" was adopted at birth and his adoptive father consistently reminded him of his failings and how he never wanted Robert as a son. Shep: "I will go to my grave believing that his downfall was related to the fact that he was not accepted by his *supposed* father." Even at the execution, Robert's father told Shep that "he knew right off the bat it was a mistake to adopt him." Robert was so angry with his life as an adopted child, he waived several optional appeals toward the end. He just wanted to end it.

"Sebastian," a decorated firefighter, also exemplifies the anger found in some. His father deserted him as a young child, and he pledged never to do that to his own son. When his wife divorced him and gained custody of their son, Sebastian tried to kidnap him. He was sentenced to forty years in prison. He wanted to kill his ex-wife and talked openly about what he would do if he ever escaped. Shep: "Sebastian was an EMT person and knew how to torture someone over a long period of time. He wanted to peel her skin back slowly." Sebastian escaped from prison and, in route to his son's home, was recaptured. From a holding cell in a county jail, he convinced a young female officer to help him escape. He eventually murdered a police officer with three shots: one to the hip, one to the chest, and one to the head. Because he claimed that no prison could hold him, Donaldson placed him on total lockdown for the six years he was on death row. When Sebastian was transferred to Holman for execution, it was the first time that Shep got more than just a glimpse of him through his tray slot. Shep: "Damn, Sebastian! You *do* have a body!" Sebastian was so angry with his life that he opted to waive appeals. He, too, just wanted to end it.

Two Kinds of Hope In the death cell, there are two kinds of hope. The first is hope of avoiding execution. Bubba: "You always live with the expectation of something *positive.* If you say 'goodbye,' it is a sign of giving up. You hope that something's going to happen—that you will come out of this thing unscathed." The second kind of hope is to leave an impact on others—similar to the lesson taught by the chaplain from *John* 11. Bubba:

> You looked at the fact that death *is* a possibility. But you don't even want to pass that on to your family because you don't want to place any further burdens on them than you already had. You have to more or less suck it up and try to put forth that image where "I'm not worried about it. It's gonna be all right. And if it don't, I'd still be all right."

Execution Thursday When the chaplain enters Holman each morning at 8:00 a.m., he walks past the visitation yard to get to his office. Normally there is no one in that room at that time, but this is not necessarily the case during the execution week. The condemned man and visitors see the chaplain pass by in his normal casual attire. As he walks past them on Execution Thursday, however, they notice something different: he is wearing a dark gray suit, or what he calls his "funeral suit." They see him carrying the coat on a hanger over his shoulder and, if they look closely, the tie is folded neatly in the front pocket of his starched white dress shirt. Later in the afternoon, during the last visitation, the condemned man and friends will see him in full regalia—underscoring the significance of this day.

Still there is hope on Execution Thursday, some of which is valid and some a bit pretentious. There is always the possibility of a stay of execution. For instance, in August 2008 one man learned late in the afternoon that the Alabama Supreme Court issued an indefinite stay due to the state losing DNA evidence which might have caused doubt about his guilt. Most condemned men hold out hope for this kind of postponement.

But some are given *false* hope. Until 3:00 p.m. (executions were performed at midnight at that time), Orlando was certain that he was not going to be executed because, according to Shep, "some idiot minister told [Orlando] that God had promised [that pastor] that Orlando would have a long life." By 3:00 p.m. Orlando finally realized that, after eighteen years on death row, he would be executed.

Grace and Comfort Anthony: "What I've witnessed is God's grace bringing you a long way quickly. You might have questions, doubt in your faith, but when your back's to the wall like someone being executed, they *find* the strength through God."

Once Jimmey D learned that there would be no stay of execution, a sense of relief came to him. And while a part of him questioned deeply the existence of God, Anthony recalls, he did not worry about it any more. He talked a lot about his daughter and his grandchildren and how much he loved them. He worried about their future.

Noticing that the Kairos volunteers looked tired, Abe insisted they return to their motel to rest for a while. When the news came that the final appeal was denied, Abe continued to show compassion. Anthony: "His lawyers fell apart, but he just looked down and then looked up at all of us who were standing around him, having hands on his shoulder, telling him it was to be OK. He said, 'well, that's all right. I appreciate what everybody's *done* for me. I appreciate your help. And it's alright. I'm gonna be *OK*.'" Then Abe began to comfort his visitors. Anthony: "He asked *me* how *I* was doing. He asked if there was anything *he* could do for *me*."

Shep also saw much grace from Orlando in his last few hours. "He didn't *want* to die, but knowing that's what's going to happen and there wasn't anybody that could stop it, his trust was in the Lord, and he was willing to go through whatever he had to go through." As soon as he realized that there would be no delay in his execution, he started ministering to his family in the visitation yard. He told them their lives were leading "straight to hell." He told them that "God had a better plan and they needed to get with it." They accepted Christ on their last visit with Orlando prior to his electrocution. With the help of Kairos volunteers, Orlando baptized his family on his Execution Thursday.

Last Meal If the condemned man is hungry, breakfast is delivered to the death cell around 4:00 a.m. Lunch is usually not an issue if he is in the visitation yard. There, he normally chooses to eat from vending machines with loved ones and Kairos volunteers. Between 1:00 p.m. and 3:00 p.m., the man receives a last meal. If no visitors are present, it is delivered to the death cell. Given the involvement of Kairos volunteers, if not family members, the condemned man is most likely to have visitors and thereby take his last meal in the visitation yard.

Unlike in the movies, Alabama condemned men cannot order anything they want. It must be items in stock and cooked in Holman's kitchen. Only one tray of food is allowed, which is more than sufficient. Anthony:

> the men typically do not eat that last meal. They just don't have the appetite. It is a reminder of what's to come: "here's your last meal, enjoy it." They think, "Well, thanks for reminding me that in three to four hours, I'm gonna be dead." And at that point, they really don't want it. [Some] just dump it in the trash can.

Jimmey D requested fried green tomatoes, corn on the cob and two cans of Coca-Cola. He ate some of it and threw out the rest with little fanfare. Abe had an orange-flavored drink, black-eyed peas and pepper steak—a mainstay of bland meals back at Donaldson, but at Holman it had some taste. Abe also ate just a little of it.

Occasionally humor prevails. When the warden asked what was desired, one condemned man, "Charley," responded "seafood. Can I go to *Capt. D's* in Mobile?" The warden just shook his head, smiled and said, "Charley, you know you can't do that." Charley replied, "Warden! You *know* I'd come back!" Charley's humor was followed by more humanity and compassion. When the warden brought in his last meal, fried fish sticks and tartar sauce from the canteen, Charley asked if he could pray for him. Glenn:

> So we all gathered up in a circle and Charley prayed this really beautiful prayer for [the warden]. Of course, the first thought I had was the prayer, "Father, forgive them for they know not what they do," but Charley didn't do that. He prayed *for* the warden, not *about* the warden. It was an amazing thing to see a man who is about to be executed to pray for his executioner.

Final Goodbyes About 4:15 p.m. each man must say goodbye to those in the visitation yard. He hugs his family and loved ones for the last time. Anthony: "the hardest part for me in an execution is watching the moms say goodbye." He saw one such mother "laying across the trunk of a car in the parking lot, crying uncontrollably, because she knew she'd never see her son alive again."

Then cuffed and shackled, he leaves through the shakedown room and returns to the death cell via the infirmary as he has done all week. This time, however, the chaplain is in the visitation yard and, with the spiritual advisor, reassures the man that they will see each other back in the death cell. Then the chaplain and spiritual advisor go out the front of the visitation yard, walk through the clearance station and leave their drivers license and car keys—standard operating procedure for further entry into any part of Holman Prison. They walk through the general population area and meet the condemned man at the infirmary. They escort him, along with the two members of the execution team, back through death row.

Once back at the death cell, the man realizes that there are now a growing number of execution team members in the narrow hallway. In a gesture to give as much privacy as possible, the chaplain and spiritual advisor stand in the death chamber for a few minutes in case the condemned man wants to take a final shower and change into another set of crisply ironed prison "whites." When the condemned man is situated and ready, the chaplain and spiritual advisor exit the death chamber and return to the death cell. The time is now about 4:45 p.m.

Shep: "The celebration is over then. Believe me, it's *over*." Abe had to defecate again in the commode that is just feet away from three execution team members who, at this point in the process, are now concerned about suicide attempts. They stand in readiness to open the cell bars if needed. Abe says to Shep: "They ain't got to worry about *that*. I ain't going to do anything to *me*."

Abe wanted a cigarette and one team member handed him some *Bugle* paper and tobacco, and he rolled one while another team member logged that activity into the book on the table. Abe asked Shep: "You mind?" Shep nodded his acquiescence. Abe joked: "Well, I *know* you don't smoke!" Shep joked back: "I don't mind you killing *you*, I just don't want you killing *me*!"

Abe smoked a couple of cigarettes in rapid fashion. Shep and Abe talked, and finally Abe asked, "do you mind if we pray?" Shep: "So we held hands and prayed for a *good* time. And then we sat there for a while." The chaplain was just outside the cell. Abe asked, "Chris, would you like to join us?" The officers opened the cell and the chaplain came in. Now all three men held hands and prayed.

With each condemned man, the chaplain offers a reminder about what was discussed earlier in the week: that he has a choice to be fully engaged in the practice of life until he is dead—that his choice can center either on his own life or the healing that he can offer to others. He reminds the man that the warden is an obedient servant of the Lord and is doing the job of being God's representative with the sword. Soon the warden comes by to see if the man wants to talk and gradually he discovers that there are now six members of the execution team in the small hallway.

The Last Five Minutes At 5:30 p.m. the execution team leader motions "FIVE" with his hand—meaning there are only five more minutes of fellowship. Anthony told Jimmey D, "it's getting close to the time that you need to go." They hugged and prayed together one last time. Anthony:

> I told him that I really appreciated his friendship. He was an example to me as a friend. I encouraged him. I told him everything was going to be OK. He was *strong* in doing what he was doing. He wasn't going to be in *pain* anymore. He was going to be *free*. And we would always have a part of him with us. Then I left the death cell.

Shep was the spiritual advisor for Abe and, from his perspective, the last five minutes are the fastest five minutes of life. "Every morning I sit on my patio watching the sun come up over the river and drink my coffee." On the Tuesday morning before Abe's execution, the sun came up so fast it was like "it's britches were on fire. If that damn sun is going that fast for *me*, how fast is it going for *Abe*. I cried like a baby. Sat right here and cried like a baby." And indeed, the last five minutes for Abe expired swiftly and uncontrollably. Shep: "The next thing I knew, they opened up and said, 'Abe, it's time.' He got up. I hugged him. Walked down the hall."

By about 5:40 p.m., the chaplain reminds the man what Jesus said to the sister of Lazarus in *John* 11: 26, "He who believes in me will never die. Do you believe this?" He then asks his own very simple question: "are you ready?" Certainly it is a rhetorical question, but one that also announces a new phase in the process. He must now enter the death chamber.

In the last decade or so, no one has defiantly protested and had to be pulled and carried, kicking and screaming, out of the death cell. Most of the emotions are gone by that time. Once a condemned man announced, "Fellows, I'm not hostile and I'm not going to do anything that harms anybody. But I'm gonna let you know that I do not believe in the death penalty and I am not going to go willingly." In this particular case, the execution team had to carry the man. To assist them, however, he voluntarily squatted so they could use a "fireman's" hold to lift him up.

But normally this is not the scenario. The condemned man is handcuffed, shackled, and walks out of the death cell to the death chamber under his own power and control. They consider this the manly thing to do. A few go limp once in the death chamber and are somewhat aided toward the gurney. Jimmey D's knees began to buckle, for instance, and he was assisted at his elbows. All others, including the chaplain and spiritual advisor, remain at the furthest end of the death cell hallway while the transference occurs.

The Death Chamber

Abe and Jimmey D each walked the fifteen steps on their respective death days. Each exited the death cell and turned left, took five steps and turned left again. Then another three steps, and a right turn through the door of the death chamber.

As the death chamber door opens, the condemned man encounters perhaps the brightest room he has ever seen.[9] It is almost blinding, with twenty-eight fluorescent ceiling tubes literally flooding the room. It goes beyond a clinical feeling; it is more heavenly in texture—the brightness gives a sense of relief that a comforting end is sure to be near. The floor has white tiles, similar to the death cell and hallway. The walls are also painted eggshell white. Because the thermostat is in the death cell hallway, and the cooling is unevenly distributed, the temperature in the death chamber seems particularly brisk—goose bumps easily form on your arms.

The death chamber is not an exceptionally large room, although it somehow feels spacious. It is seventeen cement blocks wide, twelve cement blocks high and fourteen linoleum squares deep. The room angles at the center so the deepest part affronts the DOC witness room. In addition to the control room window and slits for the IV and EKG lines, the wall behind the gurney's head has a clock, three air ducts, and a microphone cable which is extended when the warden reads the death warrant and if the man has any last words. Another clock is on the opposite wall where the man can easily see from the gurney.

There are now just seven steps left to take—from the death chamber's door to the gurney's edge. Then, with his back to the gurney, two or three members of the execution team (depending on obesity) hoist the condemned man onto the gurney. Two other members simultaneously uncuff either arm and, without relinquishing control, strap each arm into fixed positions on the gurney. Two other team members unshackle him and strap each leg into position. Two paramedics, who enter the death cell hallway after the man is extracted, now enter the death chamber. They insert a fourteen-gauge catheter (the largest sold commercially) into each arm (in case one vein causes the drugs to back-up) and connect the EKG lines. A physician is waiting in the death cell area to cut into a main-line vein if both arms fail to produce a viable option. The paramedics then exit the death chamber and, shortly thereafter, so do all but two of the execution team members. The former wait in the death cell hallway while the latter assume posts outside each of the three witness rooms and at the outside door which leads all witnesses into the death chamber.

The chaplain enters. The job of the chaplain, as it has been all week, is to maintain emotional control of those involved in the execution. He whispers to the man the procedures as they are being implemented. The gurney is slightly tilted so that the feet are lower than the head to increase the comfort of the man and permit him to see the witnesses and they, him. The chaplain points to the man's left to designate the witness room where his spiritual advisor and loved one will soon be positioned. With Abe, this is where his brother once sat. It is the same room where Jimmey D's daughter and Anthony also sat. It will someday hold Lawton's son.

The chaplain then points at the center to indicate the DOC witness room and then to the man's right to show the victim's witness room. With Abe, this is where relatives sat who survived his torrent, just as it occupied relatives of the old woman that a much younger Jimmey D shot three times and called it suicide. Someday it will seat the daughter of the man who was murdered by Lawton's actions.

Throughout this time, as he has done for days and weeks, the chaplain reassures the condemned man that he is not alone—that this process is not unlike dying at a hospital where loved ones are near his side. He also assures the man that he is surrounded by caring people who take his life not out of animosity or revenge. He tells the man that there is an officer on either side of the gurney, that the deputy warden is standing between the gurney and the victim's witness room, and the warden will be standing at the foot of the gurney. The chaplain reassures the man that, during the reading of the death warrant and his opportunity for last words, he will be standing just to the left of the witness room containing his loved one and spiritual advisor. Once again, he reminds the condemned that he still has time in the "here and now" to offer healing to those in the witness rooms as well as in the death chamber.

There is occasionally humor in the death chamber, which tends to calm the condemned man. One man strapped down on the gurney blurted out: "*Damn*! These lights are *bright*!" The seasoned members of the execution team broke into laughter, knowing this man's humor which they had come to enjoy for over a decade. They joked back with him. A DOC administrator, first time in the chamber, sharply questioned the propriety of such banter. The chaplain thought in his mind that it was very appropriate to joke and still maintain the dignity of the process. It was, after all, what the condemned man wanted.

All the procedures, from the last seven steps to being affixed on the gurney, take place in rapid fashion. Once on the gurney and the other members of the execution team are in position, the witnesses enter by assigned room through an outside door. While all can see shadows and hear mumblings, the curtain remains closed. At about 5:50 p.m., the curtains are drawn open. At this point the warden enters and reads the death warrant.

Last Words The man is given the opportunity to speak. In most cases, he says nothing because he is now truly that "deer in the headlights" which was first felt so many years ago after coming off Z-1 status. Most cannot muster words that would make sense. This was the case with Abe; all of his words were expended in the death cell a few minutes prior to walking to the gurney. The entire week Jimmey D kept reminding Anthony and his daughter, "if I don't say anything, it's not because I don't care about y'all or don't want to say anything to you. I just don't want to say nothing because I don't want it in the paper." In the final analysis, most men are so anxiety-driven by the task of that day, or too anti-social after so many years on death row, they do not know how to say anything of importance.

A few, however, apologize to both the victim's family and to their own loved ones. Shep: "The men feel the pain and they know they caused pain." Some say their last words in other ways: a wink of an eye or a nod of a head. Jimmey D told his daughter and Anthony, "I might look at you" and on the gurney he mouthed one final "I love you." Orlando, who was so certain of a reprieve hours before and who baptized his family shortly before his final goodbyes, had no final words.

Fewer try to use the opportunity to make speeches about the inhumanity of the death penalty or restate a claim of innocence, or use the time to prolong life. For instance, one complained that the straps were too tight and asked if they could be loosened. He also began to ask a lot of questions about the IV lines. At this point, the chaplain walked over and quietly reminded the man of his relationship with the Lord and everything about which they talked earlier in the week: the need to use the "here and now" for healing. He assured him that everything was going to be fine—that he was on the verge of being with the Lord.

Death It is about 5:55 p.m. The warden and deputy warden exit the death chamber and enter the control room through a door at the end of the death cell hallway. They are accompanied by two additional physicians.[10] The warden inspects each of the seven large syringes, as do the physicians. Prior to plunging them, now around 5:58 p.m., he calls out the words "code blue" over the intercom and one of the remaining COs exits the death chamber.[11] The execution team leader and the chaplain are now the only ones remaining with the condemned man. The chaplain grasps the hand of the condemned and places his other hand on the man's knee. He then kneels next to the gurney and prays. Quite often prior to unconsciousness, the condemned man either joins in with the chaplain or prays independently.

At 6:00 p.m. the warden administers sequentially the contents of the seven syringes. The two doses of sodium pentothal and one dose each of pavulon and potassium chloride are separated by doses of saline. The execution team leader checks for signs of consciousness after the two doses of sodium pentothal, flicking the man's eye lashes and pinching his cheek and, once affirmed, the process plays out. The chaplain continues to pray.

With lethal injection, the condemned man appears to shut his eyes and go to sleep after the first dosage of sodium pentothal. Shep: "It's not inhumane what they're doing. You think of something gory and it's not *that*. Basically, all you as a layperson see is the same as if your kid was fixin' to have his tonsils out or appendix out."

At about 6:20 p.m. the two physicians exit the control room and enter the death chamber to determine death. After its pronouncement, the curtains close and COs begin to escort the witnesses out of the facility.

Witnesses for the now-deceased are returned to the nearby hotel. Witnesses for the victim and DOC representatives are escorted to a press conference in a small building called the "club house" at the neighboring prison ranch.

Once the curtains close, members of the execution team return to disengage the IV tubing and EKG wiring. The body bag, hidden between the sheets and the gurney's mattress, is pulled out and zipped up. The contents are then transported to the University of South Alabama hospital where a state forensics expert conducts the autopsy.

Lessons about the Real of Murder and Capital Punishment

The purpose of the *citizen-nachahmer's* exploration into the intimate consequences of public action is to see, in Bonhoeffer's words, "how something really is" (Bethge, 1997: 158). That is, we try to capture each day as it is created by God and as we present it back to Him. This task is no less difficult with the taking of life from developed human beings than it is with the taking of life from unborn human beings. As with abortion, part of the challenge is there is one dimension of the real that can never be fully explicated: the views of the murdered and the executed.

It may seem trivial and strange to say we lack the opportunity to discuss death with the dead. Yet Dietrich Bonhoeffer reminds us through poem that death "lay[s] waste the burdens of chains and walls which confine our earthly bodies and blinded souls, that we see at last what here we could not see" (Robertson, 1999: 74). Our task is to minimize those "chains and walls" in this lifetime so that we may at least approximate that which we otherwise "could not see."

The real of murder must be the most traumatic experience of one's life—just as the real of walking those last fifteen steps and being strapped to a gurney. Certainly there are other ways to die which, though painful, are less abusive. The old joke about the man given a choice of execution methods—he chooses very old age and sleeping in his own comfortable bed—is how each one of us would like to die. This is not the case with the murdered and, at least in light of that slender mattress with scribbling that it belongs to the warden, it is not the case with capital punishment. Murder and its consequences rob individuals of worldly expectations.

Simplicity of the Real

The real of taking the life of the developed human being appears simple in at least two ways. First, murder has been a "fact of life" since

Cain killed Abel, and it shows no sign of dissipating in the twenty-first century. Murder has always been considered a crime and, throughout most of the American experience, a relative straight line has been drawn between the theocentric moral foundation and capital punishment. Despite (or perhaps because) of the morality of the social gospel, the Founders desired other moral principles that would regulate public action in its most extreme and destructive form. The moral principle of "thou shall not murder" fits the bill.

Second, executing murderers is an act of simplicity. It stems from *lex talionis* or *Al-Qisaas*, which requires little supposition on the part of the citizen. It is based on scripture which, in one form or another, calls for believers in the God of Abraham to simply "show no pity: life for life, eye for eye..." (*Deuteronomy* 19:21). Its simplicity is aided by concrete logistics and methods: build prison structures in secluded areas and use technologies to rid outward expressions when one life is extracted for another life taken.

Truth is, politics on both sides of the capital punishment debate denies the complexity of the real. The presentation is always dichotomous and, therefore, static: the condemned is either innocent or guilty, pain is felt by the victim's family or by the condemned man's family; the murdered is a saint or the condemned man has evolved into a caring and responsible human being. Killing the condemned is supported by Founders, like Thomas Jefferson, or opposed by Founders, like Benjamin Rush. Killing the condemned is morally justified, based on scripture, or it is morally misplaced, based on scripture. The real of murder and capital punishment is never so simple.

Complexity of the Real

First, the complexity of the real demonstrates the fundamental tragedy of what the world has missed from the lives of both the murdered and the executed. The man that Lawton murdered left behind a daughter. How would that man have shaped the little girl's life? Perhaps in similar ways that Jerry had shaped Sue's life prior to her murder. Michael wanted to marry his fiancée and give Leigh treasured grandchildren. How many lives might have been touched by his offspring? The respective store clerks, who unfortunately had Bubba and Perkins as customers, certainly would have changed someone's heart.

Yet this was also the case with Abe and his Christian influence over other death row inmates for almost three decades. It was true of Charley who prayed *for*, not *about*, the warden. It was true of Orlando who led his family to baptism. Like all sinners, murderers can be touched by the hand of the God of Abraham, regardless of the wretch they were. Wicked men can find the intimacy of the social gospel and learn to be *citizens-nachahmer*, even if their geographic portion of the political community remains confined for the rest of their lives. Founding thinkers, especially Thomas Jefferson, had to believe this deep down inside or else why rely so much on the moral teachings of Jesus of Nazareth?

Second, murder complicates the lives of *all* survivors, and it brings in *equal* measure unimaginable misery to loved ones on both sides of the ledger. Leigh is destined to relive her nightmare in front of parole boards. In the meantime, she must calculate daily travel routes which best minimizes unrelenting pain. Most likely she will battle alcohol just as Angela battles unending debt incurred while her son was on death row. On alternating Mondays, the families of men like Lawton must choose between their usual routine and death row visitation. Like Bubba's family before them, they will stand in line and be treated more or less as second-class citizens for crimes they did not commit. For everyone, holidays and birthdays will never be the same again.

Third, complexity of the real shows that, whereas murder gives way to pain and suffering, execution renders little relief. The children of Abe's victims were glad for his death but disappointed in the dignity he maintained. Abe's brother appeared proud of that dignity, but suffered with the execution of a police officer's sibling. The daughter of the man who Lawton murdered, as well as his own son, will experience that same kind of complexity on a future Thursday evening. She will somehow feel robbed at the seemingly peaceful price paid and, because of that, will continue to hurt long afterwards. He will learn to endure the transition from suffering caused by decades of letters, prayers, and visits to the ultimate suffering caused by the death of his father.

Fourth, whereas execution provides little relief to the survivors, it does end misery for the murderer. Lawton will eventually feel the same bewilderment as did Jimmey D at his last Kairos Christmas gathering. He will gauge the difference between twenty-three hours of lockdown at Holman for a limited number of days prior to execution and the additional hours in the Donaldson day room playing dominos and chess at the same table with the same partner each day for decades. He will conclude that such choices are Kafkaesque at best. As so many men before him, Lawton will lose the glimmer of life in his eyes as he ages exponentially just like the "old man" in the wheelchair at Holman. Just like Jimmey D, Lawton will come to listen eagerly for the sound of his own "bus" finally arriving. Execution will become a long-lost friend.

Finally, a complicated relationship with God comes part and parcel with the real of murder and capital punishment. The chaplain at Holman says that "death row is like a foxhole in a battle. In it you find absolutely no atheists." While this may be true, sometimes we err in leaving our foxhole and forsaking the comfort offered by God.

For all loved ones, the conflict begins the moment one hears about the bullet entering the chest or head, the knife slashing the throat, or the extension cord curtailing breath. Carolyn and Angela, on opposite sides of the equation, have damned and praised God for identical reasons. For the murderer, the conflict begins at least with Z-1 designation and ends only with walking those last 15 steps. All men on death row pray that they can end their lives like Orlando, saving souls and singing hymns, but they fear they may complete the walk questioning God's existence and love, as did Jimmey D. A conflict with God certainly must involve the warden, execution team members, and the even chaplain—especially during the week when a man is mandated to be strapped to a gurney and they are required to help and watch.

* * *

It is the illusion of simplicity that clouds the real of murder and capital punishment in the American political community. Parsimonious eloquence in calling for "an eye for an eye," while anchored firmly in God's moral word, leads citizens and public servants down a path of *civic cheap grace*. That path offers illegitimate civic communion because it denies civic confession. It convinces, we need only follow the legality of the community and never witness the intimacy of its acts.

Albert Speer (1997), rationalizing his sins committed during the holocaust, notes that technique can distance us from the intimacy of public action. Bonhoeffer agrees:

> Man has learnt to deal with himself in all questions of importance without recourse to the "working hypothesis" called "God." In questions of science, art, and ethics this has become an understood thing at which one now hardly dares to tilt.... As in the scientific field, so in human affairs generally, "God" is being pushed more and more out of life, losing more and more ground (Bethge, 1997: 325-26).

It is not the different moral paths found in the first source of truth—the word—that pushes God out of the life of the American political community. Rather, it is the absence of will to take deliberate action and explore the second source of truth—the world as it is intimately offered to us each day and as we intimately return it to God—that exchanges purposeful costly grace for unexplainable cheap grace. We have no inclination to seek the intimate consequences of murder and capital punishment. Satisfied with summaries found in newspapers and e-mail bulletins, we feel more comfortable limiting discussions to matters of technique: how long does it take and how much will it hurt? This makes it easy to ignore *Imago Dei.* As a result, believers in the God of Abraham unintentionally lend credence to the wicked who seek to reinforce de Sade's (2006: 24) contention: "God is merely the *ne plus ultra* of human reason ... the product of fear or weakness."

Recall the "minimally decent Samaritan" scenario proffered by Judith Jarvis Thomson (1971) as a moral justification for abortion. Ask yourself, "what would I do if the person I was asked to sustain were a convicted murderer and not a world class violinist?" Would you be a Good Samaritan and let him live? Or, would you be a minimally decent Samaritan and, after weighing the facts about his crime, disconnect him so that he dies? Is *Imago Dei* different when the real becomes complex? Truth is, the answer comes not from the *Imago Dei* we see in others. It lies solely in the *Imago Dei* we find in ourselves.

Notes

1. The fourteen states without the death penalty are Alaska, Hawaii, Iowa, Maine, Massachusetts, Michigan, Minnesota, New Jersey, New York, North Dakota, Rhode Island, Vermont, West Virginia, and Wisconsin. The District of Columbia also does not have the death penalty.
2. For hanging, see Seitz, 2003; Bohm, 2003; Duff, 2001. For firing squads, see Seitz, 2003; Bohm, 2003, Gill, 1996. For electrocution, see Seitz, 2003; Mansi, 2003; Dow, 2002; Lifton and Mitchell, 2000. For gas chamber, see Bohm, 2003; Seitz, 2003; Harries and Cheatwood, 1997.
3. If measured into an *Ezy-Dose* medicine spoon, with the limit at 10 mil, or 1 cc, you would have to fill it up ten times for both dosages of sodium pentothal, five times for the single dosage of pavulon, six times for the single dosage of potassium chloride.
4. Whereas it was once done mechanically, Warden Culliver manually pushes the plunger because he feels a machine cannot determine, as well as the sensitivity of a human hand, whether a vein is "backing up" due to aqueous pressure.
5. Figures are current as of February 2009.
6. Under most circumstances, there is no visual, verbal, or physical contact between a death row inmate and one from the general population. The primary reason is that, when an inmate is handcuffed, he cannot protect himself. Consequently it is the CO's responsibility to protect the handcuffed inmate. The easiest way to do this is to clear from the area all other inmates.
7. Kairos Prison Ministry volunteers bring in the best food possible because of the belief that they are visiting Jesus: "I was in prison and you came to visit me" and "whatever you did for one of these brothers of mine, you did for me" (*Matthew* 25:36, 40).

8. Upon occasion COs from Donaldson transport the condemned man to Holman Prison. In these instances, a chase car is not typically used unless the Donaldson COs feel uncomfortable with him. Typically they have known the condemned man for many years and feel comfortable anticipating his behavior. Regardless of the transportation, the vehicle contains a portable facility for urination and defecation, hence avoiding the need to take restroom breaks for the condemned man.
9. The room is so bright because of the potential need to insert the IV into a "main-line" vein in the neck if smaller veins in the arms do not work. The light is needed because a physician would have to perform surgery to open up the vein.
10. There are three physicians. One remains with the paramedics, and two are in the control room with the warden and assistant warden. The two in the control room certify the death of the condemned man.
11. The term "code blue" is used to extract the last CO that leaves because it is a common code to indicate an emergency elsewhere. It will not seem unusual to the condemned man and, therefore, will not contribute additional stress to his final environment.

5

The Real of Misery: Prison without Parole

What to do with a murderer? Thesha (pro-life): "Lock'em up until they rot ... for forty or fifty years and every day of their life they gonna think about what they did." Sarah (pro-choice): "put them in prison for the rest of their life, and to me it would be a living hell." Christopher (pro-choice): "I think we should make prisons a lot less comfortable." Jessica (mixed about abortion): "Sitting in a cell, watching TV, and having three square meals.... I know people who have been in and out of jail, and jail is not that big of a deal."

Dietrich Bonhoeffer reminds us that truth, in addition to coming from the word of God, is a matter of "correct appreciation of real situations and of serious reflection upon them." Further, "the more complex the actual situations of a man's life, the more responsible and the more difficult will be his task of 'telling the truth'" (1995: 359). As it is with a man's life, so too is it with intimate consequences stemming from complex public actions. Prisons are an example of this. The focus is on the intimate consequences of sentencing murderers to life-without-the-possibility-of-parole (LWOPP). While the locus is Donaldson Correctional Facility in Alabama, the reflection is that of any maximum security prison in the United States.

A Prison's Story

Donaldson is the state's only "super-max" prison. Specializing in repeat and/or multiple violent crime offenders, it has 300 cells dedicated to segregation—the largest segregation unit in the system. Originally named "West Jefferson" when opened in 1982, reflecting its location in a north-central Alabama county, the prison was rededicated eight years later when inmate Patrick Carr stabbed to death Correctional Officer (CO) William E. Donaldson. While Carr eventually hung himself in a

Holman Prison death row cell, the Alabama Department of Corrections (DOC) renamed West Jefferson in honor of the fallen officer.

Donaldson consists of six diamond-shaped blocks, each containing ninety-six cells identical in size to those on its death row, and each with a similar narrow access-way that leads from a main hallway to an officer cube. There are two nine-foot wide main hallways—West Side and East Side—and between them are the law library, infirmary, canteen and kitchen, barber shop, education rooms, two gymnasiums, and the store. The West Side hallway provides access to the chapel—an exterior building which offers inmates an air-conditioned reprieve from the Alabama heat and humidity and, because of its hardwood floors, a break from the constant concrete slab. Past the chapel's entrance is 1 Block, which is divided into two self-contained units of forty-eight cells. One side includes the small percentage of inmates who have jobs: kitchen crew, plumbers, painters, electricians, and lawn keepers. The other side houses the faith-based "New Beginnings" program where men with good behavior benefit from a safer environment and access to special educational and religious activities. Walking further down West Side is 3 Block, which contains mental health and segregation units. Beyond that is 5 Block, which includes death row.

Off the East Side hallway are cell blocks containing inmates with the worst behavior— men who could not be controlled at other prisons and men who choose that same conduct at Donaldson. Mixed with these inmates are others who, because no space is available on the West Side, must also live there. In addition to another segregation unit (6 Block), it is on the West Side that you find 2 Block and 4 Block—which COs and inmates sometimes call the "Jungle" and "Whore Block," respectively.

Each main hallway is 315 steps long and concludes at locked metal exit doors which open to the South Side. There you find five dormitories, each resembling a blend of old army barrack and deteriorating warehouse structure, where men with the best behavior are permitted to live with more freedom.

Overcrowding

Built for 992 inmates, currently 1,679 men call Donaldson "home." It will accept as many as 1,945 inmates. Some inmates (in the death row and segregation units) live in single cells and all South Side residents live in open spaces, but more than half the population share cells with other inmates. In each cell, two metal bunk beds are attached on top of the original concrete bed slab. Given that the height of the cell is only seven cement blocks, the top bunk nearly scrapes the ceiling. Each cell has a 12" by 4' strip where a window might be expected. Slats, however, cover up many of these windows because of obscenities shouted or drug deals conducted or death threats communicated. On others, all but the top part is covered up. Hence, at worst there is no air circulation and, at best, only the top bunk has a chance of getting a little relief. Ventilation is exacerbated because, unlike death row cells, there are no open tray slots in the solid metal doors. Given the space needed for personal property boxes, the amount of room for each cellmate dwindles to what his mattress offers. All cells are locked each evening and re-opened in the morning, meaning there is a substantial amount of time in extremely close confinement with cellmates. The fact that lockdowns occur after acts of violence means that three men per cell in the Jungle and Whore Block could easily remain behind a solid door for days and even weeks with the exception of trips to the canteen. Overcrowding is felt further when, in that small confinement, two men smoke cigarettes and the third has lung or heart problems, or two have sex and the third has no desire to watch but no where to go.

Bathroom accommodations also reflect overcrowding. While every cell has a commode and sink, there are only four or five shower heads in each 48-cell unit. In the Jungle and Whore Block, where three men share each cell, this means one shower for every thirty-six inmates. Even on South Side, where barrack style allows for greater ventilation, there is a high ratio of bathroom facilities to residents: one sink for every sixteen men; one shower head for every twenty-two men; one commode for every thirty-two men; one five-foot long urinal trough for all 130 men.

Understaffing

COs at Donaldson are dedicated public servants who perform the best they can under extraordinary circumstances. Understaffing happens to be one of those circumstances. While authorized for 244 positions, low wages and poor working conditions (which often include six 16-hour work shifts each week) means that Donaldson has been able to hire only 166 COs—146 men and twenty females. On the surface the number of COs may seem adequate—one officer for every 10.1 inmates. However, prisons never shut down, even if inmates appear to be sleeping, and so the 166 men and women are divided into three shifts—about fifty-five COs per shift, or one for every thirty-one inmates. Given that a few COs are full-time administrators and some from each shift are either on sick call or vacation, coupled with shifts requiring the stationing of COs in watch towers and at shift command posts—the actual number of COs in close position to inmates (for the purposes of protection and regulating behavior) is about fifteen per shift, or about one for very 112 prisoners.

Underfunding

As with most prisons, Donaldson is a cheap and costly proposition. Only $12,000 a year is needed to warehouse each inmate, a cost of just $32.88 per day, which includes clothing, meals, healthcare, exercise and training/educational opportunities for inmates who are not LWOPP. The fact that the price tag does not include annual flu shots for all inmates results in additional health care costs which can surpass $7 million annually. It is not uncommon to receive an extra monthly hospital bill of $500,000 for treatment of stab wounds, or debilitating illnesses, that are too severe for the infirmary to handle. The minimal budget means the safety and health of inmates, as well as COs, can be placed in jeopardy for a variety of reasons.

Intimate Consequences of Public Action: Sketches from the Real of Life in Prison

A CO once described the culture at Donaldson as being like Chinese water torture. "The first 100 drops on your forehead will not bother you. The second *one million* drops begin to make you crazy." Intimate consequences begin to accumulate, and this appears unavoidable given the conditions of overcrowding, insufficient budgets, and an inability to recruit and retain an appropriate level of COs. While everyone, including each CO, feels the pressure that is brought to bear, it is the LWOPP inmate who becomes increasingly aware of the real of their lives as days drag into years, and years into decades.

Institutional Intimacy

No one would argue that Donaldson is a pleasant place to spend the rest of one's life— that is not its intent. A stranger to Holman's pastel colors, Donaldson launches an assault on your senses.[1] Although the walls have recently been repainted (white and rust red), years go by between paintings and the walls tend to resume a soiled look after just a year or so. Years have also gone by when less than half the hallway light fixtures worked. The concrete floor is unpainted and dark, and it seems to absorb all available light.

A function of overcrowding, understaffing and underfunding, the word that best describes the kitchen and canteen is "distasteful"—surpassing the conditions of fourth rate eateries in third-world countries. The food for the general population is the same as that served on death row: on a good day, it is bland and, on a bad day, intestines flare to multiple bowel movements. While the current warden attempts to improve conditions, rust and fallen paint flakes have set the mood for years. Ovens and burners reveal inches of blackened grease, and dirt and discarded food seem permanently pressed into patterns on the concrete floor. Newer spills, and occasionally bodily fluids, moisten the floors. Flour in the large mechanical mixing bowls, where prized fresh bread is made daily, appears to be somewhat off-color at times. It sometimes stinks in the kitchen, pure and simple, bringing a feeling of nausea to the unconditioned stomach. There are days when odor gags the back of the throat, and it lobbies your nostrils even after leaving the prison. You long for a nice hot shower.

General population inmates eat in the canteen, which matches the kitchen in filth and surpasses it in despair. The floor is slippery from grease and waste. As accurately noted in a letter to the state governor from the president of the inmate advisory committee, "holes exist in the ceiling causing not only old and rusty rainwater dripping into inmates' food, but falling ceiling particles as well" (Rutland, 2007). Two dining rooms, one with twenty-seven 4-person stainless steel tables and the other with thirty-two such tables, serve between 1,200 and 1,400 inmates each meal. Given the shortage of seating space, coupled with the need to protect inmates from the libertines living in the Jungle and Whore Block, serving meals require segregation and time. Inmates from one unit must be out of the hallway and locked back in their block before inmates from another unit can proceed to the canteen. This is why breakfast call begins between 2:00 a.m. and 3:00 a.m., lunch around 10:30 a.m., and dinner around 4:30 p.m. Each inmate is given no more than fifteen minutes to eat, and most men take just a portion of that time to complete the ordeal.

The Living Room. Each unit's day room is twice the size of death row's because each is a half (not quarter) of the "diamond" holding forty-eight (not twenty-four) cells. A general population day room has seven wooden benches, each seating three inmates comfortably, plus two metal tables and chairs similar to the ones on death row. There are also two large non-cable TVs in opposite ends, one for movies and the other for sports. Near one TV is a coffee pot of hot water and a microwave oven. There are two land-based wall phones next to either TV set. In the summer time, there is also a large beach chest filled with ice.

The New Beginnings' day room is clean and quiet. The floors are mopped daily by inmates and litter is forbidden. DOC prohibits cigarette smoking anywhere inside buildings, and this policy is enforced in the New Beginnings day room but not necessarily in its cells. In addition to the benches and tables, there are more than enough white plastic patio chairs to accommodate all inmates and visitors. TVs have sufficient antenna wire to ensure adequate reception of all local channels. Everyone watching TV has purchased head phones so that the volume is low and other inmates, taking courses or reading in the library area, are not disturbed. There are industrial-size portable fans, purchased by the Kairos Prison Ministry, that moderate the summer temperature a bit.

It is aesthetically pleasing in New Beginnings. Over the entrance door is a painting of two globes, showing both sides of the earth, and two hands (one black, one white) reaching toward each other. Column supports are painted to look like tree trunks, as are sections of the vast wall separating it from the cube. The four-foot walls around the showers are painted to look like stones, as is the wall around the block's library. On the wall at the entrance is a large mural, a vision of a country road leading to a groom and bride entering a church. Vintage automobiles line the church's parking lot: 1957 Chevys, 1964 Corvettes, and classic MGs and Austin-Healeys. On the road leading to the church is a green interstate sign, "Information," with an arrow pointing out of the mural to the actual information desk at the entrance door of the day room. There are mountains over the church and, to its left, are sail boats on a large, blue lake. The mural ends on the other side of the lake with a large city skyline.

The environment in the Jungle and Whore Block stands in stark contrast to New Beginnings. Cleanliness and color are estranged concepts; floors are filthy, strewn with litter, spit, and snot. The smoking policy is not enforced in either the cells or the day rooms and, as a result, smoke clouds make breathing difficult for the visitor in just a matter of minutes. Even quicker, the eyes begin to tear. Clothes reek of second-hand smoke, as does your breath. Antenna wire has been stolen and, hence, various make-shift contraptions—typically involving aluminum foil and empty soda cans—are used to leverage reception for the TV sets. No auxiliary fans placate the summer heat and humidity, and the microwave ovens and coffee pots appear well tested by time, filth, and a lack of civility. The wooden benches are laden with filthy towels that serve the dual function of seat cushions and "reservation warnings"—either for an individual inmate or for a particular gang. No plastic patio chairs are provided which means that, given there are forty-eight 3-man cells, only about thirty out of the 144 inmates can be accommodated. This places extra value on day room seating, giving way to a pecking order with one basic rule: "sissies never sit."

It is unbelievably loud in the Jungle and in Whore Block. Basketball arenas, packed with fans screaming at the top of their lungs when the opposing team tries to make a winning foul shot, do not compare. You have to shout to have a conversation with someone just inches away, and the noise is constant: your ears numb after a twenty-minute visit. The noise starts around 2:00 a.m. with breakfast call while inmates stand in the day room waiting to exit the block. It resumes upon their return from the canteen and continues throughout the day. The volume accentuates when TV programs, such as day-time *The Tyra Banks Show*, include sexy women in scant clothing. Men scream, and some run solo or in tandem to the confines of a closed cell. Shouting continues into the night, with momentary lulls only during a major sporting event or for the two favorite TV shows: *24* and *Prison Break*. Otherwise it continues until evening lockdown, at 10:30 p.m. on week nights and 2:00 a.m. on weekends.

The Jungle and Whore Block are unbearable and, the longer you live there, the harder it is to cope. LWOPP inmate "Mark," a thirty-nine-year-old who has been in Whore Block for ten years, attests to this fact. He wanted to commit suicide with his belt from the upper balcony and no one tried to stop him. In fact, many cheered him on. He could not figure out how to get the belt around his neck and tied to the railing and, out of frustration, began to cry. This provoked further prodding from inmates. He screamed: "God, help me! I can't take this anymore."

In both blocks, chipped and smoke-stained paint is marred only by graffiti. In Whore Block, various gangs have contributed: Bloods, Crips, Vice Lords, and Disciples (for black inmates) and the Aryan Nation and Skin Heads (for white inmates). Scratched on the walls are the words,

"Fuck you" and "Kicking Ass Time." The Jungle offers similar graffiti, along with dismal signs searching for relief. A dingy poster next to a TV quotes *Yermiyah* (*Jeremiah*) 29:11, except the word "thoughts" is substituted for the word "plans":

> For I know the *thoughts* I have for you, declares the Lord. *Thoughts* to prosper you and not to harm you. *Thoughts* to give you hope and a future.

On the wall next to the filthy microwave is another hand-written poster:

> Brothers we stand at the Cross Roads to Heaven or Hell.
> We have a choice to make: Jesus = heaven. Devil = hell.

De Sade's Boudoir. Whether there are two men to a cell (New Beginnings) or three to a cell (the Jungle and Whore Block), the six- by ten-foot parameters point to misery at every turn. Question: Where do you hang wet towels? Answer: Inmates typically find hooks to pound in the cement walls and run a string around the bunks. Especially in the summer humidity, however, this is not an effective solution. The one towel per inmate, issued weekly, reeks with mildew by the third or fourth day. Question: What do you do when a cellmate has gas or defecates in the commode? Answer: Given there is no ventilation system, you have three options: (1) Convince cellmates to flush repeatedly when defecating, hence eliminating as much odor as possible. (2) Push together the towels on the line so that they shield some of the smell. (Naturally the towels will absorb the smell especially when this is done more than once per day by each cellmate.) (3) "Submarine"—bury your head underneath the blanket and use it as a gas mask. Farting while not on the commode is more challenging because the only option you have is to submarine. "Grand Daddy," a fifty-seven-year-old LWOPP inmate who looks much older, has tolerated the passing of gas by cellmates for the past three decades. "Some of these guys could go to Iraq and lay down some gas that would *end* that conflict."

Interpersonal Intimacy

Unlike men on death row, bonding around a shared destiny is a harder task in general population. No inmate can escape interacting with others, and it typically translates into constant fear. Men either project it, act to minimize it, or react to its ugly thrust. Fear about the kind of inmate who is warehoused inside Donaldson is the fundamental reason the political community constructs such facilities in the first place. Fear explains the electric fence, razor wire, and guard towers. It justifies the night sticks and mace carried by each CO. Fear is why so many inmates seek to spend time in the chapel because it means less time in the cell blocks. It is why gangs are sustained, violence occurs, and some inmates beg for transfer into the safety of single cells in segregation. Fear is the reason why traffic in the two main hallways is regulated through three lanes separated by yellow, fading lines.

"Dean," a forty-five-year-old who has been LWOPP for sixteen years, says that young black inmates "fear not being accepted, and that's why they join a gang or get involved in Islam." He adds that young white inmates have their own sets of fears, ranging from stolen property to rape to murder. Mark calls it the "boo game"—a team sport where groups of inmates try to "scare you into doing things you don't want to do. They will scare you with knives in your face. Steal things out of your box. Rape you or just beat you."

LWOPP inmate "Joel," a thirty-nine-year old who has lived in the Jungle for the last twelve years, comments on his first day at Donaldson:

> [It] was dim because there was no windows, and there was a feeling of evil and foreboding hanging in the air. You know the feeling that you get when you are leaning back in a chair on two legs and you start to fall, but catch yourself right before you do? That was how I felt.

Ten-Foot Stare. As with any free-world individual, an inmate wears a "game face." The difference is that free-world folks have a variety of game faces: perhaps one for the boss, another to scold our children, still another for watching our favorite football team. For most inmates, the game face remains constant to match the unvarying situation: dealing with fear. It is designed to either perpetuate fear or to mask its effects. Faces are without expression—even anger is missing. Rather, the game face is cold and mechanical, regardless of the man's personality prior to incarceration.

LWOPP inmate "Eli," a forty-year-old incarcerated for the last twenty-three years, says that "emotions are in the proverbial closet." Men stash them away and never bring them out. There are inmates who have not smiled in decades because smiling is considered a sign of weakness, and weakness invites fear.

It is a game face similar to the "thousand-yard stare" affixed to combat soldiers as they constantly scan the horizon regardless of setting and, hence, seemingly look right through the person talking to them. At Donaldson, it is called the "ten-foot stare" for the same reason. The only time the game face may be removed temporarily is in the chapel or in the infirmary. Perkins, who was once on death row, is now an infirmary runner. He says sometimes "you see real tears, real prayers, and real Godly conversations. Some in the infirmary just want someone to talk to them in ways that are uncommon in the blocks."

Impression, Manipulation, Intimidation. According to Mark, "I always look over my shoulder. You don't know who is going to *try you*—play games to see how tough you are." A Jungle inmate in a Bible study group once told me that you have to be *unafraid* to live here. Fear will lead you to being someone's "boy." You have to be *strong*—physically and emotionally to serve time here.

"Steve," a seventeen-year-old Jungle resident in his first year, is not very strong. He is an effeminate homosexual who professes his Christianity by sashaying around the block greeting his sex customers with the words, "God is *Sweet*! God is *Sweet*!" Inmates claim that he was neither gay nor effeminate when he arrived.

"Shorty," who is fifty-eight years old and about five feet and four inches tall, lives in the Jungle. While his teeth are green with rot, he remains in muscular condition reminiscent of his time as an Airborne Ranger. In the Jungle, his *raison d'être* is to generate fear. When he talks with you, he invades your space by standing just inches away from your face. At the top of his lungs, he recites incredibly vicious poems about murder and mutilation—all of which he authored. Especially when others are listening, he refers to his fists as "peace makers." He claims to be a Christian, calling himself the *Holy Spirit Hit Man in Hell's Kitchen*. He screams so that those close-by can hear him: "Where there is no danger, I go looking for danger." Shorty claims fear is the basis of the three stages of what he calls "the prison game." (See Figure 1)

One day Shorty approached me looking quite agitated. He was just denied parole (for the fourth time) because of bad behavior. "Because I can't behave in prison, they don't think I can behave in the free-world." To add insult to perceived injury, Shorty's cell was searched for contraband earlier that day and, in the process, a CO allegedly destroyed his only copies of poems he had written in the past thirteen years.

Figure 1
Shorty's "Prison Game"

Stage 1: Impression. You make an impression, either as a man or as a woman. Shorty says that he came to Donaldson as a man, and he intends to leave as a man.
Stage 2: Manipulation. You manipulate inmates to get their property. This is accomplished through deceit, theft, or convincing someone that you can be trusted.
Stage 3: Intimidation. You either create fear or you become afraid. Shorty says this is the stage he likes the best.

As Shorty likes to say when others are listening, his job in the Jungle is to *provoke*, and that is how he vented after the parole denial and destruction of his poems. He threw an inmate's Bible on the cement floor and poured coffee on it because "the man was a hoax." As he talked *at* me, he began poking his finger into my stomach—inmates are not allowed to touch COs or free-world volunteers, not even in the Jungle. He was probing my level of fear and intimidation by those pokes and, quite frankly, the test had some success.

Shorty then shouted to me, making sure others could hear, that he intends to kill the CO who destroyed his poetry. He has a bet with other inmates on whether he can dropkick the CO from the top of the stairs, missing all seventeen steps on the way to the floor. He invited me to the top of the stairs as he explained how this task will be accomplished. (I went with him, but I stayed in plain view of the cube.) At the top Shorty demonstrated in the air how he will kick the CO's throat, catching him by surprise, with enough power to launch him to the floor.

A betting pool was created with differing odds of difficulty based on who Shorty ultimately kicks in the throat. Odds were based on the ease of potential victims: another inmate, a CO, a ranking CO, or (the prize) the CO who allegedly destroyed his poetry. The bet was not *whether* he would dropkick someone—his reputation was on the line and his ability to generate fear would be greatly threatened if he changed his mind. Rather, the bet was *who* he would ultimately dropkick in the throat and land at the bottom.

Daily Violence. According to "Paul," a former LWOPP inmate—now paroled—who as a child was adopted by Satanists,

> the biggest challenge is to stay alive. You can get '"clutched out"' which means five or six of the inmates will get on you. It's so easy [for them] to turn up at your cell

> and slam the door and there's no getting out. So it's so easy to take their life and wait about twenty or thirty minutes for the guard to not be looking and walk out the cell and shut the door.

Based on the projected $500,000 monthly bill from area hospitals, it should be of little surprise that violence is commonplace. When Bubba's death row sentence was changed to LWOPP, "the warden told me that I needed to either get me a *knife* or get me a *man*."

Muayyad," a fifty-four-year-old Muslim serving LWOPP for the past twenty-six years, had a gold necklace stolen from his bed when he took a shower. Furious about it, he put out the word of a $50 reward for information about who stole from him. Having discovered the culprit, "I jumped him and whooped him." When Marion got off death row and was sent to Donaldson, he had $30 worth of items and laid them on his cell bunk. He then shouted: "Anyone takes one thing, I will kill one of you. I'm going to dinner." A cellmate once wanted Mark's bunk, and a knife fight looked eminent. Mark, whose about six foot tall but weighs only 150 pounds, successfully rebuked the cellmate. With a collapsed nose from countless encounters, Mark says, "when you defend yourself, you have to make them think you're tougher than them." He once used a pencil to prove his point. Joel:

> The first time I heard that someone got stabbed, I was like, My God! I hope they are okay and I was perplexed for quite a while. Now, whenever I hear of someone being stabbed, I'm like, Man, I hope they'll still feed us on time because we are having french fries today!

The majority of fights and stabbings occur in the summer time because of the heat and cramped quarters, as well as in lockdown. In hot months the penalty for violence—time in a segregation cell—is a welcome reprieve because it means being in the same-size cell without cellmates. At any time of the year, that punishment is known as "taking a vacation"—an opportunity to do something different for a while. Paul:

> you got three men in a couple of feet of walking or standing space and so you got all that testosterone. You might have two guys that are homosexual and one guy that isn't and doesn't want to see that stuff. Something is going to *happen*.

Violence does not discriminate in terms of sentence length. Paul had an eighteen year-old friend in Whore Block who had only fixed-time to serve for repeated DUIs, the last offense resulting in a traffic fatality. On his first night, five inmates ran into his cell and raped him. When he recovered, the lad purchased a shank (a home-made knife) and killed one of the rapists. That was twenty-seven years ago, the same year Donaldson opened for business, and he has since been serving LWOPP in the same block.

Packing. How many inmates are armed? According to LWOPP inmate "Bud," a forty-year-old living in Whore Block since being evicted from another prison in 1997, it is a myth that so many have weapons: "80 percent don't have knives and 50 percent wouldn't know where to find one." According to most inmates, however, weapons are quite common. According to DOC, a few corrupt COs are mules for drugs and, therefore, they probably also smuggle in razors or metal objects. But inmates gain access to weapons in other ways as well. Paul: "I've seen homemade knives made out of spoons to concrete nails to a piece of bone. I've seen them make even homemade cross-bows." Inmate trustees working in maintenance can covertly provide materials for a price, and some of the pre-fabricated wood is stripped off the metal tables in the day rooms. Zip guns, firing .22 caliber bullets, are made from pieces of pipe, and bullets are smuggled in typically on visitation days. Paul:

> A lot of guys will put stuff in a balloon and swallow it. And then as soon as you come in, you take a little tooth paste cap full of shampoo and you drink it and it makes you throw up instantly. So the balloon is thrown up, too. Or, they've got homosexuals "dinging it"—sticking it up their rear end and bring the stuff in.

Living with Homosexuality. Some inmates mistakenly think that physical strength is more important than mental or emotional stamina. Marian: When this occurs "a big man can be made to dress up as a little girl." And if this can happen to a "big man," it certainly does not bode well for a weak adolescent, like Steve. Prison homosexuality is a dangerous activity. There are no condoms and, therefore, the risk of STDs and HIV/AIDS is great. But the dangers exceed long-term health issues because it can lead to one's murder. Bubba: "You can get killed if you don't participate. You can get killed if you participate and then stop."

Between one and ten percent of the male population in America engage in homosexuality (Kinsey et al., 1998; Hite, 1991). It is more prominent in prisons (Buffum, 2004), with estimates ranging from 30 to 65 percent (Hensley and Tewksbury, 2005; Hensley, 2000; Hensley, et al., 2000). Estimates are even higher at Donaldson, ranging between 50 and 80 percent. From all accounts—inmates, COs, and the chaplain—well over 1,000 inmates (out of 1,679) engage (or have engaged) in homosexual practices.

Sissies. Dicks. Buddies. Kings. Queens. Boys. There is a whole vernacular to sex in most prisons, and Donaldson is no exception. The words are meant to describe and rationalize one's involvement. "Sissies" are "receptive" partners. Inmates with petite physiques, or those who display fear, automatically become prime sissy candidates. Others may also become sissies because of debts incurred through betting or loans from "store men"—inmates who purchase pantry supplies from the prison store and then sell those items with high interest rates to others who run out of goods during the week. Still others become sissies for the sake of friendships. The truth is, sissies want others to be sissies to rationalize their own way of life. Grand Daddy:

> They pull the other guy in. You want to be with your friends in prison. If they get involved with homosexuality, then you have a choice to make about having them as your friends. If you want them as friends, then you have to have sex with them.

"Dicks" are the "insertive" counterpart to sissies. They do not regard themselves as homosexuals, nor are they viewed that way by other inmates. Dicks are either heterosexual men needing sex in an all-male environment or "businessmen" collecting on transactions—perhaps a third-party sexual payment for work completed or restitution for a delinquent debt over last month's store items or this year's Super Bowl outcome.

"Buddies" are dicks and sissies who pair up strictly for sex with no long-term emotional connection. They look for a reliable sex partner and nothing more. A "king" is a dick who engages in a long-term monogamous relation with a sissy. In this amorous situation, the sissy becomes a "queen." Kings and queens try to arrange transfers so that they live in the same cell. They eat meals as a couple, watch TV together, and care for each other.

"Boys" are either prostitutes to be rented or whores to be used at one's pleasure. These sissies may be "owned" by a gang on a long-term basis, have a pimp for protection, or simply be a dick who got into debt and, at least temporarily, must don the catcher's glove in this "ball game." Mark has a friend in Whore Block, a "tough guy" when he first entered Donaldson, who now shaves his legs and buttocks daily and wears lipstick, blush, mascara, and eye shadow. Once a proud man, Mark's friend is a sissy and, rather than being a queen, is relegated to the lowest echelon—the boy. Inmates like this are discretely displayed in the Jungle and openly paraded in Whore Block. There, many boys who cannot afford nylons and cosmetics choose to wear only a towel around their waist as they prance about the day room talking either to perspective customers or clients directed to them by their task-masters. The towel permits them to entice prospective partners, and it makes it easier to disrobe during the conduct of business back in the cell once a partner has been secured.

One evening in Whore Block, a new CO came running down the stairs from the second tier of cells. Shaking with fright, his screams were so loud that they even silenced the shouting conversations in the day room. A CO from the cube rushed to see what had happened to the inexperienced CO. He frantically shouted that he had just opened a cell door and found six men inside. In the spirit of De Sade, five were geometrically positioned on the three bunks so they could simultaneously participate in oral and anal sex. The sixth inmate, sitting on the commode, was masturbating at the scene. Because such a display is the norm, the cube CO and many inmates in the day room broke into uncontrollable laughter at the inexperienced guard.

An Ice Cream Social. Near the central shift station and the law library is the prison store, where once a week items can be purchased as long as the inmate has sufficient funds in his account. It is not a store as we envision in the free world. It is neither a supermarket nor a Wal-mart, but more like a concession stand where inmates line up in the West Side hallway and purchase items through a window. Next to that window is a sign:

> ICE CREAM CALL
> Blocks: Tuesdays and Thursdays
> South Side: Mondays and Wednesdays.
> Store slips for ice cream will be
> passed out around 7 a.m.
> and will be picked up around 10 a.m.
> No Slip, No Ice Cream

Especially on hot summer days, ice cream is a treat that can either be enjoyed by the purchaser or it can be used to pay off debts. However, one CO discovered that ice cream can also be used for other purposes. One afternoon in the faith-based New Beginnings block, a CO randomly inspected cells on the second tier. Opening one door, he came upon two men enjoying ice cream in a peculiar way that would have excited De Sade. One inmate had buried an entire ice cream cone up the other inmate's rectum. He jammed it in so deep that the top of the cone was flush with the dentate line. As the CO opened the door, he saw the inmate digging with his tongue, licking and sucking out the ice cream through the other man's anal canal. This was not an inexperienced CO, so there were no frantic screams of horror. However, those who heard about the incident—from the chaplain to COs to many inmates—lost their appetite for ice cream during the remainder of that long, hot summer.

Living with Heterosexuality. Like most prisons, Donaldson is filled with younger men with overflowing testosterone levels as well as middle-age men who share with their youthful comrades a level of dreadful daily boredom that is beyond the imagination of most free-world people. These two phenomena—primacy of sex and dullness of routine—provide some explanation (but not moral justification) about the dicks and sissies. They also give some insight into the seemingly uncontrollable urges of inmates who have not completely forgotten their heterosexuality.

While sissies and dicks are either ignored or excused, men caught in acts of heterosexuality are typically punished. An inmate I know was justifiably punished for one such incident. He lived on South Side and, because of the greater level of freedom offered there, he liked to walk around in the evening hours. Eventually he got into the habit of visiting with a female CO who worked the late shift, and for several weeks they chatted at various times. He began to fantasize about a sexual connection between them. One evening he tested that hypothesis by gently caressing her buttocks as he walked past her.

That inmate quickly found out about null hypotheses. He was arrested and found guilty of sexual molestation. He spent the next forty-five days in segregation and, upon release, was evicted from the comfort and safety of South Side and sent to live in a three-person cell in the Jungle.

Masturbation. Masturbation is practiced by the incarcerated as it is by free-world people. The differences, at least at prisons like Donaldson, are three-fold. First, it is done quite a bit—estimates range between 60 to 80 percent of all inmates masturbate at least once each day, and around 40 percent masturbate anywhere from four to eight times in any twenty-four-hour period. Second, masturbation by necessity occurs in semi-public forums because few have single cells. Third, for some—perhaps as many as a quarter of the inmates—masturbation is also performed in totally public areas. Public masturbation is a phenomenon which typically involves the more youthful inmate. Muayyad:

> We have had a cultural shift in our views of sensitivity in society—much more permissive now. The younger guys coming into prison *now* have no inhibitions about masturbating in public. It is a twenty-first century version of *acting-out.*

Gunners. Public masturbators are called "gunners." They masturbate whenever a female CO is in the vicinity and where ever the mood strikes them, but normally they restrain themselves when free-world volunteers are near by. Joel talks about his first time in the exercise yard:

> I saw four guys standing real still and facing the guard tower. They just kept standing there because of a female guard in the tower. Now the tower was quite a ways off, and I couldn't see anyone in it. I figured out that these gunners must have one hell of an imagination. For all they know, it could have been a male guard in the tower or perhaps a hat hanging on a broom stick!

Public masturbation occurs in every cell block. I frequently arrange for my college classes, including both male and female students, to tour Donaldson. On one tour of a segregation block, an inmate slid a "flip-flop" sandal under the door, extended a wire through the air vent in the door, and tried to hook the sandal in a way so that it would unlatch the tray slot as it was pulled up to the air vent. Unsuccessful, he wanted to show the class his erected penis and kept shouting to the female students: "Wait! Look what I have for you!"

Masturbation happens occasionally in the kitchen as meals are being prepared. Sometimes an inmate will begin to masturbate, stop to complete a food preparation task, and then resume. This is done without hand-washing. It happens in the main hallways, especially around the central station where female COs and non-uniformed female secretaries are often located. Inmates walk quickly by and peep into the station, then walk down the hallway and masturbate. It happens in the faith-based New Beginnings block where, some inmates argue, female COs are posted as a reward for good behavior. It happens so frequently, and without the habit of hand-washing, that the common act of shaking hands can have hygienic repercussions.

Public masturbation even occurs during Sunday worship services in the chapel. Typically sitting in the back row of plastic patio chairs, the inmate unbuckles his pants and adjusts them for comfort. Staring at the female CO, he unzips his pants and covers his exposed penis with the shirt tail. Or, he inserts one hand into a front pant pocket, rearranges his underwear, and massages his unexposed penis. Chapel workers discourage the practice, but fear a fight might break out if they tried to stop a masturbator during church service. Besides, as one chapel assistant asked: "What can you do when someone is masturbating through their pocket?" The chaplain is not present for Sunday services, and volunteer pastors seem not to have a clue about back-pew activity. Masturbation has not yet become a problem during the Friday Muslim worship services in the chapel, perhaps because the chaplain is nearby, but their sergeants-at-arm are aware of the potential and maintain a watchful eye.

The Art of Fine Dining. There has always been a connection between manners and the political community. Stephen L. Carter (1998) refers to it as one indicator of our ability to demonstrate a "sacrificial" civility toward each fellow citizen. As many times as I have visited the canteen, the level of etiquette speaks poorly about the nature of such sacrifice among inmates at Donaldson. It is loud—harmfully loud—with men shouting to each other in conversation. With exceptions, men chew with their mouths wide open and some, because of lack of teeth, gnaw at their food. It appears that tables are cleaned only after the last inmate exits and, in the mean time, many men choose simply to sit in filth rather than take the time to clean off a portion of the table and chair prior to their use. It is reminiscent of Norbert Elias' (1982) observations about European customs prior to the acceptance of the fork as a civilizing utensil. Unlike Elias's sixteenth century patrons, inmates do not defecate on their seats. However, they fart and belch, food flies out of their mouths, and many eat with their fingers. Some sneeze openly and care not about the direction or density of their discharge. Cooks add *savoir-faire* by occasionally urinating in the ice tea. Eating in this setting three times a day for the rest of your life adds misery beyond repair.

Personal Intimacy

Each day offers reminders of one's station in life. "Clyde," a sixty-seven-year-old who has been LWOPP for the last twenty-five years, recently had influenza. It reminded him that, unlike men his age in the free-world, he could not get up in the middle of the night to get a second pillow or a cooling can of ginger ale from a refrigerator to douse the flame in his throat. Clyde had no bathroom cabinet filled with cough drops and aspirins. After evening lockdown, he had to lay in his fevered sweat and wait for a "pill call," which occurs four times a day: 3 a.m./p.m. and 9 a.m./p.m. At those moments he is especially mindful that his "senior" years are qualitatively different than others his age. Clyde looks at a treasured reminder of the past: a "baseball card" which was printed in celebration of his father's eighty-ninth birthday. On the card is a picture of his father with the inscription: *Happy 89th Birthday, Paw. From your kids and grand kids*. His father died more than a decade ago, and Clyde is aging. He talks about an appeal, but realizes he has been talking about that for the last twenty-five years. Decades go by quickly and slowly in the cell, a fact noticed more in moments of sickness. Clyde: "It's hard to believe that I can maintain my senses."

Grand Daddy tries to avoid reminders of his station in life. He used to live on South Side, but he would start fights just to go to segregation lockdown. He now resides in Whore Block. Why?

> I don't like seeing the outside. It's depressing. On a nice summer day, the grass is green and I start thinking about my lawn needing cut. I'd see trees in the distance, the smell of fresh cut grass in the air—it depresses me. In the dormitories, I'd see stars at night and then look down at the razor-top fence. So I don't like to go outside much.

Hotel California. Sometimes the problem is *finding* a routine, as in the case of prolonged lockdowns. Grand Daddy: "You just have to figure out how to pass your time. Most stay up all night, talking to each other or shouting to friends in other cells." Although card games are contraband, many make sets of playing cards out of cardboard from instant soup containers. Others play chess or checkers in their cells. Still others turn to sex, with or without help from a cellmate, and make that part of their lockdown routine.

Even on days with no lockdown, the routine becomes unbearable. Figure 2 illustrates a typical day for Clyde in New Beginnings. Not much has changed in what he does over the past twenty-five years and very little will be altered until he is buried on the family's homestead in northern Alabama. Figure 2 also shows a typical day for Bud in Whore Block. Nothing will ever change for him, except an occasional softball game in the exercise yard. He knows that, at forty, life is passing him. He fully understands that "prison cappuccino" and endless packs of cigarettes are not substitutes for raising his teenage son, who is unaware that Bud is even alive, or ending his aging mother's relentless efforts to rescue him from his hell—she takes $60 a month out of her social security check to save for the $40,000 needed to pay a lawyer to make one more fruitless appeal. Deep down inside, Bud is aware that he will die at Donaldson.

The routine is more flexible in South Side's Honor Dorm where 130 open bunk beds dispel dingy cells. One can venture outside any time of the night to be blessed by bright stars and sultry breezes. Nevertheless the hopelessness and despair brought on by prison life is no less harsh. Dean summarized the anguish succinctly.

> Yes it is nice to walk around, but do you see that fence? Do you see that guard tower? You can never go past them. They will shoot me if I try. My world begins and ends here. You can never go home.

A World of Bartering and Debt

For the inmate, prison is a costly proposition in more ways than time and stamina. It is costly in terms of financing the "amenities" to make prison life bearable, and this is especially true at Donaldson where few have jobs and no jobs earn wages. As a result, economics is based on bartering and debt management. If an inmate desires those "extras," he is dependent upon the receipt of money into his prison account from outside sources. Bud receives a monthly stipend of $59, and a Christmas bonus of $100, from a cousin who is a physician in Atlanta. He started writing her a year ago; money was the only thing that he requested. He also receives $100 a month from his aging mother, and $30 a month from his aging dad—both on fixed incomes.

Grand Daddy received money from his father until he died, and now he receives $200 a month from his brother. The fact that his brother is

Figure 2
Routine of LWOPP Inmates

Time	"Clyde" New Beginnings Block	"Bud" Whore Block
Before 2:00 a.m.	Sleep	Wake up, drink a shot of instant coffee, an "8-ball," and a serving of hot chocolate. "It's like a cappuccino." Then have a smoke in the cell.
2:00 a.m. - 3:00 a.m.	Breakfast call: 15 minutes to eat. Not a big breakfast eater.	Breakfast call: 15 minutes to eat. Likes pancakes, which are served three times a month.
3:00 a.m.	Pill call. Waits in day room for cells to open. Lockdown.	Waits in day room for cells to open, lockdown.
3:00 a.m. - 6:00 a.m.	Goes back to sleep. His one cell-mate also sleeps.	Smokes cigarettes, another "cappuccino," as his two cellmates try to sleep.
6:00 a.m.	Sleep	One cell-mate goes to trade school, but not Bud because he is LWOPP (state does not pay training for LWOPP inmates). Bud goes into the day room.
6:20 a.m.	Sleep	Head count, which means all must go back into the cell for lockdown until count is correct.
7:00 a.m.	Head count, which goes quickly in New Beginnings.	Head count continues.
7:00 a.m.	Takes a shower/shave	Head count continues.
7:30 a.m.	Reads or watches the news on TV	Goes into day room/smokes/TV.
8:30 a.m.	If yard is open, goes for a walk.	Stays in day room.
9:00 a.m.	Pill call.	Stays in day room.
10:00 a.m.	Works information desk (until 1 p.m.).	Stays in day room.
10:30 a.m.	Lunch: 15 minutes to eat.	Stays in day room.
11:30 a.m.	Works information desk.	Lunch: 15 minutes to eat.
noon	Works information desk.	"Get comfortable, put on some shorts and talk with friends" in day room.
3:00 p.m.	Pill call.	Stays in day room or goes to yard, if permitted.
4:30 p.m.	Dinner: 15 minutes to eat.	Stays in day room or in yard, if permitted.
5:00 p.m.	Goes into day room and visits.	Dinner: 15 minutes to eat.
6:00 p.m.	Watches news on TV in day room.	Showers and shaves.
7:00 p.m.	Mail call (week days).	Mail call (week days).
7:30 p.m.	Reads	Watches TV: *24* or *Prison Break* or *American Idol*.
8:00 p.m.	Goes to bed.	Watches TV.
9:00 p.m.	Pill call.	Watches TV.
10:00 p.m.	Institutional movie on Friday and Saturday nights. (Clyde still goes to bed at 8:00 p.m.)	Institutional movie on Friday and Saturday nights.
10:30 p.m.	Mandatory lockdown (Sunday through Thursday)	Mandatory lockdown (Sunday through Thursday).
2:00 a.m.	Mandatory lockdown on Friday and Saturday nights. (Clyde still goes to bed at 8:00 p.m.)	Mandatory lockdown on Friday and Saturday nights. Final cigarettes in cell, and perhaps a card game.

aging means ultimately that source of income will disappear. He now writes to younger nephews and nieces and their children—planting the seeds of future family welfarism on his behalf. He writes as many as twenty letters a week.

Eli gets between $100 and $200 a month from his mother and step-dad. From a trust fund left by his parents, Mark receives $75 a month. Muayyad receives about $70 a month from his two sisters. Clyde's parents are dead but he inherited property. In 1992, he sold his share of the homestead to his brother for $25,000 and, from that pool, he receives $200 a month. "Shaheem," a forty-eight-year-old Muslim serving LWOPP for the past twenty-two years, receives money occasionally from his family, but

> I manage to have what I need. Actually you don't need much finances in prison. *They* need money on the outside. There is no reason to get hundreds of dollars each month. There is no need for me to walk around with a $150 pair of shoes.

These men are clearly exceptions at Donaldson because most inmates do not have contact with loved ones in the free-world after about eighteen months of incarceration. Hence, if an inmate wants to supplement amenities not provided by DOC, he must take chances on gambling or get a loan from another inmate, or provide some kind of service—perhaps in a gang or as a boy—to those who have money in their accounts. Much of the fear and violence, as well as homosexuality, stems from limited means of satisfying desires for immediate gratification.

The Cookie Standard

Once a week, inmates are allowed to place orders from the prison store. What amenities are available? About what you would find at a convenience store, and every good is broken down into a measurable unit, called an "item." A package of *Al's Oatmeal Cookies*, containing ten individual servings, costs $5.20. Each cookie in the package is valued as one "item." The cookie has been used so often as a measurement of worth that it has become the basis of the block economy—it is the equivalent of the one dollar bill. If a cookie is worth one item, then everything sold or loaned is compared to that one cookie. A package of eight *Snickers* bars costs $4.56, and each of the eight bars can be resold individually for a negotiated amount which is based on the "cookie standard." It may be worth three items or, if I am desperate for a candy bar and it is not "store day," it may be worth four items or more. A 3.5-ounce jar of coffee costs $3.38. Inmates transform its contents into eight coffee balls, placed in little sacks typically made out of old nylon panty hose. Each "eight ball" can be traded for as many as seven items. An inmate, desperate for coffee, might barter an $8.80 book of stamps for an entire jar of coffee—thus rendering the recipient of the twenty stamps a valuable commodity which he can barter for as many as five items per stamp. Name brand products always have greater value, perhaps as much as an additional nine items, compared to the generic barter price.

A price tag is also attached to every service rendered. Depending on the quality and reputation of the giver, sex normally costs just two or three items per trick. Managing a betting pool, say for the Super Bowl or the NCAA basketball tournament, comes with a set commission of items based on the volume of bets. Extemporaneous betting, like Shorty's odds on dropkicking someone over the railing in the Jungle, also brings in a take for the pool. Providing tattoos, a service of necessity in the blocks, comes with a cost of about ten to fifty items—given the nature of the design, the need to secure ink from the outside, and the need to bribe an attendant or nurse for needles from the infirmary. Illegal drugs like "cocaine shots," a concoction of cocaine and water, cost a great deal more—perhaps one-hundred items per shot—because of the need for needles and cooperation of third parties in the free-world. However, the inmate who scores cocaine from the outside on just a one-time basis is financially secure for the rest of the block fiscal year.

There are other services provided. For instance, Paul used to gain items by applying what he learned from his adoptive Satanic family. He taught inmates about witchcraft, and his services of casting Black Magic spells were in great demand.

> If an inmate had a crush on a guard or nurse, I could get them to bring me something that she's touched: a piece of paper or whatever. They couldn't touch it with their hands, so they'd have to use a tissue or something to bring me that item. Then I'd sit down with 'em and I would chant certain things over it. And then in a couple of days, all of a sudden the nurse or the guard would start being nice to them: bringing them *food*, offering stuff like that.

The social gospel also renders a price tag. For example, Paul talks about one inmate who could not feed himself because he "had no arms. He was born with just these little stub fingers at the sides of his shoulders." The infirmary runners, who agreed to feed him each day, were charging this man a $30 store draw each week.

Interest on a Loan

As with free-world loan sharks, and some high-priced Wall Street bankers, prison loans come with interest which must be paid in full. At Donaldson, the interest rates are as follows: one item = two items, two items = three items, three items = five items, five items = eight items. Marian: “Borrowing is nurtured by addictions: homosexual addictions, betting addictions, drug addictions, and eating addictions.”

The negotiated price of a trade is one thing, but what if you have nothing to trade? You may rely on a friend or acquaintance, but most inmates go to the “store man” because he buys in bulk from the prison store each week. When others run out during the week, or cannot afford amenities in the first place, the store man is available to help remedy the problem. Joel estimates that 80 percent of Donaldson’s general population deal with one store man or another throughout the week. This is how debts mount up and, as long as debts are paid, borrowing continues and the block economy flourishes. Bud says he borrows but has a good reputation for repaying on time.

> I’ve owed over $1,000 and wasn’t worried about someone killing me. They don’t *want* to kill you. They just want their *money*.

What if you cannot pay? Some inmates beg the COs for safety via eviction to the segregation unit. Others try to con their free-world friends and loved ones into sending more money. Some will sell their portions of Sunday’s fried chicken dinner—the only meal to which inmates look forward—and fast for that day.

Quite a few inmates, however, get into debt and cannot repay the loan. Marion: “When you get into debt, the penalty ranges from no more loans to being sexually loaned out.” Dean: “They will take your radio, take your shoes, take any property you have. Some will beat you up. The extreme consequence is sex.” Perkins: “Nobody will take state-issued boots because everyone has them. But if you have expensive tennis shoes—$200 *Air Jordans*—then those will be taken.” Joel: “I’ve seen people get killed for eighty-five cents.”

Control

Shaheem: “You are a man, but you have no control.” Muayyad: “this is a place where they tell you when to eat, sleep, get up, go to the bathroom, take a shower." Prisons represent the *Absolute Time Out* for adults in the American political community. It is similar to punishing a small child by forcing her to sit in the living room corner chair for ten minutes of her short life. The LWOPP inmate, however, must sit in that chair for the rest of his life. And rather than being in a comfortable living room, his "time out" chair is placed far away in a cold, concrete setting. It is there that control is exerted until death.

Rules

Rules are one way to control inmates, both physically and mentally. They teach behavior about three basic life lessons which should have been learned a long time ago. First, patience is required in any process involving machines or humans. Second, nothing ever centers strictly on the self; one man's desire becomes another man's burden, and one's action becomes another's consequence. Third, rules governing punishment—however fair and compassionate—are still a reflection of *lex talionis* and *Al-Qisaas*.

If you wish to consume prison meals, and thereby limit store purchases and debt, then you must eat according to the prison schedule and not according to the whims of your appetite. Just as a child, you are not allowed to bring meals to your bunk bed. Grown men have a bed time curfew. (My teenage children, when studying for tests, are permitted to stay up later on week nights than are inmates at Donaldson.) Even on South Side, the inmate must never slouch casually in a plastic white patio chair as he watches a college football game or an episode of *Prison Break* prior to having to go to bed.

Unofficial rules also control behavior and enforce *lex talionis* or *Al-Qisaas*. A CO does not have to let an inmate attend chapel if she feels he is undeserving. A CO can place the entire block in lockdown if he feels such action is warranted. On hot steamy summer afternoons, the cube officer has the discretion to open or close the yard door and, hence, control the amount of relief inmates receive from a potential breeze. Due to understaffing and overcrowding, he can truncate or eliminate time in the exercise yard. A CO can destroy personal property, like Shorty's poems, in an honest and thorough search for contraband. The end result of all activities is control over the inmate.

Control by DOC has a ripple effect on power asserted by inmates over other inmates. As noted above, very few seats are available in the Jungle and Whore Block and, unlike New Beginnings and South Side, there are no plastic patio chairs. Seating becomes a scarce resource which adds value to the available spots. The pecking order is based on fear, violence, and a willingness to go into debt to pay for a seat. Those at the top of the hierarchy sit throughout the day. Those at the bottom, the sissies, sit on the concrete floor next to their dicks. Those in the middle stratum just stand all day. All this is based on an unofficial rule that plastic patio chairs, which are stacked in abundance in chapel storage areas, will not be distributed in the Jungle and Whore Block.

Controlling the Little Things

Because of the potential for making weapons, there are no glass mirrors. In the chapel bathroom, plywood covers the spot over the sink where a mirror was mistakenly affixed by free-world workers. On South Side, there are tin plates attached to the bathroom area walls. These are sufficient for shaving, but offer only a distorted reflection of the whole face. In the cell blocks, your image is reflected only off the stainless steel commode and sink or perhaps a piece of contraband metal. The intimacy of growing older—graying hair, sinking eyelids, lines and sagging facial skin—things that most people use as highway markers in their lives, simply go unnoticed by most inmates. Prison controls the basic intimacy of what a man sees of himself.

The Best Seat in the House

As long as you are in your cell, bowel movements are your own business. What is controlled, however, is the commode itself. The best seat in the house is found in any death row cell because it is private and used by only one person. The next best seat is found in the dorms. While shared by many, South Side rules require regular cleaning and, unlike those in cells, these commodes are made of porcelain with raisable seats. The next best place to defecate is in a New Beginnings cell, where men also have incentives to be neat and clean. While stainless steel and without a raisable seat, these are private and shared only with one other inmate. The worst seat in the house is found in the cells of the Jungle or Whore Block, where inmates have absolutely no incentive to be clean. Shaheem: "I get tired of telling people to flush the toilet and to clean off the urine from the seat." Quite often these commodes flood because some inmates are not in the habit of flushing their refuse and, therefore, it piles up with each usage. Others use their commodes as trash cans. Still others use the toilets as repositories for drugs or "julep"—an alcoholic concoction made of fruit smuggled out of the canteen. Sometimes the plastic bags containing the contraband break or leak, causing a two-fold problem: the toilet eventually clogs and foul toilet water seeps into the julep.

There are several commodes outside each cell block but, as another form of control, only a few are available to inmates. The worst toilet at Donaldson is located in the East Side gymnasium. There is no privacy barrier between the commode and the basketball court, and the left side of the raisable porcelain seat is broken off. When you sit down, you do so only with your right cheek hitting the seat. The left cheek sits in the squalor left on the rim.

The best "public" toilet for inmates is in the air-conditioned chapel. The lavatory is larger than any single space at Donaldson, and it is totally private with a door which the inmate controls. Located in the back of the chapel, it is twenty-one 2-inch tiles wide and twenty-eight tiles deep. The door is metal with peeling black paint, and the vent at the bottom of the door is filthy. The handle over the commode is broken off. For years, you used the handle's "nub," but even that is no longer in tact. Now a string hangs from the top of the bowl with a piece of wood tied to it. The other end is tied to the bowl dam which regulates flushes. The porcelain seat is black and, while it tends to wobble, must bring back memories of other times and places. There are no paper towels to wash your hands, but there is a well-used rag hanging over the wash tub in the outer room. Given privacy and porcelain, the commode is another reason inmates attend so many functions in the chapel: many of those who attend the Muslim services on Friday also attend the Christian services on Sunday as well as the various Bible study groups throughout the week. There is often a line to the bathroom, and this bothers some members of the chaplain's staff who view that commode as their own special perk. One staff member: "This is the chapel's bathroom. It *ain't* for dumping in. It really pisses me off."

Toilet Paper

In 2001 SCA-Tissue, a Swedish paper-product firm, purchased an American company in Reenhah, Wisconsin and is now a leader in the institutional markets of North America with its "Main Street" toilet paper. Donaldson purchases the two-ply paper, although you would be hard pressed to find the second ply, at $74.03 per each 96-roll case.

Given that each inmate gets only one 500-sheet roll per week, less than $65,000 is spent annually on toilet paper.

One roll of toilet paper per week may seem adequate, given that the average free-world person uses fifty-seven sheets daily (www.toiletpaper-world.com). This means that a roll of toilet paper will normally last about eight days. However, it is important to remember that this estimate is based on two assumptions. First, the diameter of each sheet is 4.5 inches square. Second, a person has only one bowel movement per day.

These assumptions do not hold at Donaldson. Each sheet is only 4.5"x 3.75"—meaning the average person would use 15 percent more sheets. This increases the daily average to about sixty-five sheets per day, and the roll now lasts around seven-and-a-half days. Further, most inmates have two or three bowel movements daily as a result of the nature of food and drinking water, as well as the occasional urination in the ice tea. But let's be conservative and argue that there are only one-and-a-half daily bowel movements (not two or three) for each inmate. This results in using ninety-eight sheets per day, and now we are down to having enough toilet paper for just a little over five days.

Naturally there are consequences to controlling access to toilet paper. Stretching five days into seven exacerbates flu and cold seasons. Most inmates do not purchase facial tissue and, because of the need to conserve toilet paper, use nothing to blow their noses. They tend to just flick snot with one finger, and it remains on the concrete floor. Then each sissy who sits on the floor, and each inmate who is touched with the hand that flicked the snot, is subject to virus or infection. Toward the end of any seven-day cycle, the value of toilet paper increases. An inmate steeped in debt may be quite willing to sell portions of his roll to reduce the amount of items owed. He might then defecate without cleaning himself, and this too adds to the misery inside the cell as well as threatens the health of cellmates and those who may shower after him.

Lessons about the Real of Life in Prison

Dietrich Bonhoeffer was in prison for only two years and most of that time was spent in cell 92 at Tegel Prison. His celebrity status buffered him from the core horrors of Nazi incarceration and, if not for the Russian march onto Berlin and the imminent end of the regime, he would have remained in prison indefinitely rather than executed on April 9, 1945. While conditions at Tegel did not nearly compare to future hardships he would face in the Gestapo basement on Prinz-Albrecht-Strasse or at the

Buchenwald and Flossenburg extermination camps, he fully understood the *edgeless life of prison* (Bethge, 2000: 894-928). Bonhoeffer's fiancée, Maria von Wedemeyer, recalled that on her first prison visitation "his emotions showed only in the pressure with which he held my hand" (Bethge, 1997: 414). In November 1943, he wrote her about prison cells, where one "does various unessential things, and is completely dependent on the fact that the door of freedom has to be opened *from the outside*" (Bethge, 1997: 416). While never diminishing the consequences of Dean's crime, if Bonhoeffer were alive today he would certainly empathize with Dean's lament about the Donaldson fence and guard tower keeping him from ever going home. In December 1943, Dietrich wrote Maria: "You can hardly imagine how I long for everyone: after these long months of solitude, I have a real hunger for people" (Bethge, 1997: 417). He certainly would cry for the vast majority of Donaldson inmates who, after just eighteen months of incarceration, typically receive no further correspondence from loved ones. If alive today, he would even empathize with Mark's desire to receive money from loved ones to purchase store items. The Gestapo did not operate a "prison store," so Bonhoeffer had to rely directly on loved ones for routine, but special items—as indicated in a letter to his parents (Bethge, 1997: 401):

> Now for a few more requests: unfortunately there were no books handed in here for me today.... There were no matches, face-cloths, or towel this time. Excuse me for asking.... Could I please have some toothpaste and a few coffee beans?

More than sixty years after Bonhoeffer's death, the fears felt by Grand Daddy and Bud in Whore Block would echo his assessment of the human condition: "Man cannot live without hope ... men who have really lost all hope often become wild and wicked" (Bethge, 1997:372). Even Clyde in New Beginnings and Dean on South Side live within the ink of Bonhoeffer's poem, *Nachtliche Stimmen* (*Voices in the Night*), which reads in part (Robertson, 1999: 57):

> Stretched out upon my prison bed,
> I stare at the empty wall.
> Outside, a summer evening,
> regardless of me,
> goes singing into the country.
> Softly ebbs the tide of the day
> on eternal shore.

The argument has been made throughout this book that, in addition to scripture, truth comes from the real which is given to us by God. "The purpose of our words," according to Bonhoeffer, "is to express [that] real." He adds, "the assigned purpose of our silence is to signify the limit which is imposed upon our words by the real...." (1995: 364). Certainly some aspects of the real are unpleasant enough to make us speechless, and others are sufficiently shocking to make us want to pretend they do not exist. The task of the *citizen-nachahmer* is to find the real of public action—in its most intimate and consequential human form—so that its exposure might shrink our limitations and, thus, clarify our obligations to the political community. In doing so, our actions will truly find voice and become courageous in reconciling the real with the word and presenting it back to God.

The Real of "Regardless of Me"

Bonhoeffer's phrase, "regardless of me" is central to the lives of LWOPP inmates. Imagine returning to the town in which you grew up after an absence of many years. Dirt roads might now be paved, new shops built, and old businesses relocated. Different people might have purchased homes in which you once had great familiarity. Then again, perhaps not much has changed except the color of paint on those houses and the age of people who still dwell in them. Either way, you still have to "catch up" in some fashion because, after so many years, town life continued without you and, in fact, it continued *regardless of you.*

Such is the real of LWOPP. Beautiful spring evenings and crisp autumn days, as well as the lives and deaths of loved ones in the free-world, all exacerbate the punishment delivered onto LWOPP inmates. They talk about their hometowns, to which you might have recently visited, as if nothing has changed in them for the last three decades. Truth is, they know better and the fact that they can never return kills them quietly each and every day. Life goes on while the LWOPP inmate remains stagnant in that Absolute Time Out. In the end, the tide of his day ebbs softly yet agonizingly onto the "eternal shore," and does so *regardless of him.*

The Real of Hopelessness

In the fourteenth-century epic poem, *The Divine Comedy*, Dante Alighieri (1321; 2006) wrote about the gate to hell: "All hope abandon ye who enter here." The real of prison is not unlike Dante's hell. It is without free-world hope that these men must live, and this truly can turn quiet souls into wild ones, and wild souls into wicked ones. It is not just a loss of hope about getting out of prison and resuming old ways. New cars, fast women, and bar scenes are not core issues here. Much more central is the loss of hope about everything that is truly precious. You see, most of these men have actually learned the "meaning of life"—and this is one reason I visit and learn from them. The problem is, they acquired the "great *a-ha* effect" too late to apply it to their own free-world selves. Hopelessness prospers in such a quandary.

So there they sit and, like Bonhoeffer, do all the unessential things in life. Grand Daddy will never meet the children and grandchildren of his brothers and sisters. He will attend neither baptisms nor weddings, birthday parties nor little league games. The same with Eli: "I can't pick up and hold my nephew. I can't pray my mother to sleep." He may someday be notified about his mother's death before the funeral service takes place, but he will never have a chance to give her that one last hug and say "I love you, mom." As she awaits the eternal closing of her eyes, he will not be able to confess "I'm sorry to have put you through this, mom."

Hopelessness has some pretty complex corners where loneliness can always find a home. Muayyad says that, regardless of the inmates you claim as friends, eventually and permanently "you become lost." When free-world volunteers talk about their outside activities, it does not bother Eli because it gives him a chance to live through their lives. Stories from the outside are his only lifeline. Bud sends more than a dozen cards to loved ones at Christmas time, and few if any return the gesture. Shaheem, a devout Muslim, grows excited during the Christian season of Lent because his Christian sister might send him an Easter card. He says it's wonderful just to be remembered. Mark makes a special treat on each birthday: a moon pie with thick cocoa mix as frosting and a smiley face fingered on it.

The Real of Minimally Decent Samaritans

Who can you trust in an environment that, at best, is a collection of "minimally decent Samaritans" (Thomson, 1971) and, at worst, is the house that de Sade (1795; 2006) built? A sissy who was initially raped in prison, and whose older sister was raped years before his incarceration, once posed the question: What is the difference between free-world rape and prison rape? Answer: With free-world rape, you do not necessarily have to see the rapist ever again. With prison rape, you have to sit across the canteen table from him each and every day. You have to watch TV with him in the same day room. When you are a LWOPP inmate, you must do this for the rest of your life. How do you ever trust that rapist? Can you trust those in the block who knew in advance about the rape? How do you trust those who did nothing to stop the rape in the hope of gaining just one more "boy" in the block?

The "minimally decent Samaritan" philosophy is the reality found in most interactions among inmates. You simply weigh someone "giving" you an item with the prospect of having to repay it in some fashion at double value. A needed hug is withheld after weighing how it might be interpreted as a sign of willingness to engage in homosexuality. A friendly smile is withheld because it might be considered a sign of weakness. How do you find compassion in a kingdom of store men? Furthermore, what does it mean to be friends with a minimally decent Samaritan like Shorty? Certainly his calculations about the relationship will be quite thorough, but for you the weight of consequences will always be uncertain. Uncertainty, after all, is key to Shorty's "prison game," the rules to which become the skewed foundation of a de Sadean social gospel.

The Real of Misery

There is misery in maximum security prisons (Carceral, 2004; Bruton, 2004). At one level, misery is often nurtured from a mixture of institutional environment and human interaction. It is typically found in the intimate yet seemingly insignificant pockets of the day. For instance, a world of misery can be found in the square footage of one's life. The average size bathroom in America is one hundred square feet. At Donaldson, a cell is only sixty square feet. To grasp the real of this kind of misery: choose two loved ones to share six hours with you in your own bathroom. Have each bring a box of personal items, as well as a fishnet of clothes. Shut the door and do not open it. Blacken the window so you cannot see out, and close off the air-conditioning and heating ducts. Tape over all mirrors so that no reflection can be seen. While you lack two additional bunks, everyone sit on the bathtub rim. Do not sit on the commode—assume it has no cover or seat. Do not sit on the floor; assume it is filthy. Do not leave the room when someone urinates or defecates. Do not turn on the exhaust fan. Enjoy your time together.

Now picture doing this in an even smaller space (sixty square feet) with two strangers who are not compelled to show courtesy, civility, or compassion. They may urinate on the floor and masturbate into the sink. They will belch and fart at their own pleasure as a sign of power, control, or simply ill-manners. When illness strikes, the ventless stench of the space will be sweetened with the soured aroma of vomit and diarrhea.

If your cellmates choose to purchase toothpaste and brush their teeth, they will still be unable to clean their gums properly because dental floss is banned due to its potential use as a weapon. The lack of mirrors means they will be less conscious about decaying teeth which you will see in their mouths as each word is uttered. Foul tasting canteen food will decompose slowly between their teeth. Coupled with fungus formed from microbial deposits in the back of their tongues, these two men will have the worst breath imaginable. It is a breath from which there is no escape—the intimacy of the cell and the decibel level in the day room both require conversations that violate normal boundaries and that must be conducted from inches away. Each man will exhale the raunchy odor approximately sixteen times per minute, 960 times per hour, 23,040 times each day, and 8,409,600 times annually—that's just one of them, so double the number to include the other cellmate and triple it to include yourself. The aftertaste of your own breath will gag you.

Now, think about the inmate's breath as he tries to kiss you when the cell door slams shut each night. Just like Bonhoeffer, you discover that "freedom" can only "be opened *from the outside*."

But "institutional" misery is not the worst kind. Even without it, the misery that comes from within the heart and soul poses the greatest nightmare. Eli sometimes is irked by free-world volunteers saying they understand the pain suffered by LWOPP inmates. He responds politely, but thinks to himself: "how in the world are *you* suffering? Are you learning *anything* when you come out here?" Free-world volunteers just don't understand the reality of the intimate misery which each LWOPP inmate harbors. Eli: "The whole concept is being missed. You can give me a TV, but the bottom line is I still have no freedom."

The inner misery stems from self-imposed fantasies reinforcing the "what if" and the "what might have been" in life—things that Perkins thought about on death row and, to his horror, still thinks about each day with LWOPP. This kind of misery pops up at the drop of a thought and consumes every synapse of the brain. The pain is constant and felt with escalating intensity and magnitude as each year slowly passes.

Perkins wanted to be an accountant and earn an MBA degree. He still wants to earn that degree but knows that DOC would not pay the tuition for an LWOPP inmate, even if the courses were offered at Donaldson. Part of Perkins' private misery is knowing that he will never fulfill that dream in this lifetime. Marion misses the simple "smiles on children's faces when they discover something." He will never see that kind of smile again. Mark misses having a family of his own. "Every time a birthday comes, I realize that my life is passing and I still don't have a wife or child." He knows he never will. Each night Clyde thinks of the days when he once walked through his father's woods. He fantasizes: "I lie down on the leaves. I listen to the breeze going through the trees. I see up through the branches, a squirrel is looking at me." His misery stems from the fact that he will never walk on his father's land again. Eli wrestles with thoughts of petting dogs and simply touching the bark on trees. To me he says: "When you go home tonight, let your basset hound jump on you, and think of me. Go in your back yard and touch one tree, and think of me." Eli will never again do those things, and this comprises the greatest punishment bestowed on him. He compares his day to what he imagines mine to be:

> You get up and see your children off to school and kiss your wife goodbye. I get up and see the same faces everyday and see no one leave and kiss no one. You go to work and cultivate lives through teaching. I step outside my cell and see the same behaviors for the last twenty-three years with very little growth. You eat lunch with many choices. I get a meat patty with the same individuals day-in and day-out on a filthy table or a soaking wet table. You get back from lunch to your students. I get back from lunch and get counted to make sure I didn't miss lunch. You leave work and go home to see your children and wife and the investments you have been trusted with. I stay in my pod and see no investments and outcome.

Eli continues:

> You eat dinner with your family and discuss your day. I eat dinner and discuss nothing that has not been already discussed in the past twenty-three years. You watch a little TV or go to track practice to watch your son. I go back to my cell and wonder how my nieces' and nephews' track practices are going. You shower, kiss your kids and wife good night and reflect on your day. I shower and lay down to sleep but not to reflect on the day for it is redundant and I pray for a long sleep because come morning, it will be Tuesday, Wednesday, or is it Thursday? Maybe it is my mother's birthday or is it Christmas? It doesn't matter because every day is the same except for Sunday, where mercy is shown in here as they only serve *two* meals, not three.

Imagine living with this kind of misery for the rest of your life. The real is both the simplicity and complexity of hell. Its hopelessness and misery are shackled to the heart and soul of each inmate serving a sentence of life-without-the-possibility-of-parole.

* * *

We began this chapter with a very basic question: What do you do with a murderer? Given our exploration of Donaldson, coupled with the earlier review of scripture, that question can now be addressed.

Remember Nicole who had an abortion while in college? She tells of an African tribal "pro-choice" ritual (similar to that found in Islamic law) that determined punishment for murderers. Members of the tribe bound the murderer with rocks and tugged him into the middle of a lake. There he was left as they swam back to shore. As the rocks began to drag the murderer underwater, the victim's family had to choose either to grant mercy or practice retribution. Granting mercy forced the victim's family to take *deliberate action* because it was their obligation to swim out and rescue him. Practicing retribution also required *deliberate action* by the victim's family. If they chose to let him drown, they had to join the entire tribe in watching the execution from the water's edge.

In some ways punishment in the American political community is similar to this African fable. Members render sentencing recommendations and, when the collective wisdom points toward death, it is the jury which takes deliberate action by tugging the convicted man to the middle of the lake. It is not only the defendant's family who has the option to plea for mercy at sentencing, like Angela did for Wes. The victim's family also takes deliberate action by testifying for mercy and thereby swimming out into the lake, or pleading for the death penalty and remaining on the water's edge. They can even take further deliberate action by standing near the shore in what we call the victim's witness room next to the death chamber.

Sadly we also differ from that custom in that there is no obligation for every member of the political community to witness the intimate consequences of that public action after the guilty verdict is rendered. We make it difficult to find the lake, and nearly impossible to watch from its shore. Even the victim's family is not obligated to observe the execution. In a democratic political community that chooses to execute murderers while advocating an intimate social gospel as its center piece of morality, much more should be expected of the *citizen-nachahmer*. We all need to swim out or stand and watch attentively.

The word of God provides a choice between mercy (*rahmat*) and retribution (*lex talionis* or, in Islam, *Al-Qisaas*). God gives us permission to travel in either direction based on which scriptures we choose to follow. If we choose to grant mercy, it is out of *rachamin* (compassion) or *chesed* (acts of loves). We grant mercy because of the primacy of human life demanded by the Judaic-Christian concept of *Imago Dei* and the Islamic tradition of regarding human life as the most precious gift given by the God of Abraham. If we choose retribution, we do so because the murderer has violated the sanctity of life and that justifies his elimination for the sake of everyone else. Either way, we are called to take deliberate action in applying theocentric morality, especially the social gospel, and to do so intimately to all concerned.

As we have seen in the previous chapter, the damage that the murderer inflicts is both devastating and irreversible. It surpasses the victim's life and engulfs the lives of surviving friends and loved ones on both sides of the equation, victim and murderer. Because we don't know whose lives might have been touched one day by the victim, as well as how other lives will never be touched as a result of the pain relived daily by the survivors, the damage inflicted by the murderer is so ravaging that it must be felt by everyone. Hence, the believer in the God of Abraham can impose the death penalty in the American political community, and do so with all moral conviction. This conclusion is affirmed by scripture and was widely practiced in the time of the Founders as it has been throughout our history.

It is also a conclusion supported by Dietrich Bonhoeffer. He wrote about the "right to bodily life" (1995: 154-164) as an end in itself, and that "the first right of natural life consists in the safeguarding of the life of the body against arbitrary killing" (p. 158). He continues: "One must speak of arbitrary killing wherever innocent life is deliberately destroyed.... And, of course, there is nothing arbitrary about the killing of a criminal who has done injury to the life of another" (p. 158).

However, Bonhoeffer challenges us to go much further than simply accepting his view of the real. He encourages us to explore the intimacies of the real as we see it. He professes only that the words which we use to express that intimacy must be truthful words and, therefore, reflect the world God presents to us. When the intimacy found within the presented world is not consistent with the moral expectations of scripture, it is the real—and not the word—that must be reconciled or changed. This is how God expects us to return the real to him each day—reconciled with His morality.

We have explored the intimacy of the real for LWOPP inmates. The real of hopelessness and misery, consequences of public action pertaining to murder and life in prison, calls into question the moral relevance of the death penalty as a punishment tool. As discussed in Chapter 1, a political community with the social gospel at its moral core must have sound and extreme cause for deviation. After all, how we treat the least of His is how we treat Him. Yet while the real may seem in need of reconciliation with scriptures that speak to the social gospel, it is important to remember that the intimacy found calls not for an unharnessed license for mercy. Mercy from death, yes, but mercy from punishment, no.

For the *citizen-nachahmer* led singularly toward the God-granted moral path of *lex talionis* or *Al-Qisaas*, this exploration of the real of prison life begs that he answer some questions. Which punishment is more retributive? Should we remove an "eye for an eye" by having the murderer fall softly asleep on a gurney and thereby relieve him of the sight of what he's done and the thought of what he is missing? Or, should we force that eye to remain wide open for constant reflection throughout each of the remaining days in the murderer's life? Is it more satisfying to execute the murderer after a ten- to thirty-year stint in a single cell, or insist that he endure thirty to fifty years in conditions of constitutional misery with multiple cellmates?

The *citizen-nachahmer,* who is led solely toward the morality of *lex talionis* or *Al-Qisaas*, might think that the solution lies in quicker executions. In this way, the murderer cannot enjoy the luxury of the single room for a prolonged period of time. That response begs another question. Which has a greater retributive calculus: a year on death row or a lifetime in the Jungle or Whore Block? A quickened pace toward the gurney also questions our commitment to the sanctity of *innocent* life. What about Wes who was eventually vindicated of the capital crime?

It is understandable that the *citizen-nachahmer* seeking the morality of *lex talionis* or *Al-Qisaas* fears many slippery slopes when it comes to eliminating the death penalty. He might reply that the murderer's sentence can change from LWOPP to life-with-parole, then to parole, and then even to a pardon—as in the case of Bubba. He might ask, are there no guarantees for lasting imprisonment? The truthful answer is, sentences change primarily because of trial errors and district attorneys who are more concerned with the efficiency of plea bargains than the effectiveness of democratic deliberate action via retrial.

For every *citizen-nachahmer*, supportive of the morality of mercy or supportive of the morality of retribution, the problem (and therefore solution) lies in holding the justice system's feet to the fire. Defense lawyers and district attorneys alike must be armed adequately with resources and steeped equally with inclination. Families and schools must affirm the theocentric moral foundation so that children grow up free of bigotry and fully prepared to be responsible *citizens-nachahmer* and, hence, qualified jury members as well as citizens who do not murder. Just as members of the American political community embrace *costly grace*, its government must also pursue *outward justice*. Only through outward justice can we nurture a well-educated citizenry that will eliminate judicial error and consequently permit sentences of "life without parole" to actually translate into "absolutely no parole" for the few who choose to murder.

It is possible for the *citizen-nachahmer* yearning for *lex talionis* or *Al-Qisaas* to accept the alternative strategy of "life without parole" because he understands the fallacious dichotomy of execution versus forgiveness. Mercy does not mean freeing the murderer at the water's edge. Unlike the African tribe, modern prisons provide a third option—one that is underscored in the *Evangelium Vita* (Chapter III at 56) of the Roman Catholic Church. We can incarcerate the murderer indefinitely and thereby guard against the taking of further life in the political community. We can warehouse the murderer forever in Absolute Time Out, and we can do this as a God-granted moral punishment regardless of rehabilitation and remorse. If he chooses to murder while in prison, hence placing in jeopardy the "first right of natural life" of other murderers, he can be placed in a special segregation cell that has perhaps only forty square feet of space, such as death row cells at Holman Prison, to live in solitude for the remainder of his despicable life.

The *citizen-nachahmer* desiring the morality of *lex talionis* or *Al-Qisaas* might fear the argument that a theocentric political community, with its core values found in the social gospel, must never take away hope from anyone—including the LWOPP inmate. He may remind us of Bonhoeffer's concern that the absence of hope leads to wickedness. This is true.

We must distinguish between two kinds of hope: *this-world* hope—for what can be accomplished in this lifetime—and *next-world* hope—for forgiveness and redemption by God in order to enter into His Kingdom, whether that vision of heaven be a part of Jewish, Christian or Islamic traditions. Both kinds of hope are quintessential in avoiding Bonhoeffer's concern about wickedness. Most everyone grasps desperately for *next-world* hope, but it is *this-world* hope which must be reshaped for the LWOPP inmate. In his case, we need to distinguish between two subsets of *this-world* hope: (1) *free-world* hope—of someday being released from prison—and (2) *my-world* hope—of what might be accomplished in the remainder of this lifetime as lived entirely in the "here and now" of prison—just like the "here and now" offered to condemned men by the chaplain at Holman.

Violating the sanctity of life—the act of murder—demands the surrender of *free-world* hope, just as every kind of *this-world* hope was seized without pity from the victim and extracted ruthlessly from the victim's family. To encourage otherwise simply invites a cruel and unusual dimension to hope—a burden similar to that which was added to Orlando's last few hours on this earth by that "idiot" pastor who swore that he would never be executed. Hence, the same kind of mercy that emanates from the death chamber also mandates an exchange of *free-world* hope for *my-world* hope for each murderer spending the rest of his life in prison. What could have been accomplished in the outside is now moot. The real of hope must center on what the murderer might accomplish through the spreading of the social gospel in his cell and in his block.

Our efforts as *citizens-nachahmer* must quell the misguided legitimacy of *free-world* hope for murderers and, in doing so, convince others who seek the morality of *lex talionis* and *Al-Qisaas* of the virtue of eliminating capital punishment. Our focus should be on deliberate action to instill *next-world* hope so that the murderer receives eternal forgiveness and redemption. This will help instill *my-world* hope because true salvation will lead him to take deliberate action in spreading the social gospel and thereby touching intimately the hearts of other murderers. Even that kind of "this-worldliness" requires the intimacy about which Bonhoeffer wrote (Bethge, 1997: 370): "living unreservedly in [my-world's] duties, problems, successes and failures" and throwing oneself "completely into the arms of God, taking seriously, not [my] own suffering, but those of God in the world" of this prison. In this way, we eliminate Dante's draconian warning because we are no longer at the gates of hell. Perhaps we will even see the word "thought" revert back to "plan" in the *Yermiyah* (*Jeremiah*) 29:11 verse that graces that dingy poster in the Jungle.

The *citizen-nachahmer,* searching for assurances that *lex talionis* or *Al-Qisaas* will never be neglected, might wonder about the motives of others who, in the name of outward justice, demand reform in the Whore Blocks and Jungles of every prison system. Will there still be sufficient misery for retribution? Yes, but certainly a political community based on a firm foundation of social gospel, and a government which recognizes its primary task of outward justice, seeks to end the prison atrocities of rape, murder, and other acts of violence. Atrocities, after all, do not constitute the intended *lex talionis* or *Al-Qisaas* which comes strictly from legal time spent and constitutional misery felt.

For a political community seeking outward justice, *rahmat* and *lex talionis* become a two-edged sword. Mercy requires the *citizen-nachahmer* to make the prison safer by eliminating the causes of violence, fear, and debt. Bonhoeffer (2003:282) reminds us that:

> those who create their own god and their own world, those who allow their own desire to become their god, must inevitably hate other human beings who stand in their way and impede their designs. Strife, hatred, envy, and murder all have the same source: they spring from our own selfish desire.

As part of reform, therefore, the block economy must be detached from the murderer because it contributes to the most evil consequences of selfish desire. Murderers should survive mercifully, but only at the level and condition of the poorest *free* member of the political community. They should receive nothing more than what the state provides: generic shoes and clothing, standard toiletries, and three meals a day from the canteen. Murderers should be segregated into their own block, and they should have no jobs. Prison stores should be off limits to them, and no money or goods should be brought in from the outside. Money from external sources, like Clyde's family inheritance, should be directed to the victim's family or to the state's effort to provide outward justice for the *citizen-nachahmer* who lives in poverty or without education.

Ultimately the mercy of eliminating the causes of debt, and thereby reducing much of the concomitant violence and fear, underscores the other side of the sword—the God-based path of punishment toward those who have murdered. Life without parole should never be "cruel and unusual," but reform should never ease constitutional misery. Public masturbation and "ice cream socials" must be eliminated for civility's sake, but air-conditioning should never replace the need for fans and ice buckets—unless the poorest of the poor in the free-world community enjoys that amenity. Even if reform brings an end to three-inmate cells, that sixty-square-foot space remains smaller than your bathroom. Even if the quality of food improves, it will be the same menu until death—eaten in the same place and with the same men every day. Hips, knees, and feet will continue to feel the same cold concrete floor—inside the cell and everywhere in the block—from the early morning breakfast call to the final evening lockdown. Prison routine can never be reformed. That is the basis of constitutional misery.

Reform will never remove the harshest kind of constitutional misery: the self-imposed misery of "what might have been." After all, it is the intimacy of that misery that makes murderers like John Henry and Tag want out so very badly. It should give grieving parents, like Leigh and Carolyn, great comfort knowing that the likes of those men will remain steadfastly bound to this lifetime. The potential of a prolonged life with absolutely no chance of parole is what Lawton fears more than those fifteen quick steps to the gurney. His ultimate nightmare is not public action which takes life-for-life, but rather public action which imposes misery-for-misery. He does not want his misery to match in duration the life-long misery felt by the daughter whose father he murdered. Hence, the challenge for the *citizen-nachahmer* is to get Lawton off death row but never out of prison.

Truth is, the real of LWOPP approaches moral unity with scriptures advocating mercy because it recognizes the sanctity of life. Truth is, it also approaches moral unity with scriptures calling for retribution for those who destroy *Imago Dei* because it is a reality of absolute time and unrelenting constitutional misery—an existence that will certainly drag on "regardless of self." The real of LWOPP reflects mercy and retribution not as dichotomous concepts but rather as the "X" and "Y" axes of a moral-algebraic continuum. How much *lex talionis* and *rahmat* are needed for the crime of murder? The data points, representing each murderer, must lay toward the top of the retribution axis while not falling too close to the bottom of the mercy axis.

The task of *citizens-nachahmer* becomes one of translating the moral-algebraic notation into public action. It will take proponents of the morality of *lex talionis* and *Al-Qisaas* to accept the elimination of capital punishment in exchange for the commitment of retribution through unending time and non-ending constitutional misery. It will take proponents of mercy to accept the covenant of "no parole," regardless of rehabilitation and remorse, in exchange for the preservation of human life. This challenge, well grounded in Bonhoeffer's two sources of truth, confronts each member of the American political community who adheres to its theocentric moral foundation and is thereby committed to the sanctity of human life. The *Imago Dei* we see in the murdered is no different than the *Imago Dei* we must see in the murderer. Its preservation, through mercy and misery, reshapes a public reality worthy of presenting back to God.

Note

1. Since his arrival in 2008, Warden Gary Hetzel has tried to improve Donaldson's environment. Hallway lights are now turned on, and many walls have been repainted. He is attempting to enforce the no-smoking policy in Whore Block and the Jungle, and he is trying to use technology to combat violence. Improvements in the kitchen facility are to the point where the stench has been reduced. Certainly some headway has been made, at least in the short-term. As with any prison, however, a warden's tenure is always uncertain and budgets are even less certain. Policies and priorities change with each warden and with each new budget cycle. Given the current economic recession, the odds of Donaldson resuming fully its customary climate cannot be overlooked. In 2009, Donaldson inmates sued in federal court Governor Bob Riley, Corrections Commissioner Richard Allen, and Warden Hetzel for prison conditions—specifically overcrowding, understaffing, violence (more than fifty *reported* incidents in 2008, the majority of which were stabbings), and the lack of work opportunities.

6

Outward Justice and *Imago Dei*

We began this journey of seeking truth about the intimate consequences of taking life by noting two contemporary caricatures of the American political community. One is a neo-theocratic community where interpretation of disparate scripture dominates government decision making and public action. The other is a postmodern secular community where religious thought represents an illegitimate moral compass unworthy of shining light on neither government nor individual. Either caricature thrives in the hearts of too many Americans. Advocates of the former tend to oppose abortion yet support capital punishment. They defend the life of an unborn baby, but pray for a death of crucifixional savagery for men who commit the act of murder. Advocates of the latter tend to support abortion yet oppose capital punishment. They believe in a world of "minimally decent" Samaritans (Thomson, 1971) who opt for sucking and scraping the life of the unborn burden into sterile-room jars and rejoice in the gospel of "saint" de Sade (1795: 139) which proclaims "it is an equally major or minor evil to kill an animal or a human being."

Either caricature envisions a community that is anchored by peculiar *license*—theocratic or secular—costuming as promised *liberty*—scriptural or constitutional. Advocates of both perspectives walk away from the God of Abraham because they turn their backs on the *Imago Dei* presented by Him in this lifetime. The Founding words of John Adams (1793: 13), used to rebuff Thomas Paine's desire to separate God from community, also apply to the advocates of these caricatures: they have "departed altogether from the principles of the Revolution." Neither caricature reflects adequately the kind of theocentric moral foundation envisioned by the Founders: one that shuns equally the urge toward theocratic tendencies and the presumed sovereignty of secularism.

In addition, advocates of either caricature do not use the two sources of truth proffered by Dietrich Bonhoeffer: the word of God and the *real* which God presents to us each day. Therefore, neither represents a comprehensive exploration of scriptural morality, nor affords an intimate exploration of reality, because no one is looking through the eyes of a *nachahmer des Gottes*—no one is making the effort to imitate God in terms of what He would do in this lifetime. All this makes it impossible to reconcile the real with the moral word of God.

Taking Life

Truth discovered in this journey leads us to conclude that abortion is morally wrong. It is murder, and the real of that murder destroys the lives of many who survive. Pro-abortion supporters tend to neglect the real by framing the embittered fruits of public action as nothing more than libertine choice and, in order to make that argument stick, hide the intimate consequences of abortion under a bushel of ideology. The American Psychological Association (APA) denies the existence of abortion-derived consequences. In order to sustain this great myth, the National Organization of Women (NOW) fails to lobby for federal funding to research the null hypothesis. NOW's website demonstrates a concern for economic and political issues, but is silent about abortion alternatives like abstinence, parenthood, or adoption rights. Many course syllabi found in Women's Studies programs across American college campuses validate the ideology of abortion: it is portrayed as a political right and the only "true" consequence seems to stem from the fear of losing that right if it is not exercised absolutely and abundantly. The arrogance of Zoloth's (2003) call for creative scriptural interpretation, for the sake of finding abortion's theocentric moral justification, is surpassed only by the selective pedagogical and scholarly inventiveness offered in some circles of academia. The phenomenological essence of truth is often cluttered by ideological pretentiousness found under the auspices of terms like "scientific method" and "hypothesis testing" This seems especially the case in the social sciences where myopic, neo-alchemic findings filter to the level of the abortion counselor and gravitate as "fact" to the girl or woman contemplating ending the life of her child.

Another part of the real of abortion deals with its alternative: giving life to the unborn. Far too many pro-life supporters neglect this aspect of the real by choosing not to take deliberate action in spreading the social gospel. Rather, they acquiesce to the pressures of political correctness, or perhaps to the routine of contemporary church life, and thereby choose not to stand with a moral eye toward the raging storm. As a result, many do not seek the battle lines drawn on street pavement in their own towns. They forget their obligation to sustain the theocentric moral foundation of the political community.

The truth discovered in this journey also leads us to profess that the murder of a fully developed human being remains an immoral act, just as it was when Cain killed Abel. We also must confess that capital punishment for the murderer, while not morally wrong, becomes morally unnecessary because of the institutional security and constitutional misery afforded by contemporary prisons. The real of murder and execution is that both inflict life-long and unimaginable suffering on the survivors. This is certainly true for the loved ones of the murdered and the murderer, but both acts also leave their marks on others: residents in the neighborhood where the murder occurred, prison officials who must terminate life, and all members of the political community who profess a theocentric moral conscience. The only person who finds relief through capital punishment is the murderer because execution becomes a welcome escape from the long-term constitutional misery found in prison. The alternative of life-without-the-possibility-of-parole (LWOPP) removes the need for executions and thereby brings an adjusted reality closer to unity with the scriptural morality of both compassion and retribution. Suffering continues within the hearts and minds of all surviving loved ones, as it will throughout their lives, but now the murderer joins them in rank with his own sense of misery and with unlimited time to think and to regret. It is this *justice of misery-shared* that will accompany the murderer to the grave.

As with abortion, significant aspects of the real of murder and capital punishment are neglected by members of the American political community. People tend to seek a clean solution to the consequences of a singularly vicious act, and this kind of hygiene simply does not exist. Many who favor capital punishment ignore the possibility of change in the condemned man—that he might turn towards God as so many have done before him and, coupled with the salvation gospel, seek to spread the social gospel in the real of prison life. Hence, he can still be an instrument of God for the remainder of this life and in this unique part of God's world.

On the other hand, far too many opponents of the death penalty tend to discount the murder itself as if its intimacy is unworthy of acknowledgment and, much less, repeated memorialization. They forget what was experienced by the human being extracted from this world through the act of murder, as well as the unimaginable and unending pain incurred by the victim's family and loved ones. They downplay the human potential—regardless of its state and quality at the time of unexpected death—that the act of murder robs God of someday using in the real of this world.

Both sides tend to miss the moral mark because of an unwillingness to explore the intimate consequences and potentials of the real and, in doing so, choose to look elsewhere rather than at the full frontal view of *Imago Dei*. Truth is, the murdered looks no less like God—is no less a special gift from God—than is the murderer. The same applies to the murderer whose image of God is equal to that of everyone else. Those who fail to recognize this truth also walk away from God.

The *Citizen-Nachahmer* and Outward Justice

We tend to ignore those aspects of the real which conspire to permit the act of murder, whether it be the taking of life from the unborn or born. This is not to say that social forces cause anyone to violate *Imago Dei.* Jessica was never conscripted to murder her unborn baby at Omega Breeze, despite her rationalization of being a first-generation college student with an end-game of earning a Ph.D. As Nancy Reagan might have urged, she could have just said "no." In similar vein, nothing forced impoverished Jimmey D—not his lack of education nor his state of drunkenness—to take the life of the lady who helped him in so many ways. He, too, could have simply said "no." Even in the poorest environs and the most dreadful circumstances, the morality of the God of Abraham—specifically, "thou shall not murder"—is known by all in the American political community.

So concern about background circumstances does not stem from an assumption of cause-and-effect. Rather, it is an admission that, within the context of free will, conditions help create situations which may contribute to poor judgment in our search for desirable outcomes. Too many times, those situations speak so loudly that we fail to hear the simple whisper of morality. Perhaps it is from this realization that Bonhoeffer encourages us to reconcile the volume of reality with the serenity of scripture.

Stephen L. Carter (1997; 1998), an admirer of Bonhoeffer, reminds us about society's proverbial "three-legged stool"—family, church,

Figure 1
Bonhoeffer's Elaboration of the Envisioned Political Community

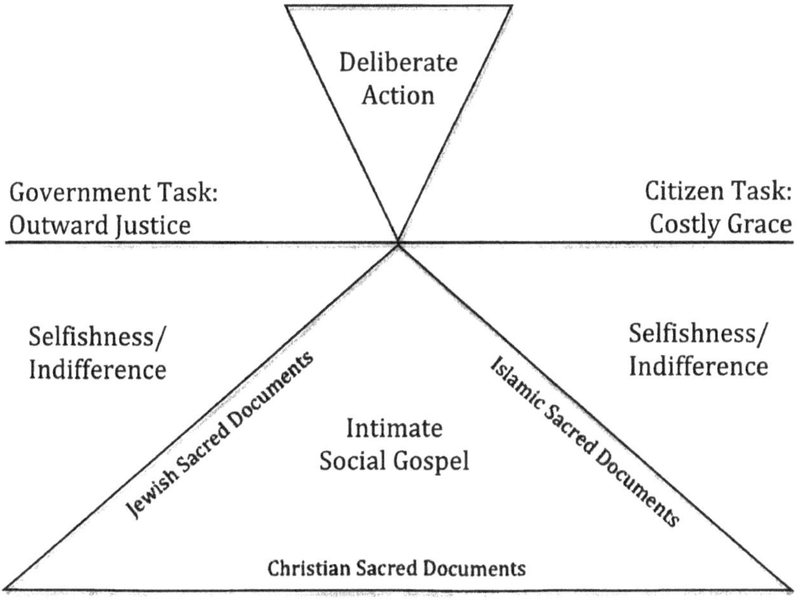

school—and notes that each is equally important in maintaining a moral foundation. Too often we focus myopically on the church leg of that stool and perhaps only on our *immediate* family and our *own* local school system. We tend to place insufficient focus on the intimate realities of families and schools in other parts of the political community. Certainly we help individuals through a variety of distant missions which spread the social gospel, but we are less attentive to resolving in a more systemic fashion the challenges which confront *all* families and *all* schools.

We tend to forget about the role of *outward justice.* Its purpose is not to acquire some sort of absolute socialistic leveling. In the American adaption, outward justice has a Lockean theme of ensuring a reasonable (not necessarily equal) balance of strength, or a reasonable balance of vulnerability, among all members of the political community. A dearth in outward justice was, after all, the root of the American Revolution, as underscored by the Declaration of Independence: "our repeated petitions [*about what?—imbalances of strength and vulnerability*] have been answered only by repeated injury." The promise of reasonable balance assures each individual a fair share of *this-world* hope for a future of security and prosperity. It frees each member to serve God in this lifetime and, subsequently, to assist in maintaining the theocentric moral foundation of the political community. But because some reject the notion of the social gospel on the basis of secular selfishness, while others focus strictly on deliberate action by the individual, we often renege on our daily obligation to guarantee outward justice—a guarantee that is suppose to benefit all families, all schools, and each individual.

Remember that the citizen's task of *civic costly grace* and the government's task of *outward justice* rest tenuously at the apex of the social gospel—the core of our moral foundation (see Figure 1). A balance between the two is required or else government will either dominate or be ineffectual and, conversely, individuals will either be impotent or carry unyielding license. Individual effort is quintessential to the spread of the social gospel, but it cannot be successful in a *democratic* political community without an equal effort on the part of government to guarantee outward justice. Hence, *citizens-nachahmer* must insist that government not remain aloof on issues pertaining to outward justice because such distance by government ultimately places in jeopardy *Imago Dei*. Part of civic costly grace, therefore, requires the *citizen-nachahmer* to support government in its mandate to provide *this-world* hope through ensuring outward justice which, by the way, can be rendered either through Democratic or Republican means and through conservative or liberal visions.

From the perspective of outward justice, therefore, the pro-choice movement poses a valid question. If we cannot afford to nurture the children currently born, how could we have nurtured the fifty million babies aborted? My question is about the future. How can we change the scope of *this-world* hope so that the next fifty million girls and women, thinking about taking life, might have hearts and minds calmed by a new kind of real that permits the quiet pleas of morality to be heard loud and clear?

Here the problem lies on the pro-life side of the equation. Far too many pro-life supporters ignore the real of young girls and women who, temporarily lacking moral courage, make choices about death based solely on narrowing parameters of *this-world* hope. According to Christopher, Wendy "didn't *want* to bring a baby to term because she was trying to get her career on track." Jessica: "I did drugs (cocaine) when the child was conceived so there was a possibility that the child might have been born with nerve or brain damage. I knew I couldn't deal with *that*."

Both Wendy and Jessica lacked moral courage which might have been reinforced if only the pro-life side recognized their intimate reality.

An exchange between the trenches on Court Street underscores this point. Shouter: "What are *you* doing to help these women? You don't care *anything* about them as long as they get an abortion! If they change their minds, what are you gonna do for them?" Cheerleader: "What are *you* gonna do for them?" Shouter: "We do a lot for them: pre-natal, hospital, adoptions, counseling…." The cheerleader interrupts: "*Pre-natal*! I wanna know what you're gonna do for them when they're fifteen? You gonna put underwear on their ass? What about when they're in high school and they don't have the shit they need?" Another shouter: "Man, that argument does not fly. You're in America…. There is more food here, there is more clothes here...." Cheerleader: "You have no idea about poverty in America, do you?" Shouter: "There's *no* poverty in America!" Cheerleader "What about the homeless people in [South Amherst]? Are they not *poor*? Someone who has no food on their table and can't afford anything, *that's* not poverty?" Shouter: "They are homeless because they *want to be* homeless. There's *no* poverty in America." Another cheerleader jumps in:

> That's not very *Christian*! You complain about women who choose not to bring children into the world because they can't support them, and you have no feelings about the reasons they do that! You're not being ethical at all.

The cheerleaders are right. Even though abortion is a middle-class phenomenon, too many pro-life advocates ignore the real which is experienced each day by pregnant girls and young women who feel alone and without hope. Who *will* put underwear on their children and prepare them for high school? Too many pro-life advocates are concerned about the *birthing* of life but not necessarily with the *raising* of life. Too few are prepared to spread the social gospel through civic costly grace and, as a result, many choose to be minimally decent Samaritans once *Imago Dei* is expelled from the cervix.

Recall Bonhoeffer (2003: 44-45): "costly grace is the hidden treasure in the field, for the sake of which people go and sell with joy everything they have." Spiritually he is referring to the kind of sacrifice necessary in order to be a disciple of God. In the secular realm—in the realm of the *citizen-nachahmer* and government pursuing a civic social gospel—costly grace represents the kind of deliberate action needed to protect and enhance the sanctity of life. It is for *Imago Dei*, unborn or born, that we are expected to willingly and gladly "go and sell with joy" everything we have. This is why babies are supposed to live. Yet there are 850,000 abortions each year and only 125,000 adoptions.

The Unborn and the Need for Outward Justice

Faced with the silence of government, those who choose not to abort tend to be blessed only with the costly grace expended by loved ones. They tend not to feel the comfort and security of outward justice. Three examples underscore this point.

Donna

"Donna," a single twenty-four-year-old with a master's degree, grew up in a small town north of Montgomery, Alabama, and lived with her father after her parents' divorce. She got pregnant at the age of fifteen and wanted an abortion because she feared she "would never get to do anything again, ever." She didn't have to tell her dad about the pregnancy because "I had this look on my face and I think he just knew." Unlike the fear that causes many girls to abort, she did not suffer from the tempestuous wrath of her father. "He *did* drive around the block for a couple of hours. Around and around, I sat at the window watching him." Finally he came back in the house and confessed that his second wife (who had since passed away) wanted an abortion when pregnant with Donna's younger sister. He resisted, and eventually she agreed to give birth if he would raise the baby so she could concentrate on her career. A firefighter by profession, he took that baby with him each day to the station and everywhere else he went. His love of human life is why he would not permit Donna to abort.

Keeping her baby was a struggle for Donna. She resented being pregnant and had trouble initially bonding with "Ellen." "I didn't pick a name for like three days after [the birth]." Donna's fears of missing out on many high school activities were also realized. She no longer had time to participate in sports, and she had to take care of Ellen on the weekends which preempted socializing with friends. School officials were not empathic with her situation; clerks never approved Donna's sick-day absences when she had to stay home to nurse Ellen through infant illnesses. Teachers treated her differently. Although she qualified for the National Honor Society, the principle tried to keep her from participating in the induction ceremony.

Nevertheless Donna made excellent grades and, with the help of her parents, raised Ellen. They continued to live with her father, even during college, and did not worry about food or clothing. Her mother baby-sat so that Donna could study and earn spending money with a part-time job. Most importantly, her parents made sure Donna did not forfeit *this-world* hope. "There was never a question of whether I could still go to college." She didn't have to worry about getting help from the government for either sustaining Ellen's life or giving both of them opportunities to pursue *this-world* hope.

Paige

Giving away a child through adoption in America also relies more on family than outward justice offered by government. Living near Charleston, South Carolina, "Paige" became pregnant at the age of fourteen from a date rape. Unlike Jessica and so many others, Paige did not have to hide the incident from her mother. "I took off a few days of school and mother took off work. We went to a few pregnancy crisis groups [to find out about options]." Abortion, however, was never an option.

> We don't believe in it due to our religion. But personally, I don't see how you can kill a baby. I mean even if its not your fault—even in the case of rape—I still knew in my mind that having an abortion wouldn't be right because it wasn't [the baby's] fault for my being raped.

In addition, Paige's aunt had several abortions as a teenager, and it was Paige's mother who was the escort to the abortion clinic. "Both suffered. They both told me [abortion] brings closure for a short period of time, but in the end you start to think about what that baby might have been." Her aunt and mother reinforced in her that abortion was not the answer.

Paige also knew she could not keep the baby. Divorced, her mother would have to quit her job to take care of the baby or Paige would have to drop out of school. With her mother's help, they chose a California adoption agency and, after selecting the adoptive parents, Paige moved in with them for the last four months of pregnancy. "I *know* [my baby] has a good life. I know that they're financially able to give him a better life; that their family is a good family." She also realizes that she "gave [that family] a gift that not many people can give—the gift of being parents." She is now a college student and plans to someday open a business in Charleston. Through family, not government, Paige was able to do what was morally right and maintain *this-world* hope—for her baby and herself.

Elizabeth and Richard

Unfortunately becoming adoptive parents relies more on the costly grace of family than the outward justice of government. "Elizabeth" and "Richard" live in Birmingham, Alabama and have been married for twenty years. They always assumed they would eventually adopt. Elizabeth: "There are enough children in the world that need to be adopted." Both are white and decided to adopt part African-American children, first "Courtney" and, three years later, "Kirby." Courtney's birth mother was fourteen years old, and Kirby's was seventeen years old. The white fathers of both pregnant girls refused to have a black child living in their respective homes and forced the abortion option. Each birth mother resisted, however, and Kirby's actually walked out of the examination room just prior to the start of the abortion.

As all parents know, raising kids is a challenge. As Elizabeth and Richard know, this is true regardless of skin pigmentation. They raise Courtney and Kirby, not as black kids or white kids, but rather as Christian kids. Their children are embraced by their extended families as well as their predominantly white church. While they are financially secure, government did nothing to assist them in the adoption process, the cost of which totaled $32,000 out of their own pockets.

These three examples—a girl who kept the baby, another who chose to give away her baby through adoption, and a couple choosing to adopt babies—underscore the need for costly grace on the part of family members. But what about people who do not have a family support system like Donna or Paige, or the personal financial capabilities of Elizabeth and Richard? What if Caoimhe could have received help and thereby was able to give birth and become that great violinist? What if help was available so that Hannah did not think she had to abort her son, or KC did not think she had to abort her twins? What if Cynthia's aborted babies might have lived and one of them discovered a cure for breast cancer? Christopher is right in that some of the aborted children might have found a home on the death rows of Donaldson or Holman, but what value has been lost because we acted as a "minimally decent" political community?

Hillary Rodham Clinton (1996) has a point: sacrificial deliberate action must come from the *entire* concept of "village." It is not enough just for citizens to rise above being minimally decent Samaritans. Each day government also awakes in that same metaphoric bed and finds *Imago Dei* attached to its organs of outward justice. Because we benefit so much from the potential of *future* life—whether that potential is the unborn, new-born, teenager, or adult—we cannot tolerate a "minimally decent" government when it comes to the issues of sustaining life and instilling *this-world* hope. The core moral value of the intimate social gospel in the American political community requires individuals *and* government to be *Great* (not just "good") Samaritans.

We forget that civic costly grace requires a *regulatory* dimension so that government can maintain outward justice. We also forget that civic costly grace entails a *financial* dimension and some of that must come from government sources, through taxation, as well as from the charitable and tithing pockets of *citizens-nachahmer*. If the *raison d'être* of democratic government is to guarantee outward justice for everyone so that individuals can be liberated to serve God in this lifetime as each is called, then *citizens-nachahmer* must support government through regulation and taxation so that it can accomplish this task.

Wanted: Government assistance in providing affordable and safe child-care facilities in sufficient number to allow access for each working mother, as well as the teenage mother trying to stay in school. *Desperately needed*: Government subsidized night-care facilities because *this-world* hope of single moms sometimes hinges on evening study sessions and night courses leading to diplomas, as well as swing shift assignments in factories that offer better paying jobs. *Wanted*: Federal and state laws that nurture and facilitate adoption for all mothers who wish to give up their children and for all individuals desiring to become adoptive parents. *Desperately needed*: Government regulations requiring insurance companies to cover expenses associated with adoptions at the same level they cover the cost of pregnancy for birth families.

Outward justice should be financed in part through a combination of volunteerism, faith-based and non-profit initiatives, and corporate incentives. When it comes to government's obligation to protect *Imago Dei*, however, the issue of adequate regulation and taxation cannot be overlooked. Ah, but here lies the rub, doesn't it? What is an adequate level of government involvement in a democratic political community that ascribes to the social gospel as the center piece of its theocentric moral foundation? What price should we place on *Imago Dei*? Like the shouters on Court Street whose eyes fail to see the bankrupt reality of *this-world* hope, too many pro-life advocates reject any role of government when it comes to preserving *Imago Dei* beyond the womb.

In part this is due to a disconnect between scriptural morality and the socio-economic reality of this world. Many pro-life women and men believe that the remedy to abortion is found solely in one's Bible and never in one's checkbook. Others simply have a distrust of those whom they elect and re-elect into government office. Few concur with Michelle's pro-life friend, Marge:

> If you could guarantee that there would be no more abortions if my taxes were tripled, then I'd say "yes"! It's worth saving those children ... some of the money needs to go toward education and programs to help with their self-esteem ... [without such programs] the increase of taxes could be a band-aid. You gotta put money *deeper* before the women get to that clinic in the *first* place.

The Born and the Need for Outward Justice

If Marge is right about the need to "put money deeper" before the girl or woman enters the abortion chamber, there is also a need to "put money deeper" prior to when a boy or man commits the act of murder and has to spend either the rest of his life in prison or walks fifteen steps into the execution chamber. Advocates and opponents of capital punishment argue over what to do with a murderer, but too few want to bridge the gap between outward justice and the prevention of murder.

The real at Donaldson is similar to the real of prisons in every part of the American political community. There is relatively little which government does to ensure the kind of outward justice needed to sustain the sanctity of life. Before a *non*-LWOPP inmate is released, either on parole or at end-of-sentence (EOS), the Alabama Department of Corrections (DOC) provides pre-release training on how to cope in the free-world. This includes how to complete a job application, obtain a driver's license, and establish a checking account. If the inmate is released as part of parole, he is transported to a halfway house and stays there six months for further training or to a minimum custodial work center where he earns $2 each day. Whether through parole or EOS, the inmate receives only the clothes he is wearing: one pair of pants, one polo shirt, underwear, socks, and shoes.

If the inmate is EOS and has no one to drive him home—and remember, most do not hear from loved ones after the first eighteen months of incarceration—DOC transports him to a bus station with a one-way ticket to the county where the crime was committed. In addition to funds that may exist in his prison account, which typically is at best minimal due to having limited or no contact with loved ones, he (like the paroled inmate) is given a cash sum of $10. For the EOS ex-con, this ends government involvement in pursuing outward justice.

What happens to an EOS ex-con who, say, has spent a decade in prison for a crime which did not involve the taking of life? With $10 in his pocket, wearing all the clothes he owns and holding a one-way ticket, DOC escorts him to the bus station. There he may walk across the street to a convenience store and perhaps purchase a pack of Marlboro cigarettes. This costs him $4.53 with tax, and he now has $5.47 left. Because he ate breakfast in the prison canteen, he is not hungry and either boards a bus or attempts to sell the ticket and remain in the neighborhood surrounding the station. Assuming he takes the bus trip, he arrives at his destination and is now hungry. He goes to a McDonald's restaurant and orders the "Big Mac Meal"—a Big Mac hamburger, french fries and a soft drink. If he is watching the cash register, or if he remembers his pre-release seminar, he understands that the state of Alabama has a nine percent sales tax. Altogether his lunch costs $5.09. It is now mid-afternoon on his first day in the free-world, and he has just 38 cents in his pocket. What to do about dinner? Lodging? Tomorrow? What to do about *this-world* hope?

An ex-con with less than two quarters in his pocket may not hear the whisper of morality over the growl of his own stomach. He may not listen to its plea when his prospects for *this-world* hope appear so drastically pale in comparison to that of others who now surround him in the free-world. Certainly old habits may quickly re-surface which can lead to a reinvestment in criminal activity. Such activity turns into "special circumstances" if committed in association with an unanticipated act of murder, like in the case of Bubba or Perkins. Unanticipated or not, *Imago Dei* is taken and the debate over capital punishment is refreshed.

Wanted: Better preparation for inmates who reenter the political community. *Desperately needed*: More public funding for training, prison jobs that instill a work ethic, more assistance in job placement, and adequate release-funding so that even EOS ex-cons can acquire driver licenses, clothing and lodging during the first week of freedom.

This is also part of the real: too many inner-city public schools cannot offer *this-world* hope. "Olivia" is a fifth grade teacher at an excellent elementary school in a Birmingham, Alabama suburb. Recently named one of the top history teachers in the nation, she started her career at an inner-city elementary school. "Fighting was nothing uncommon in the school. I could get out of my car and pass by a couple of fights on the way inside each morning." This is not surprising because violence was a part of her students' lives. One came in crying because, on the way to school, "she had seen a dead lady in the gutter with no arms or legs." Another watched a man murder her own mother and sister. Violence was common in her classroom but, even in its absence, the threat of violence was omnipresent. Olivia:

> One [fifth grade] boy who was in a gang, and hardly ever made an attempt to do any work, was actually sitting at his desk with paper out. We were doing long division. I stopped by his desk and asked if I could show him how to get started with the first problem. He said, "If you come near me, I'll knock you through that wall."

Even as a talented professional on her way to national acclamation, she could not do anything to change the learning climate and its consequences. As an individual teacher, there was little she could do to instill *this-world* hope in her students. When Olivia and her husband became pregnant, they agreed she should resign her position in that school for the safety of their unborn child. The loss to one inner-city school was another victory for a suburban school.

"Leonard" is the only music teacher (a percussionist) at one inner-city kindergarten through eight grade school in the Birmingham area. The budget has not allowed the purchase of musical instruments in thirty-five years and, therefore, Leonard quietly spends about $3,000 annually out of his own salary to repair existing instruments and to purchase used ones for the benefit of his students. Last year he was instructed to teach seventh-grade math, in addition to music for all grades, because no public funding was available to replace the math teacher who had resigned. Leonard: "I scored a composite nine on my ACT test, and it was because my math score was so low." Despite this frailty, the principal was more interested in Leonard's reputation for controlling the kids. He tries to stay a week ahead (in preparation) of the math students but, despite his sincere efforts, there is very little *this-world* hope for children who might have developed dreams of someday becoming engineers or professors of mathematics.

Similar to Olivia's experience in the inner-city schools, the threat of violence is always present in Leonard's world. Seventh graders will "walk up in your face and bump you with their bodies and they have their chests sticking out and they stand there looking at you. What they're doing is threatening you, wanting you to take the first strike." Actual violence happens daily and, when extreme, classroom lockdowns occur which sometimes last for weeks—perhaps as a precursor of prison lockdowns to come. Leonard's seventh grade math students do not fear the possibility of prison and, as Donaldson's Grand Daddy suggests, many look forward to it because of friends and family members already incarcerated. Leonard: "I have taught thirty to forty students in the last ten years whose fathers or brothers or uncles are in prison for *murder*. For *murder*!"

Now let's revisit Court Street. There is no poverty in America? What planet do the shouters live on? Bob Dylan once sang, "you don't need to be a weather man to know which way the wind blows." We do not need standardized regression coefficients to understand the real of poverty. It is presented intimately each day either in our own backyard or in close-by neighborhoods which desperately seek from the rest of us something more than a "minimally decent" relationship. To see how much outward justice is lacking, we need only to look around.

About forty percent of the residents, adjacent to the middle class neighborhood that is home to Omega Breeze, live below the poverty line. Not surprisingly nearly forty percent of the young adults, between the ages of eighteen and twenty-four who attended Olivia's inner-city school, do not possess high school diplomas. If lucky, they will work the rest of their lives for minimum wage at fast-food restaurants. If unlucky, they will work in fast-food places where ex-cons eat and perhaps become enticed with plans of crime. Nearly 60 percent of the neighbors next to Leonard's inner-city school live under the poverty line. About 24 percent of Alabama ex-cons live near Leonard's school, and on a fast late-night drive in a stolen car with perhaps only thirty-eight cents in pocket, anyone of them can be within a matter of minutes deep into the affluent and unprotected neighborhoods which surround Olivia's current elementary school. The cycle of crime, and the chance for murder, is reborn.

This is the real of *hope eliminated*, and it is due in part to the lack of outward justice. It is difficult to keep *this-world* hope alive when the whisper of morality is drowned by the constant roar of need, comparison, and greed. *Wanted*: Better schools for all students. *Desperately needed*: Great schools in the inner-cities of the American political community, and this will require a magnified level of public funding. If the social gospel is important to the *citizen-nachahmer*, then it is her duty to equip government with requisite tools and resources to ensure outward justice for everyone.

Sanctity of Human Life

A pro-life advocate and Kairos Prison Ministry volunteer, Anthony claims that: "you will never convince this society that killing the guilty is wrong until you convince them that killing the innocent is wrong." Perhaps, but the relationship between the intimate consequences of abortion (killing the innocent) and the intimate consequences of execution (killing the guilty) is more reciprocal than it is sequential when framed against the backdrop of the sanctity of human life. If the political community finds utility in destroying *Imago Dei (*or in Muslim verse, the greatest gift from God) through the taking of life by execution, then it must accept utility in destroying *Imago Dei* through the taking of life by abortion. If, on the other hand, it refutes the utility of destroying God's image through execution, then the political community must also reject the utility of destroying God's image through abortion. Hence, if the sanctity of human life is valued in one situation, it must be treasured simultaneously in all situations. This *quid pro quo* reflects the essence of the three religions that claim to worship the God of Abraham

While each sacred document permits the taking of life in the case of fully developed human beings who murder other fully developed human beings, the real which God presents to us makes doing so an unnecessary act against *Imago Dei*. These same sacred documents prohibit the hurting of innocent children—born and unborn—and the real, which God presents, offers the potential of so many alternative paths that one's selfishness should never reign supreme over one's duty toward *Imago Dei*. Flaws presented in the real—especially those involving the loss of *this-world* hope—must be addressed through deliberate action of *citizens-nachahmer* (civic costly grace) and government (outward justice) in spreading the social gospel and thereby protecting and nurturing the human condition within which God dwells. It is only then that the real is worthy of being presented back to God.

Given the Founders' envisioned theocentric moral foundation, members of the American political community really have only two choices. We can continue to endorse a policy of taking life—a *policy of death*—when it comes to capital punishment and abortion, or we can profess a new policy—a *policy of life*—reflecting the sanctity of the human being through mandatory LWOPP sentences and abortion-alternatives. If we choose death policy, we are forced to be hypocritical in regards to our relationship with the social gospel that lies at the core of the community's morality. The *citizen-nachahmer* may offer a certain amount of civic grace, and government may offer some justice, but this is done superficially and strictly for our selfish benefit—perhaps as a way of easing our conscience as to what we are actually doing to *Imago Dei*. The civic grace we boast as being so "costly" turns out to be just cheap grace, the same kind that plagued Bonhoeffer's world of Nazi Germany. The same is true with the facade of outward justice. After all, Machiavelli (Donno, [1515] 1984) advises us to fit morality into the specific needs of each situation. The resultant illusion of doing what we claim as morally "right" can allow everyone to sleep a little better at night—whether that bed be in 1940 Berlin or 2020 Boston. Debate will continue to center only on questions of *process*: At what week does the unborn female begin to look too much like Michelle to be destroyed? Can we make sure Lawton does not feel any pain during his execution? Bonhoeffer's 1943 theological critique finds a home in the secular world of the twenty-first century: "We're paying more attention to dying than to death" (Bethge, 1997: 240).

A policy of death means that our public actions will continue to be built merely upon a pallet of post-modern situational ethics and not upon a firm foundation of absolute morality. It is, after all, easier to rationalize the real as it is presented—or adapt it slightly at the margins—when we use a lens which magnifies situations but eclipses absolutes. The unspoken consequence, however, is that each one of us becomes nothing more than the "minimally decent" Samaritan we despise so dearly.

If we choose a policy of life, reflecting our Abrahamic belief in either God's precious gift of human life or *Imago Dei*, we are forced to exchange our pretentiousness in action for transparency in purpose. We exchange civic cheap grace for civic costly grace. As Bonhoeffer reminds us, "God is no stop-gap; he must be recognized at the centre of life, not when we are at the end of our resources" (Bethge, 1997: 312). The task is not to "pick and choose" which *Imago Dei* we happen to like today and then either protest outside an abortion clinic, or attend the funeral service of a murder victim, or participate in a candlelight vigil on the evening when the murderer is executed. Each of these disparate acts remains pretentious because of our selectivity in praying for life, and each reflects our stop-gap use of God at the end of the road of public action. By themselves, each is nothing more than the expression of cheap grace. Bonhoeffer reminds us that in politics as in religion, our task is to dare "to do what is right...trusting in God whose commandment you faithfully follow"

(Bethge, 1997:371) and that our "action comes, not from thought, but from a readiness for responsibility" (Bethge, 1997: 298).

A policy affirming *Imago Dei* means readily grasping that responsibility—through civic costly grace and government outward justice—to spread the social gospel "deeply" into every weave and fabric of the American political community. Old debates are revisited but now from a different lens, cut from the lathe of a simple question about *result*, not process. What is the condition of *Imago Dei* at the end of each day as we present the real back to God? In a political community which claims a theocentric moral foundation, a commitment to the sanctity of human life requires embracing the task of nurturing and defending *Imago Dei*—even if it costs us, to give new meaning to Founding words, "our Lives, our Fortunes, and our sacred Honor." In our public actions, it calls for nurturing the sanctity of *all* human life—perpetrators and victims, those seemingly without *this-world* hope and those blessed with earthly abundance. However, we must *act deliberately*—as individual citizens and through the instrument of government. From his Tegel Prison cell, Bonhoeffer reminds us that "there is always reasons for not doing something; the question is whether one does them nevertheless" (1997: 325).

* * *

It takes courage to pursue a policy affirming the sanctity of human life because it requires seeking truth from both the word and the real, and acting deliberately to reconcile the real with the word once that truth is discovered. It takes courage because there are those who claim that such a *search* for moral truth—as well as its application—is unnecessary in today's world due to either the religion of secularism or the secularization of religion. The neo-Hegelian philosopher Benedetto Croce (1949; 1977) argues that, while philosophers should be courageous in finding truth, statesmen and politicians should channel their own courage away from morality and limit it only to things that produce a good political outcome. The same sentiment calls into question the need for *individual* courage to do what is morally right.

In any Lockean political community, everything rests on the shoulders of the individual—either in the capacity of *citizen-nachahmer* or government official. Within the particular setting we call the American political community, there have been countless times when issues compelled citizens and leaders to become courageous and seek the intimate consequences of moral truth, tell about what they found, and take deliberate action in its remedy. The nineteenth-century Abolition Movement (Bauman, 2003) and the twentieth-century Civil Rights Movement (Roberts,

2005) offer examples of this kind of courage in defending and nurturing *Imago Dei*. Even Martin Luther King, Jr., who initially walked ever so gingerly down the path of civic costly grace (Marsh, 2005), summoned requisite courage to take deliberate action on behalf of moral truth after hearing the voice of Jesus on one particularly intimidating night in Montgomery, Alabama: "Stand up for truth. And lo, I will be with you. Even until the end of the world" (King, 1998: 78).

Like King, Bonhoeffer believed that "God can and will bring good out of evil, even out of the greatest evil" (Bethge, 1997: 11). Bonhoeffer also knew that it takes courage to "imitate" God in bringing good into the real (Bethge, 1997: 5):

> Who stands fast? Only the man whose final standard is not his reason, his principles, his conscience, his freedom, or his virtue, but who is ready to sacrifice all this when he is called to obedient and responsible action in faith and in exclusive allegiance to God—the responsible man, who tries to make his whole life an answer to the question and call of God. Where are these responsible people?

Seeking moral truth and acting upon it should never be viewed as a singular and detached endeavor. Rather, it is a continual journey into the heart and soul of the political community—into the sanctuary of intimate consequences stemming from our public action or public non-action. You might ask, why should I embark on this journey? It will take courage, and it will be costly. This is true. But Christian scripture (*John* 8:32) reminds all within any political community that, at the journey's end, the truth *will* set us free. So, how can we be free if we choose *not* to embark on this journey? In our own democratic setting, freedom is only as sound as the moral capital from which it is purchased. Moral capital is gained only along the road to truth.

Who will hear the simple whisper of moral truth about the sanctity of human life? We must all "stand fast" and become that "responsible people."

Bibliography

Adams, John. [1793] 2002. *An Answer to Pain's [sic] "Rights of Man."* London: John Stockdale.

Albrecht, Gloria H. 2003. "Contraception and Abortion within Protestant Christianity." In *Sacred Rights: The Case for Contraception and Abortion in World Religions,* edited by Daniel C. Macquire, 80-103. New York: Oxford University Press.

al-Haq, Jad al-Haq Ali Had. 1983. *Al-Fatawa al Islamiyya min Dar Al-Ifta al-Miriyya.* Cairo, Egypt: Wazara al-Awqaf/at Majlis al-A'la li al Shu'un al-Islamiyya.

Alighieri, Dante. [1321] 2006. The Divine Comedy. www.italianstudies.org/comedy. Translated by James Cotter.

Baird-Windle, Patricia and Eleanor J. Bader. 2001. *Targets of Hatred: Anti-Abortion Terrorism.* New York: Palgrave.

Barkan, Steven E. and Steven F. Cohn. 1991. "Racial Prejudice and Support for the Death Penalty by Whites." In *The Death Penalty in America: Current Research*, edited by Robert H. Bohm. Cincinnati, OH: Anderson Publishing Co. pp. 113-145.

Baumann, Roland M. 2003. *The 1858 Oberlin-Wellington Rescue.* Oberlin, OH: Oberlin College.

Beccaria, Casare. [1767] 1975. "Essay on Crimes and Punishment." Originally published in 1775, London: F. Newberry. Translated by Harry Paolucci, 1975. Indianapolis, IN: Bobbs-Merrill.

Bedau, Hugo Adam. 2004. "An Abolitionist's Survey of the Death Penalty in America Today." In *Debating the Death Penalty: Should America Have Capital Punishment? The Experts on Both Sides Make Their Best Case,* edited by Hugo Adam Bedau and Paul G. Cassell. Oxford: Oxford University Press, pp. 15-50.

Bentham, Jeremy. [1781]1982. *An Introduction to the Principles of Morals and Legislation.* (Edited by J.H. Burns and H.L.A. Hart.) London: Methuen and Company, pp. 165-185.

Berns, Walter. 1995. "The Morality of Anger." In *Punishment and the Death Penalty: The Current Debate*, edited by Robert M. Baird and Stuart E. Rosenbaum. Amherst, MA: Prometheus.

Bethge, Eberhard (ed.)(revised and edited by Victoria J. Barnett). 2000. *Dietrich Bonhoeffer: A Biography.* Minneapolis, MN: Fortress Press.

Bethge, Eberhard (ed.) 1997. *Dietrich Bonhoeffer: Letters and Papers From from Prison.* New York: Touchstone Book.

Bitler, Marianne and Madeline Zavodny. 2002. "Did Abortion Legalization Reduce the Number of Unwanted Children? Evidence from Adoptions." *Perspectives on Sexual and Reproductive Health* 34 (1): 25-33.

Bohm, Robert M. 2003. *Deathquest: An Introduction to the Theory and Practice of Capital Punishment in the United States*. Cincinnati, OH: Anderson Publishing Co.

Bonhoeffer, Dietrich. 2003. *Discipleship.* Minneapolis, MN: Fortress Press.

Bonhoeffer, Dietrich. 1995. *Ethics*. New York: Touchstone Books.

Boyle, Mary. 1997. *Re-Thinking Abortion: Psychology, Gender, Power, and the Law.* London, UK: Routledge.

Brennan, William. 1983. *The Abortion Holocaust*. Louisville, CO: Landmark Press.

Bright, Stephen B. 2002. "Discrimination, Death, and Denial: Race and the Death Penalty." In *Machinery of Death,* edited by David R. Dow and Mark Dow. New York: Routledge, pp. 45-78.

Broen, Anne Nordal, Torbjorn Moum, Anne Sejersted Botdtker, and Olivind Ekeberg. 2005. "The Course of Mental Health after Miscarriage and Induced Abortion: A Longitudinal, Five-Year Follow-Up Study." *BMC Medicine* 3:18. Online: www.pubmedcentral.nih.gov. Retrieved: 12 July 2007.

Brugger, E. Christian. 2003. *Capital Punishment and Roman Catholic Moral Tradition*. Notre Dame, IN: University of Notre Dame Press.

Bruton, James H. 2004. *The Big House: Life Inside inside a Supermax Security Prison*. Stillwater, MN: Voyageur Press.

Burke, Theresa and David C. Reardon. 2002. *Forbidden Grief: The Unspoken Pain of Abortion*. Springfield, IL: Acorn Books.

Burns, Gene. 2005. *The Moral Veto: Framing Contraception, Abortion, and Cultural Pluralism in the United States.* Cambridge, UK: Cambridge University Press.

Cannold, Leslie. 2000. *The Abortion Myth: Feminism, Morality, and the Hard Choices Women Make.* Hanover, NH: Wesleyan University Press.

Carceral, K.C. 2004. *Behind a Convict's Eyes: Doing Time in a Modern Prison*. Belmont, CA: Thomas/Wadsworth.

Carter, Stephen L. 1998. *Civility: Manners, Morals, and the Etiquette of Democracy.* New York: HarperPerennial.

Carter, Stephen L. 1997. *Integrity*. New York: HarperPerennial

Cassell, Paul G. 2004. "In Defense of the Death Penalty." In *Debating the Death Penalty: Should America Have Capital Punishment? The Experts on Both Sides Make Their Best Case*, edited by Hugo Adam Bedau and Paul G. Cassell. Oxford: Oxford University Press. pp: 183-217.

Ceaser. James W. 1976. *Liberal Democracy and Political Science*. Baltimore, MD: Johns Hopkins University Press.

Church, Forrest. 1989. "The Gospel according to Thomas Jefferson." Preface in Thomas Jefferson [1820] 1989. *The Jefferson Bible: The Life and Morals of Jesus of Nazareth*. Boston, MA: Beacon Press.

Clair, M. 1995. *The Abortion Dilemma: Personal Views on a Public Issue*. New York: Plenum.

Clinton, Hillary Rodham. 1996. *It Takes a Village: And Other Lessons Children Teach Us.* New York: Simon and & Schuster.

Cohen, Daniel A. 1995. "Homicidal Compulsion and the Conditions of Freedom: The Social and Psychological Origins of Familicide in America's Early Republic." *Journal of Social History* 28 (4) (Summer): 725-764.

Cohen, Joel E. 1995. *How Many People Can the Earth Support.* New York: W.W. Norton.

Condic, Maureen L. 2003. "Life: Defining the Beginning by the End." *First Things.* (May). Reprinted in *The Ethics of Abortion*, edited by Chrstine Watkins. 2005. Farmington Hills, MI: Thomas/Gale. pp.: 12-28.

Cooper, William. 1772. "A Case of the Caesarian Section." Medical Observations Inquiries. 4: 261-271. Cited in A.D. Farr. 1980. "The Marquis de Sade and Induced Abortion." *Journal of Medical Ethics*, vol 6. p. 7.

Critchlow, Donald T. 1999. *Intended Consequences: Birth Control, Abortion, and the Federal Government in Modern America.* New York: Oxford University Press.

Croce, Benedetto. 1949. *My Philosophy and Other Essays on the Moral and Political Problems of Our Time.* London: George Allen and Unwin.

David, Henry P. 1985. "Postabortion and Post-Partum Psychiatric Hospitalization." *Abortion: Medical Progress and Social Implications.* London: Ciba Foundation Symposium 115: 150-164.

Debate over First Amendment Language [1789] 2002. Reprinted in *The American Republic: Primary Sources*, ed. Frohnen, Bruce. Indianapolis: Liberty Fund.

Dicks, Shirley (editor). 1991. *Congregation of the Voices against the Death Penalty.* Buffalo, NY: Prometheus Books.

Diel, Stan. 2007. "Jones put to death for '78 Oneonta Murders." *Birmingham News*, 5/4: pp 1A, 11A.

Donno, Daniel, editor. [1515]1984. Machiavelli, Niccolo. *The Prince.* Bantam Books.

Dow, David R. 2002. "How the Death Penalty Really Works." In *Machinery of Death*, edited by David R. Dow and Mark Dow. New York: Routledge, pp. 11-36.

Duff, Charles. 2001. *A Handbook on Hanging.* New York: New York Review of Books.

Ebrahim, Abul Fadl Mohsin. 1989. *Abortion, Birth Control and Surrogate Parenting: An Islamic Perspective.* Indianapolis, IN: American Trust Publications.

Eisenberg, Daniel. 2007. "Abortion and Halacha." www.jewishvirtuallibrary.org/source/judaism/abortion/html. Retrieved: 19 June 2007

Elias, Norbert. 1982. *Power and Civility.* New York: Pantheon. (Translated by Edmund Jephcott). Elias' original work was published 1939 as *The Civilizing Process.*

Endres, Michael E. 1985. *The Morality of Capital Punishment.* Mystic, CT: Twenty-Third Publications.

Evangelium Vitae. 1995. (Pope John Paul II), March 25.

Farr, A.D. 1980. "The Marquis de Sade and Induced Abortion." *Journal of Medical Ethics*, vol 6. pp. 7-10.
Frohnen, Bruce, ed. 2002. *The American Republic: Primary Sources*. Indianapolis: Liberty Fund.
Fuchs, Rachel G. 1991. "Public Power and Women's Bodies: Abortion, Infanticide, and the Penal Code in the Nineteenth Century." *Proceedings of the Annual Meeting of the Western Society for French History* 18: 567-577.
Gill, James. 1996. "Going Before the Firing Squad." *Times-Picayune* (New Orleans). January 28, p. B-7.
Gissler, Mika, Elina Hemminki, and Jouko Lonnqvist, "Suicides after Pregnancy in Finland. 1996. *British Medical Journal*. 313:1431-4.
Glenn, Gary D. 1987. "The Forgotten Purposes of the First Amendment Religion Clauses," *Review of Politics* (Summer): 340-365.
Glover, T.R. (Translation). *Tertullian's Apologeticum*. www.tertullian.org/works/apologeticum.htm. Retrieved: 12 February 2007.
Golden, Renny. 2005. *War on the Family*. New York: Routledge.
Gold-Steinberg, Sharon and Abigail J. Stewart. 1998. "Psychologies of Abortion: Implications of a Changing Context," In *Abortion Wars: A Half Century of Struggle, 1950-2000,* edited by Rickie Solinger. Berkeley, CA: University of California Press. pp. 356-373.
Gomez, Lavin C. And Garcia R. Zapata. 2005. "Diagnostic Categorization of Post Abortion Syndrome. *Actas Esp Psiquiatri*. July-August: 33(4): 267-72.
Gudorg, Christine. 2003. "Contraception and Abortion in Roman Catholicism." In *Sacred Rights: The Case for Contraception and Abortion in World Religions*, edited by Daniel C. Macquire. New York: Oxford University Press. pp. 55-78.
Hand, Samuel. 1881. *The North American Review*. December. Reprinted in *The Death Penalty*, edited by Bonnie Szumski and Susan Bursell. 1986. St. Paul, MN: Greenhaven Press. p. 31.
Harries, Keith and Derral Cheatwood. 1997. *The Geography of Execution: The Capital Punishment Quagmire in America*. Lanham, MD: Rowman & Littlefield.
Hensley, Christopher. 2000. "Attitudes toward Homosexuality in a Male and Female Prison: An Exploratory Study. *The Prison Journal*. Vol. 80 pp. 434-441.
Hensley, Christopher, Cindy Struckman-Johnson, and Helen M. Eigenberg. 2000. "Introduction: The History of Prison Sex Research." *The Prison Journal* vol. 80, pp. 360-367.
Hensley, Christopher and Richard Tewksbury. 2005. "Wardens' Perception of Prison Sex." *The Prison Journal* vol. 85. pp. 186-197.
Herring, Mark Y. 2003. *The Pro-Life/Choice Debate*. Westport, CT: Greenwood Press.
Higgins-Ciddle, John C. 2000. ed. *The Reasonableness of Christianity: As Delivered in The Scriptures*. Oxford, England: Oxford University Press.
Hite, Shere. 1991. *The Hite Report on Male Sexuality*. New York: A. Knopf.

House, H. Wayne. 1997. "The New Testament and Moral Arguments for Capital Punishment." In *The Death Penalty in America*, edited by Hugo Adam Bedau. New York: Oxford University Press. pp. 415-428. (Originally published in Wayne H. House and John Howard Yoder, 1991. *The Death Penalty Debate*. Dallas, TX: Word Publishing.)

Ivers, Gregg. 1995. *To Build a Wall: American Jews and the Separation of Church and State*. Charlottesville, VA: University Press of Virginia.

Jackson, Timothy P., editor. 2005. *The Morality of Adoption: Social-Psychological, Theological, and Legal Perspectives*. Grand Rapids, MI: William B. Eerdmans Publishing Company.

Jefferson, Thomas. [1820] (1989). *The Jefferson Bible: The Life and Morals of Jesus of Nazareth*. Boston, MA: Beacon Press.

Jefferson, Thomas. [1786] 2002. *Virginia Bill for Establishing Religious Freedom*. Reprinted in *The American Republic: Primary Sources*, ed. Frohnen, Bruce. Indianapolis: Liberty Fund.

Jewish Encyclopedia. 1901-1906. See section on "Abortion." New York: Funk & Wagnalls Co.

Johnson, Robert. 1998. *Death Work: A Study of the Modern Execution Process*. Belmont, CA: West/Wadsworth.

Kaplan, Laura. 1998. "Beyond Safe and Legal: The Lessons of Jane." In *Abortion Wars: A Half Century of Struggle 1950-2000*, edited by Rickie Solinger. Berkeley, CA: University of California Press, pp. 33-41.

Kastenbaum, Robert. 2006. "Definitions of Death." *Encyclopedia of Death and Dying*. www.deathreference.com/Da-Em/Definitions-of-death.html. Retrieved 11 June 2007

Katme, A. Majid. 2007. Islam and Abortion. Muslims@spuc.org.uk. Retrieved: 24 June 2007

Kerrigan, Michael. 2007. *The History of Death*. Essex, CT: Globe Pequot Press.

King, Martin Luther, Jr. 1996. *The Autobiography of Martin Luther King, Jr.*, edited by Clayborne Carson. New York: Warner Books.

King, Rachel. 2003. *Don't Kill in Our Names*. New Brunswick, NJ: Rutgers University Press.

Kinsey, Alfred E., Wardell B. Pomeroy, and Clyde E. Martin. 1998. *Sexual Behavior in the Human Male*. Bloomington, IN: Indiana University Press.

Kirby, Peter. 2001. "Chapter 2. The Second Commandment: Grave Sin Forbidden," *Didache*. Translated by Roberts-Donaldson. www.earlychristianwritings.com/didache-roberts.html. Retrieved: 2/12/07.12 February 2007

Kirk, Peggy. 2003. *You Aren't Alone: The Voices of Abortion*. Nevada City, CA: Blue Dolphin Publishing.

Kirk, Jerome and Marc L. Miller. 1986. *Reliability and Validity in Qualitative Research*. Newbury Park, CA: Sage Publications.

Kozinki, Alex. 2004. "Tinkering with Death." In *Debating the Death Penalty: Should America Have Capital Punishment? The Experts on Both Sides Make Their Best Case*, edited by Hugo Adam Bedau and Paul G. Cassell. Oxford: Oxford University Press. pp: 1-14.

Lader, Lawrence. 1973. *Abortion II: Making the Revolution*. Boston, MA: Beacon Press, 1973

Lemkau, J.P. 1988. "Emotional Sequelae of Abortion." *Psychology of Women Quarterly* 12: 461-72.
Landrine, Hope, Elizabeth A. Klonoff, and Alice Brown-Collins. 1995. "Cultural Diversity and Methodology in Feminist Psychology: Critique, Proposal, Empirical Example." In *Bringing Cultural Diversity to Feminist Psychology: Theory, Research, and Practice*, edited by Hope Landrine. Washington, D.C.: American Psychological Association, pp. 145-163.
Levine, Phillip B. 2004. *Sex and Consequences: Abortion, Public Policy, and the Economics of Fertility*. Princeton, NJ: Princeton University Press.
Lifton, Robert and Greg Mitchell. 2000. *Who Owns Death? Capital Punishment, the American Conscience, and the End of Executions*. New York: HarperCollins.
Lightfoot, J.B. 2007. *The Epistle of Barnabas*. www.earlychristianwritings.com/text/barnabas-lightfoot.html. Rerieved 12 February 2007.
Locke, John. [1689] 1983; 1992. *Two Treatises on Government*, edited by Peter Laslett. Cambridge: Cambridge University Press.
Locke, John [1689b] 1983. *A Letter Concerning Toleration*, edited by James H. Tully. Indianapolis: Hackett.
Lonang Institute. 2006. October 7, 1801 Letter to Thomas Jefferson Sent by the Danbury Baptists Association. www.lonang.com/exlibris/misc/danbury.htm
Lovrin, Mellen. 1999. "Parental Murder and Suicide: Post Traumatic Stress Disorder in Children." *Journal of Child and Adolescent Psychiatric Nursing*. 12 (3) pp. 110-117.
Lyons, Emily and Jeff Lyons. 2005. *Life's been a Blast*. Birmingham, AL: I EM Press.
Madison, James. [1785] 2002. *Memorial and Remonstrance Against against Religious Assessments*. Reprinted in *The American Republic: Primary Sources*, ed. Frohnen, Bruce. Indianapolis: Liberty Fund.
Major, B., C. Cozzarelli, M.L. Cooper, J. Zubek, C. Richards, M. Wilhite, R. H. Gramzow. 2000. "Psychological Responses of Women after First-Trimester Abortion." *Archives of General Psychiatry* 57(8): 777-84.
Manzi, Stephanie. 2003. "Capital Punishment in the United States." In *Handbook of Death and Dying*, edited by Clifton D. Bryant. Thousands Oaks, CA: Sage Publications, pp. 368-377.
Marquis, Joshua K. 2004. "Truth or Consequences: The Penalty of Death." In *Debating the Death Penalty: Should America Have Capital Punishment? The Experts on Both Sides Make Their Best Case*, edited by Hugo Adam Bedau and Paul G. Cassell. Oxford: Oxford University Press. pp: 117-151.
Marsh, Charles. 2005. *The Beloved Community*. Cambridge, MA: Basic Books.
Martinez, J. Michael. 2002. "'Woe to the Hand that Shed This Costly Blood:' Philosophical Arguments Against the Death Penalty." In *The Leviathan's Choice: Capital Punishment in the Twenty-First Century*, edited by J. Michael Martinez, William D. Richardson, and D. Brandon Hornsby. Lanham, MD: Rowman & Littlefield. pp. 41-66.

Masur, Louis P. 1991. *Rites of Execution: Capital Punishment and the Transformation of American Culture, 1776-1865.* New York: Oxford University Press.

McCracken, Grant. 1988. *The Long Interview*. Newbury Park, CA: Sage Publications.

McKinley, Brian Elroy. 2003. "Why Abortion is Biblical. http://elroy.net.ehr/abortion.html. Retrieved: 21 June 2007.

McLouth, Gary, Lyn Seng and Arthur B. Schostaka. 1984. *Men and Abortion: Lessons in Love*. New York: Praeger.

Meacham, Jon. 2006. *American Gospel: God, the Founding Fathers, and the Making of a Nation*. New York: Random House.

Megivern, James. 1997. *The Death Penalty: An Historical and Theological Survey*. New York: Paulist Publishing.

Miles, Jack. 1995. *God: A Biography*. New York: Alfred A. Knopf.

Mohr, James C. 1978. *Abortion in America: The Origins and Evolution of National Policy, 1800-1900*. New York: Oxford University Press.

Montague, Phillip. 1995. *Punishment as Societal-Defense*. Lanham, MD: Rowman & Littlefield.

Montesquieu, Charles De Secondat. 2005. *Spirit of Laws*. Amherst, NY: Prometheus Books.

Ms. Magazine. 2006. "We Had Abortions." Fall: pp. 38-41.

Muñoz, Vincent Phillip. 2003. "James Madison's Principle of Religious Liberty," *American Political Science Review* 97 (February): 17-32.

Myrsiades, Linda. 2002. *Splitting the Baby: The Culture of Abortion in Literature and Law, Rhetoric and Cartoons*. New York: Peter Lang

NAACP - National Association for the Advancement of Color People. 2007. Death Row Statistics. www.naacpldf.org/content/pdf/pubs/drusa/DRUSA_winter_2007.pdf. Retrieved: 6/25/07.25 June @007.

Neustatter, Angela (with Gina Newson). 1986. *Mixed Feelings: The Experience of Abortion*. London: Pluto Press.

Novak, Michael.A. 2006. *Evolutionary Dynamics: Exploring the Equation of Life*. Cambridge, MA: Harvard University Press.

Nuovo, Victor. 2002. ed. *John Locke: Writings on Religion*. Oxford, England: Oxford University Press.

Novak, Michael. 2004. "Foreword: Religious Liberty." In *The Founders on God and Government*, edited by Daniel L. Dreisbach, Mark D. Hall and Jeffrey H. Morrison. Lanham, MD: Rowman & Littlefield, pp. ii-xii.

Page, Cristina. 2006. *How the Pro-Choice Movement Saved America: Freedom, Politics, and the War on Sex.* New York: Basic Books.

Percy, Walker. 1991. *Signposts in a Strange Land*. New York: Picador.

Pojman, Louis P. 2004. "Why the Death Penalty Is Morally Permissible" In *Debating the Death Penalty: Should America Have Capital Punishment? The Experts on Both Sides Make Their Best Case*, edited by Hugo Adam Bedau and Paul G. Cassell. Oxford: Oxford University Press, pp. 35-59.

Prejean, Helen. 1993. *Dead Man Walking*. New York: Random House.

Press, Andrea L. and Elizabeth R. Cole. 1999. *Speaking of Abortion: Television and Authority in the Lives of Women*. Chicago,IL: The University of Chicago Press.

Press, Eyal. 2006. *Absolute Convictions: My Father, a City, and the Conflict that Divided America*. New York: Henry Holt.

Rauch, Daniel. 2006. www.nlm.nih.gov/medlineplus/enc/article/002398/htm. 10 May 2006. Document retrieved 6 June 2007.

Reardon, David C., P.G. Ney, F.L. Scheuren, J.R. Cougle and P.K. Coleman. 2002. "Deaths Associated with Pregnancy Outcome: A Record Linkage Study of Low-Income Women," *Southern Medical Journal*.

Religious Tolerance. 2007. www.religioustolerance.org. Retrieved: 21 June 2007.

Roberts, J. Deotis. 2005. *Bonhoeffer and King: Speaking Truth to Power*. Louisville, KY: Westminster John Knox Press.

Robertson, Edwin (ed. and translator). 1999. *Dietrich Bonhoeffer's Prison Poems*. Grand Rapids, MI: Zondervan.

Rosenblum, Nancy L. 2000. *Obligations of Citizenship and Demands of Faith*. ed. Princeton, NJ: Princeton University Press.

Rue, Vincent M., Priscilla K. Coleman, James J. Rue, and David C. Reardon. 2004. "Induced Abortion and Traumatic Stress: A Preliminary Comparison of American Russian Women." *Med Sci Monit* 10(10): SR5-16.

Sade, Marquis de. 1795. *Philosophy in the Boudoir*. Reprinted with translation by Joachim Neugroschel and introduction by Francine de Plessix Gray. 2006. New York: Penguin Books.

Saletan, William. 2003. *Bearing Right: How Conservatives Won the Abortion War*. Berkeley, CA: University of California Press.

Schiraldi, Glenn R. 2001. *Post Traumatic Stress Disorder Source-Book*. New York: McGraw-Hill.

Schlesinger, Arthur M. 1946. *Learning How to Behave: A Historical Study of American Etiquette Books*. New York: Macmillan.

Schoenig, Richard. 2001. "Christians and Abortion." In *The Ethics of Abortion*, edited by Robert M. Baird and Stuart E. Rosenbaum (eds.) 2001. Amherst, NY: Prometheus Book, pp. 224-230.

Seitz, Trina N. 2003. "A History of Execution Methods in the United States." In *Handbook of Death and Dying*, edited by Clifton D. Bryant. Thousand Oaks, CA: Sage Publication, pp. 357-367.

Shaikh, Sa'Diyya. 2003. "Family Planning, Conception, and Abortion in Islam." In *Sacred Rights: The Case for Contraception and Abortion in World Religions*, edited by Daniel C. Maguire. New York: Oxford University Press. pp. 105-128.

Shamsudden, Sheikh Muhammed Mahdl. 2007. http://re-xs.ucsm.ac.uk/gcsere/courswork/outines/abortion.html . Retrieved: 6/24/0724 June 2007.

Shrage, Laurie. 2003. *Abortion and Social Responsibility*. Oxford, UK: Oxford University Press.

Simmons, Rabbi Shraga. 2007. http://judaism.about.com/library/3_askrabbi_o/bl_simmons_deathpenalty.htm. Retrieved: 6/20/07.20 June 2007.

Simonds, Wendy. 1996. *Abortion at Work: Ideology and Practice in a Feminist Clinic*. New Brunswick, NJ: Rutgers University Press.

Slane, Craig J. 2004. *Bonhoeffer as Martyr: Social Responsibility and Modern Christian Commitment.* Grand Rapids, MI: Brazos Press.

Solinger, Rickie 1998. "Pregnancy and Power before *Roe v. Wade*, 195–1970." In *Abortion Wars: A Half Century of Struggle 1950-2000,* edited by Rickie Solinger. Berkeley, CA: University of California Press, pp. 10-24.

Speer, Albert. 1997. *Inside the Third Reich*. New York: Simon & Schuster.

Stassen, Glen H. 2002. "Deliverance from the Vicious Cycles of Murder." In *The Leviathan's Choice: Capital Punishment in the Twenty-First Century*, edited by J. Michael Martinez, William D. Richardson, and D. Brandon Hornsby. Lanham, MD: Rowman & Littlefield. pp. 115-137.

Steelwater, Eliza. 2003. *The Hangman's Knot: Lynching, Legal Execution, and America's Struggle with the Death Penalty*. Boulder, CO: Westview Press.

Stevenson, Bryan. 2004. "Close to Death: Reflections on Race and Capital Punishment in America." In *Debating the Death Penalty: Should America Have Capital Punishment? The Experts on Both Sides Make Their Best Case*, edited by Hugo Adam Bedau and Paul G. Cassell. Oxford: Oxford University Press, pp. 76-116.

Stormer, Nathan. 2002. *Articulating Life's Memory: U.S. Medical Rhetoric about Abortion in the Nineteenth Century*. Lanham, MD: Lexington Books.

Surtis, Paul J. 1995. Church Teaching and the Death Penalty. The Vincentian Center for Church and Society. www.vincenter.org. Retrieved: 23 June 2007.

Thomson, Judith Jarvis. 1971. "A Defense of Abortion." *Philosophy and Public Affairs*. Vol.1, no. 1. pp. 47-66.

Throckmorton, Warren. 2005. "Abortion and Mental Health." *Washington Times*. January 21, 2005.

U.S. Centers for Disease Control and Prevention. 2007. Abortion Surveillance–United States. 56 (SS09); November 23; 1-33.

van den Haag, Ernest. 1975. *Punishing Criminals: Concerning a Very Old and Painful Question*. New York: Basic Books.

van den Haag, Earnest. 1968. "On Deterrence and the Death Penalty." *Ethics* 78 (July): 18-31.

Van Impe, Jack. 1973. *Life and Death: Abortion and Capital Punishment*. Royal Oak, MI: Jack Van Impe Crusades.

Vellenga, Jacob J. 2002. "Is Capital Punishment Wrong?" In *The Leviathan's Choice: Capital Punishment in the Twenty-First Century*, edited by J. Michael Martinez, William D. Richardson, and D. Brandon Hornsby. Lanham, MD: Rowman & Littlefield. pp. 28-40.

Voltaire. 1770. Quote attributed to Voltaire about Cesare Beccaria reprinted 1986 in *The Death Penalty,* edited by Szumski, Bonnie and Susan Bursell. St. Paul, MN: Greenhaven Press, p. 24.

Ward, Harry M. 2007. *George Washington's Enforcers: Policing the Continental Army*. Carbondale, IL: Southern Illinois University Press.

Washington, George. [1796, September 19] 2002. *Farewell Address*. Reprinted in *The American Republic: Primary Sources*, edited by Frohnen, Bruce. Indianapolis: Liberty Fund.

Wilson, James Q. 1993. *The Moral Sense*. New York: Free Press.

Witte, John Jr. 2004. "One Public Religion, Many Private Religions: John Adams and the 1780 Massachusetts Constitution." In *The Founders on God and Government*, edited by Daniel L. Dreisbach, Mark D. Hall, and Jeffry H. Morrison. Lanham, MD: Rowman & Littlefield. pp: 23-52.

Wolf, Naomi. 1995. "Our Bodies, Our Souls." *The New Republic*. Reprinted in Robert M. Baird and Stuart E. Rosenbaum, editors. 2001. *The Ethics of Abortion* (Amherst, NY: Prometheus Books): pp. 172-194.

www.toiletpaperworld.com Retrieved 1 November 2007

Yoder, John Howard. 1997. "Noah's Covenant, the New Testament, and Christian Social Order." In *The Death Penalty in America*, edited by Hugo Adam Bedau. New York: Oxford University Press, pp 429-444. (First published in H. Wayne House and John Howard Yoder, 1991. *The Death Penalty Debate*. Dallas, TX: Word Publishing.)

Zingler, Frank R. 1985. "An Acorn is Not an Oak Tree." *American Atheist*. Reprinted in 1991 as "Human Life Does Not Begin at Conception." In *Abortion: Opposing Viewpoints*, edited by in Charles P. Cozic and Stacey L. Tipp. San Diego, CA: Greenhaven Press, Inc. pp: 23-30.

Zoloth, Laurie. 2003. "Each One an Entire World: A Jewish Perspective on Family Planning." In *Sacred Rights: The Case for Contraception and Abortion in World Religions*, edited by Daniel C. Macquire. New York: Oxford University Press. pp. 21-53.

Index

For Product Safety Concerns and Information please contact our EU representative GPSR@taylorandfrancis.com
Taylor & Francis Verlag GmbH, Kaufingerstraße 24, 80331 München, Germany

www.ingramcontent.com/pod-product-compliance
Lightning Source LLC
LaVergne TN
LVHW011128300926
849160LV00008B/557